DANCING BETWEEN
—— THE ——
TOES OF ELEPHANTS

Published and distributed by Merack Publishing
Jackson, USA
www.merackpublishing.com

Library of Congress Control Number: 2025909978
Magliochetti, Michael
Dancing Between the Toes of Elephants: Clever Private Equity Idioms and Anecdotes from an Outsider's Experience on the Inside

ISBN
Paperback 978-1-964421-13-1
eBook 978-1-964421-14-8

DANCING BETWEEN
——— THE ———
TOES OF ELEPHANTS

**Clever Private Equity Idioms and Anecdotes
from an Outsider's Experience on the Inside**

Michael Magliochetti, Ph.D

To Maria, my wife, a steadfast partner through every twist and turn of my career; and to Michael Jr. and Michaela, my children, who have made the entire journey worthwhile.

CONTENTS

FOREWORD

Private equity has long had a reputation for being impenetrable to outsiders—dense with financial jargon, governed by unwritten rules, and dominated by people who tend to follow a well-worn path into the industry. I should know—I didn't follow it. I grew up in a small town in upstate New York. The first time I visited New York City was in the spring of my senior year in college. My parents didn't attend college, and I took exactly one economics class during my undergraduate years.

Like the author of this book, I entered the world of private equity from a very different starting point. I began my career practicing law. I went to law school because my father wanted me to become a "professional"—which proved the old adage that if you're not passionate about what you do, you're unlikely to succeed. I was fired from my first legal job. I never imagined that one day I'd be leading investor relations for one of the largest global alternative asset managers, founding a multi-billion-dollar fund-of-funds platform, or helping to build a world-class GP solutions firm.

But like many who find their way into this industry through the side door, I've come to realize that non-traditional backgrounds often bring a unique—and sometimes sorely needed—perspective. I stumbled into finance by accident, taking a job with the Pennsylvania Treasury Department. Much to my surprise, investments clicked with me. My challenge was that learning all the colloquialisms which I found was like trying to learn a foreign language. Investment folks have a strange habit of taking simple concepts and making them sound overly complicated. Worse yet, investment professionals are fond of using "clever" metaphors to try to explain concepts that they've already made unnecessarily convoluted.

That's part of what drew me to *Dancing Between the Toes of Elephants*. This book is not only a guide to private equity lingo—it's a deeply personal, frequently hilarious, and refreshingly honest account of what it means to reinvent yourself in an unfamiliar world.

Mike's path is anything but conventional. He started as a Ph.D. engineer, spent over two decades as a CEO in healthcare, and only then made the leap into private equity. The transition wasn't seamless—and that's exactly what makes his story so compelling. He candidly shares what it feels like to go from being the one making the final call to the one listening, learning, and adapting in real time. His evolution from player to coach, from company operator to Operating Partner, is something anyone navigating a career pivot will relate to, regardless of industry.

What sets Mike apart isn't just his technical ability or his impressive track record of creating value in portfolio companies. It's his humanity. He leads with emotional intelligence, a self-deprecating sense of humor, and a rare willingness to ask questions most others are too proud—or too afraid—to pose. He doesn't take himself too seriously, but he takes the work very seriously. That's a combination I've always admired.

Throughout this book, you'll find colorful idioms, real-life anecdotes, and moments of comic disbelief that anyone who's ever sat through a due diligence meeting or a board presentation will appreciate. But you'll also find something deeper: a reminder that PE doesn't have to be a closed club, and that leadership is as much about humility and curiosity as it is about decisiveness and conviction.

Whether you're a student considering a career in finance, a founder trying to make sense of your new private equity partners, or a seasoned investor who could use a laugh and a bit of reflection, *Dancing Between the Toes of Elephants* offers something rare: a window into the often opaque world of PE, written by someone who's lived on both sides of the table.

Mike's story is proof that there's no one "right" way to get here—and that sometimes, it's the unconventional path that brings the most insight. I'm proud to call him a friend and colleague, and I'm confident you'll find his voice as enjoyable, thoughtful, and unforgettable as I have.

So, take a breath, crack a smile, and prepare to dance.

Michael Arpey

President, Hunter Point Capital

Former Global Head of Investor Relations at The Carlyle Group

INTRODUCTION

Before transitioning to private equity investing as a full-time Operating Partner in 2012 at Riverside Partners, I spent over 20 years in private industry, serving as CEO of several healthcare companies through successful sale transactions. Originally trained as a Ph.D. engineer, I followed a highly unconventional path to get there. Given that background and the trajectory that followed, over a decade in private equity, I'm often asked, "Did you ever imagine yourself in a private equity role?" My answer is always the same: "Absolutely not."

While I believed that pursuing more education would open doors, I never envisioned one of them leading to the world of investing.

My career has involved multiple reinventions, each requiring me to take risks, leave my comfort zone, and step into leadership roles across a variety of healthcare subsectors. Each role demanded I quickly grasp new medical domains and learn how to communicate the value of products and services to both physicians and investors. Along the way, I discovered the importance of being technically sharp and intensely focused while also valuing observation, empathy, and emotional intelligence. Humor has always been my secret weapon, whether to lighten a tense moment, disarm egos, manage pressure, or just make fun of myself between setting and exceeding ambitious goals.

The shift from CEO to private equity investor has been one of the most rewarding, humbling, and educational chapters of my professional life. I had to navigate a steep learning curve and make a fundamental shift in mindset from being a "player" running companies to becoming a "coach" supporting management teams. It has been a process of constant adaptation and discovery, and truthfully, one I'm still navigating more than a decade later.

Even though I had some exposure to private equity as a CEO, this new role required me to go much deeper. I had to understand the mechanics of diligence, acquisition structures, debt instruments, financial modeling, and more. I approached it the same way I approached any new leadership challenge: I dove in headfirst, listened intently, asked a lot of questions, and relied on the wisdom and patience of my colleagues. One of my favorite strategies, listening three times before speaking, proved essential in this new environment.

I take great pride in the contributions I've made to investment teams and in helping portfolio companies define and execute value creation strategies. But I've also made it a point to bring levity, good humor, and camaraderie to my work, just as I did as a CEO. That approach has resonated not only with my colleagues in private equity, but also with the founders and management teams I work alongside, both before and after the deal closes.

Early into my transition to PE, I started keeping a personal journal filled with the colorful phrases, idioms, and inside lingo I encountered. Many of them struck me as simultaneously baffling and hilarious. It turns out I wasn't alone in my confusion. Over time, I realized these expressions weren't just colorful—they often captured complex dynamics with surprising precision, and offered a bit of comic relief in an otherwise intense profession.

Before joining Riverside full-time, I served on the firm's Healthcare Advisory Board, a group of seasoned executives with deep experience across many sectors of healthcare. Today, I chair that board as part of my role as Operating Partner. Along the way, I also established a Clinical Advisory Board composed of top physicians from a range of specialties, to complement the business insights of the Healthcare Advisory Board with clinical expertise. These two groups meet jointly several times a year.

Our meetings typically feature updates on the firm's portfolio, presentations from guest experts, reviews of potential investment opportunities, and discussions on emerging sectors. They also, as a matter of course, include a healthy dose of financial acronyms and quirky idioms, the very ones that inspired this book.

During our memorable first joint meeting, the physicians were understandably quiet after their introductions. A few with hospital administrative backgrounds chimed in occasionally, but most simply observed and absorbed. It was clear many of them were out of their element. Still, the energy in the room felt promising, and as the day unfolded, the synergy between the business and clinical perspectives began to take shape.

That evening, over dinner, several advisors remarked on the quality of the discussion and the uniqueness of the diverse and impressive group. As I reflected on the day, I found myself seated next to Dr. Stephen Zappala, a Clinical Advisory Board member, who summed up the experience with equal parts honesty and humor.

"What an incredible day," he said. "I'm learning a ton. Trying to process all of it. I do have a basic question, though. I'm almost embarrassed to ask."

"Don't be," I replied. "Ask anything."

He smiled and said, "Well, I guess once I ask, *I can't put the toothpaste back in the tube*"—a nod to an idiom used earlier in the meeting. We both laughed.

"Go ahead," I encouraged.

He rubbed his forehead and asked, "What the hell is EBITDA?"

I had to laugh. The term had come up repeatedly throughout the meeting, and his question was a perfect reminder that while I was still getting my own sea legs in private equity, the language of finance was downright foreign to many of our clinical advisors. His hesitation to ask, paired with the reference to the toothpaste idiom, captured the shared awkwardness of stepping into unfamiliar territory.

After that meeting, I followed up with each clinical advisor individually, offering feedback, context, and a plain-English definition of EBITDA: earnings before interest, taxes, depreciation, and amortization—a common proxy for profitability. Several physicians mentioned how much they appreciated the opportunity to better understand the investing world, despite its steep learning curve and peculiar vocabulary.

That moment, and many like it, inspired me to turn my journal into this book. My goal was to create an educational and entertaining guide to the idioms, jargon, and behind-the-scenes moments I've encountered both as an operator and as an investor. This book was not written for seasoned deal professionals (though they might get a chuckle or two), but for business students, early-career professionals entering investing, and executives working with PE or venture-backed companies. While many of these phrases once made me shake my head, I've come to see just how well they capture the realities they describe.

I've included personal anecdotes for color, along with weaving in bits of wisdom from mentors whose advice continues to echo in my day-to-day work. Ironically, many of the idioms I once found ridiculous have now found their way into my own vocabulary during meetings with investment teams and company leaders.

Whatever your background, my hope is for you to find amusement throughout the pages ahead and perhaps glean something useful along the way. If this book helps you navigate a new career chapter, decode the language of investing, or simply makes you smile along your journey, then the effort will have been well worth it. And above all, I encourage you to embrace personal or professional reinvention, ask the awkward question, and keep your sense of humor firmly intact.

1. DANCING BETWEEN THE TOES OF ELEPHANTS

A critical part of the pre-acquisition diligence process in private equity (PE) involves conducting a comprehensive competitive analysis of the target company. This evaluation spans a range of factors including the strength of the management team, business sustainability, growth potential, and crucially the impact of existing and potential competition. Competitive dynamics often play a pivotal role in shaping investment decisions.

My PE experience has focused primarily on lower middle-market, founder-owned companies, typically with revenues between $15 million and $60 million, and EBITDA exceeding $3 million. Despite their relatively modest size, many of these businesses compete effectively against larger private or publicly traded companies by carving out niche markets. They differentiate themselves through personalized service, higher quality standards, technical innovation, and other strategic advantages.

One common pattern is that these companies thrive by serving customer segments that are overlooked or underserved by industry giants. Their clients, often smaller in size, may be treated as "second-class citizens" by larger vendors, facing challenges such as long lead times, inconsistent service, less experienced staff, or higher pricing. Target companies, which I have analyzed by contrast, often succeed precisely because they treat these customers as top priority.

During diligence, it's not unusual to discover that a target company is already competing with much larger industry players. This can be a source of concern: while the company may have grown successfully under the radar, there's always the risk that a dominant competitor might eventually decide to pursue the same market segment more aggressively. What today appears to be a safe niche could, overnight, become contested ground.

I vividly remember one diligence meeting where I raised this exact concern: what if a leading market incumbent decided to move down market and directly challenge our target? A colleague responded thoughtfully:

"Believe me, I understand the concern. With this business, we'd be *dancing between the toes of elephants.* But I think we can do it sustainably because of the quality of service and the strength of the technology."

His metaphor captured the situation perfectly. To move forward with conviction, we needed to believe that the company could indeed "dance between the toes of elephants" to adeptly coexist and thrive even if larger players chose to enter the same space. This type of threat is a recurring challenge in lower middle-market investing. In such cases, the only way to justify the investment is to be confident that the target's competitive edge is not only real, but sustainable.

2. PLAY TO THE BACK OF THE BASEBALL CARD

In baseball, a player's statistics, achievements, and performance history are typically printed on the back of their baseball card. These statistics provide a complete review of their career, including batting average, home runs, runs batted in, and other key metrics. Instead of fixating solely on a player's recent performance or a single game, serious baseball analysts and scouts often advise looking at the entire body of work represented on the back of the baseball card to assess a player's true skill and potential.

In a memorable meeting with one of our PE portfolio company CEOs, we discussed the possibility of initiating a process to sell the company and commencing interviews with investment bankers to represent the company. Simultaneously, we were in a budgeting process for the upcoming year during which the CEO made an insightful observation, emphasizing his commitment to executing the plan, ongoing hiring, and avoiding short-term measures to artificially boost EBITDA. This tactic exactly aligned with our approach.

One of my partners stated, "I completely agree. We should stay on course and *play to the back of the baseball card*. The company needs to continue to make investments to ensure continued revenue growth and momentum."

This was the first time I had heard the phrase "play to the back of the baseball card". It was used to emphasize the significance of going beyond superficial or short-term metrics and instead concentrating on the company's comprehensive track record and performance history. My colleague's pragmatic approach, prioritizing what was in the best interest of the company, ensured that any potential acquirer during the diligence process would recognize the strength of company's record of performance, sustainability, and positioning for continued growth.

3. HALF-OF-A-SHOE-SIZE TOO SMALL

During the early stages of evaluating a potential private equity investment, we assess several key benchmark metrics: historical and current revenue, EBITDA, the caliber and commitment of the management team, sustainability of earnings, growth prospects, customer concentration, and other critical factors. For new platform investments, we typically set a minimum EBITDA threshold of $3 million. However, we're more flexible when it comes to add-on acquisitions for existing portfolio companies, where strategic goals—such as geographic expansion, customer diversification, or technology access—take precedence over strict financial benchmarks.

That said, we're often introduced to outstanding founders leading strong companies that haven't quite hit the financial milestones required for consideration as a standalone platform.

I recall one particularly memorable meeting while evaluating a company in the technology-enabled healthcare space. The business had many attributes we liked, but the numbers were borderline. During the discussion, one colleague quipped, "This is *half-a-shoe-size too small* for us. Their trailing twelve-month EBITDA is $2.8 million, and they're forecasting just $3 million by year-end."

Another added, more bluntly, "Let's be honest—once we load on the expenses to build out the leadership team, implement systems, and upgrade operations, EBITDA is going to take a hit. We'll be under water. We should pass."

I couldn't help but chuckle. The metaphor was clever, and it brought me back to a personal memory: standing in a shoe store as a kid, my foot being measured by a salesman using one of those cold metal Brannock Devices. My feet were large for my age, something I was self-conscious about. I'd always try to convince my mother to round down a half size, hoping to squeeze into smaller shoes. It never worked out. Much like in private equity, wishing a fit were better doesn't make it so.

4. STICK FEEL

This term finds its roots in hockey, where sticks are crafted from a laminated epoxy resin carbon composite with customized thickness profiles for specific flex and stiffness points along the shaft. The stick's elastic energy propels the puck when the stick is bent, such as in a "wrist shot," storing and releasing elastic potential energy akin to a slingshot. Professional hockey players prioritize stick properties like weight, length, flex point, balance, release time, and durability, all contributing to the stick's subjective "feel." By picking up a hockey stick and moving it around, they get a sense for its relative performance or "stick feel" as compared to their personal preferences.

In the realm of PE acquisition diligence, we often develop a sense, or "stick feel," to interpret and act on data analyses across various workstreams. Numerous independent variables, including market trends, product or service pricing, new customer acquisition, concentration, retention (referred to as stickiness), and attrition, contribute to this assessment.

I recall a moment which prompted a chuckle when a colleague, evaluating an investment opportunity, remarked, "From everything I've digested on this company, the *stick feel* here is not good. I don't like the high rate of employee turnover and the lack of new customer wins. It just doesn't feel right."

As diligence progresses, this "stick feel" guides us in formulating pertinent questions and provides insight to focus on specific areas to unearth key risks. Much like a hockey player's experience refines their innate sense of stick feel, a PE investor develops a similar intuition through years of diligence processes on potential targets and observing a pattern recognition.

5. YOU'LL NEVER GET A BLACK EYE ON THE PHONE

This is one of my personal favorites—a phrase and philosophy I've found incredibly fitting throughout my career, both within and outside of PE. In the post-investment phase, many of the portfolio companies I've been involved with pursue a common strategy: building out a formal business development function. This typically includes hiring key commercial leadership, such as a Chief Commercial Officer and Regional Vice Presidents of Business Development, and creating an organization that spans field sales, inside sales, and account management.

Inside sales, in particular, is a demanding discipline. These team members are responsible for hunting down new business leads, identifying and reaching out to decision-makers at potential client organizations, developing lead databases, cold calling, emailing, leveraging LinkedIn, and more. It's a grind that requires tireless effort, an optimistic mindset, thick skin, and a deep well of resilience.

As an Operating Partner in PE, I've come to truly enjoy the proprietary deal origination aspect of my role. It taps into that same business development muscle, only instead of selling a service or product, I'm pitching a partnership. Reaching out to potential acquisition candidates, often founders, is rarely glamorous. I cold call, attend conferences, send emails, and use LinkedIn to introduce myself. I usually lead with my operational background and degrees in chemical engineering, something that sometimes earns me a moment of curiosity or credibility that a more traditional finance résumé might not. Still, I get turned down far more often than not. And like any good inside salesperson, I've learned to embrace the "no's" with humility, persistence, and patience.

But when it works—when I connect with a founder, learn about their journey, and begin to build mutual trust—it's exhilarating. These conversations are among the most rewarding parts of my role. Whether the deal advances or not, hearing an entrepreneur's vision and story is always time well spent.

I was once reflecting on this with my friend Marshall, a PE veteran I've known for decades. Now in his early 90s, Marshall is still active—still making introductions, still connecting people and companies to help deals take shape. Though he's understandably slowed down, he maintains a quiet mission that gets him out of bed every morning. During a memorable conversation, he shared a piece of wisdom from his early days in investment banking that has stuck with me ever since.

"Hey," he said, "I learned early on that no one was going to call me out of the blue to give me business. I had to get over being shy or afraid of rejection. Think about it, what's the worst that can happen? *You'll never get a black eye over the phone.* Once I came to this realization, the rest was easy."

That simple line reframed the whole exercise for me. I've since shared Marshall's advice with business development teams across our portfolio companies. It's a clear and powerful reminder of the opportunity cost of not picking up the phone—of letting fear or hesitation dictate your reach. Rejection may sting, but inaction is far worse.

6. THE ACTION IS THE JUICE

I first encountered the phrase "The Action is the Juice" in one of my favorite movies, *Heat*, starring Al Pacino and Robert DeNiro, who shared the screen for the first time in this film. Their respective characters, Lt. Vincent Hanna and Neil McCauley, exist on opposite sides of the morality spectrum. Lt. Hanna is a successful police detective, workaholic, and paying the price with a string of failed relationships. On the other hand, McCauley is a stoic and determined career criminal with an icy demeanor, fully committed to his nefarious craft. Despite the dichotomy of their intentions, they share a tremendous amount of respect for each other.

In the movie, McCauley leads a crew of high-end thieves planning a major bank heist. As Lt. Hanna relentlessly pursues them, the crew contemplates whether to proceed with their plans. In a riveting scene, McCauley asks each member of the crew if they are in or out with respect to pursuing the heist. One of his partners in crime, Michael Cheritto, played by Tom Sizemore, struggles with the decision. Cheritto's eventual response is classic, "Well, you know, for me, *the action is the juice.*" For Cheritto, the thrill of the heist outweighed the risks and potential rewards.

I was amused to encounter the phrase "the action is the juice" in PE, although not as dramatic as Cheritto's situation but rather comical considering the source. In executing add-on acquisitions to existing portfolio companies, there are often degrees of synergy and redundancy conducive to integrating entities post-acquisition. These near-term acquisition synergies (back-office consolidation, vendor pricing leverage, departing executive salaries, etc.) can drive early EBITDA gains.

I recall a specific add-on acquisition where the opportunity for early EBITDA arbitrage was unmistakable. Summarizing the situation, one of my PE colleagues, "Pete," noted, "There's a significant amount of EBITDA we can capture within the first six months through integration efforts."

Another colleague, "Carl," added, "The multiple we're paying for this business is at least a full turn lower," referencing a "turn" as a multiple of EBITDA relative to the purchase price valuation.

Pete responded, "We have to be doing this deal for more than just the EBITDA arbitrage."

To which Carl, half-jokingly but making his point, replied, "Yes, but *the action is the juice*. And there's a lot of juice in EBITDA arbitrage."

I could barely control myself, thinking about how different my Ivy League-educated colleagues were compared to the nefarious characters played by DeNiro and Sizemore. I have always appreciated the idioms and resultant levity my colleagues bring, making the often fast paced and stressful environment much more enjoyable.

1. BEAR TRAP

In any context, a "bear trap" doesn't convey a positive situation. Indeed, it lives up to its name, particularly in finance, where it signifies getting ensnared in a misread future scenario. An example of this is a false indication of a market reversal from a depressed state to an upward trend or accelerated recovery, potentially deceiving unsuspecting investors. The "bear trap" scenario can manifest in various asset categories, including equities, bonds, futures, commodities, and currencies.

I first encountered the term "bear trap" amid the peak of the Covid-19 pandemic. I independently identified a potential PE platform investment opportunity in a medical device manufacturing company called "Diamond." While Diamond had faced a downturn in demand for its services due to the reduction in elective surgical procedures during the pandemic, it strategically leveraged its manufacturing capacity and technology to pivot into producing high-quality N95 surgical masks. The company secured significant government and private contracts, leading to a substantial increase in revenues and profits, surpassing any performance attributed to their medical device manufacturing before the pandemic. Diamond continued to invest capital to expand its mask manufacturing operations, including additional floor space, equipment, and cleanrooms to meet demand for masks. Naturally, the founder had valuation expectations based on the elevated EBITDA, which had a significant contribution from the mask segment.

The future demand for masks became a notable concern for this deal. While deliberating on the investment opportunity, a colleague on the investment deal team expressed, "Diamond is right in our strike zone for contract manufacturing, but the new mask business line is a bit of a wildcard. There's a finite life associated with the mask revenue trajectory. If we pay an elevated multiple based on EBITDA contribution from the mask products, then we're setting ourselves up to step into a *bear trap* when the pandemic subsides and there's an inevitable decrease in demand for masks."

I proposed valuing the business on a composite basis, applying one multiple to the non-mask EBITDA and a lower multiple to the mask-derived EBITDA. We submitted an Indication of Interest (IOI) using this approach, but ultimately, we were outbid by another buyer who anchored their offer to the inflated EBITDA that included the temporary boost from mask-related revenue.

8. CALL THE BOTTOM

My first encounter with the phrase "call the bottom" certainly elicited a chuckle. I heard this gem during diligence on a target company providing services to pharmaceutical and biotech firms. The company had experienced steady growth for several years and ended 2023 with strong revenue and EBITDA performance. However, as we dug into the details, client by client, we discovered that several were dissolving due to clinical failures. In addition, the broader market was showing signs of strain. The downturn in venture funding for pharma and biotech throughout 2023 had begun to put real pressure on outsourcing budgets.

Coming off the pandemic-fueled boom, the sector had entered a more subdued phase. Venture capital slowed, IPO windows tightened, and spending pulled back. But by the end of 2023, a flicker of optimism began to emerge. Analysts were cautiously predicting a rebound in 2024, fueled by the significant reserves of venture capital still sitting on the sidelines, growing IPO and M&A momentum, and large pharmaceutical companies needing to replenish their pipelines as patent cliffs loomed.

In private equity, when evaluating any potential investment, the deal team typically builds a set of financial cases (base, downside, and upside) to compare with management's multi-year projections. Our valuation work and investment thesis are usually anchored in the base case. In this instance, our diligence led us to forecast a revenue decline in 2024, followed by a rebound beginning in 2025. Management, however, projected uninterrupted growth, with no dip in performance.

As we reviewed our findings, a younger colleague who was not part of the core deal team posed a sincere and slightly theatrical question: "How do you *call the bottom*? What assumptions are you making?" It was the first time I'd heard the phrase used that way, but its meaning was instantly clear. His priceless delivery, somewhere between earnest inquiry and Gordon Gekko impersonation, made it especially memorable.

In this context, "calling the bottom" referred to the art and guesswork of predicting when the market for early-stage pharma venture investment would turn. A rebound would mean fresh funding for biotech companies, renewed demand for outsourced services, and a lift for our target company's revenue and EBITDA.

Getting that call right can create enormous value. Investors who accurately identify a market bottom can acquire assets at attractive valuations and ride the wave of recovery. But the risk is equally significant. A mistimed call can lead to poor performance or losses. In my experience, seasoned investors focus less on trying to time the bottom perfectly and more on long-term fundamentals, diversification, and building resilience into their investment theses.

9. HIGH BAUD RATE

In telecommunications and electronics, the "baud rate" is a fundamental measure of the speed at which data is transmitted between devices. It represents the number of signal units, or symbols, transmitted per second. While highly technical, this term took on unexpected charm when I first heard it used in a PE setting.

In both venture capital and PE, junior team members such as Analysts and Associates in particular often work at a relentless pace, with little separation between professional and personal time. Evenings, weekends, and holidays are often consumed by deadlines and diligence work. This intensity is not limited to junior staff; it tends to permeate most of the investment team.

During a conversation about the outstanding performance of "Petra", an Associate who had recently carried a heavy diligence load on a deal, a colleague commented, "Petra has an incredible work ethic. She's operating at a really *high baud rate*. She's a tremendous asset to the team."

As with many clever idioms in our industry, it took a second to sink in. But once it clicked, I found it both amusing and surprisingly accurate. Comparing Petra's focus and drive to a high baud rate conveyed that she was working in a machine-like manner at maximum throughput—efficient, precise, and seemingly tireless, much like a high-speed data transmission.

Since then, I've thought about using the analogy myself. It's smart, memorable, and technically apt. But I have to admit, it still strikes me as just quirky enough that I usually stop short. Maybe one day I'll work it into a sentence with a straight face.

10. HIDE THE BRUSH STROKES

The concept of "hide the brush strokes" reminds me of another phrase often heard in PE: "It's never a straight line up and to the right," the latter of which I describe subsequently. Both expressions capture a fundamental truth; success rarely follows a clean, predictable path. Just as an artist creates a painting with countless deliberate and sometimes messy brushstrokes, building a successful company requires a series of complex, behind-the-scenes decisions, adjustments, and recoveries from setbacks. The idea of "hiding the brush strokes" refers to presenting a polished, seamless result to outsiders—investors, clients, and potential buyers—while concealing the struggle and imperfection that went into achieving it.

In business, particularly in PE, this mindset is commonplace. Whether you're the CEO navigating operational turmoil, or a board member helping steer a company through customer issues, team turnover, or missed forecasts, the work is often messy, stressful, and filled with ambiguity. And yet, the final presentation, whether in a board deck, an investor update, or a Confidential Information Memorandum (CIM) for a potential exit tells a different story. It highlights growth, momentum, market opportunity, and leadership strength, while quietly smoothing over the detours, mistakes, and tough calls that shaped the outcome.

Having served both as a CEO and as a board member for several PE-backed companies, I've accumulated my fair share of battle scars. The journey to a successful exit is rarely glamorous. It requires relentless focus, strong execution across every function, assembling the right leadership team, and, if we're being honest, a little bit of luck. But when we recount those experiences, whether in an investor meeting or a conversation with a new portfolio company, we tend to emphasize the highlights. We don't dwell on the late night or weekend calls, the reorgs that didn't go as planned, or the near-misses on revenue. We focus on the outcome. That's the essence of hiding the brush strokes.

A colleague once put it perfectly: "Investors don't want to see how the sausage is made. They just want to know it tastes good." That's especially true in PE, where there's a strong emphasis on results. The rough edges get sanded down. The final portrait is what matters.

In the end, "hide the brush strokes" isn't about dishonesty. It's about framing. It's about communicating with clarity and confidence, knowing your audience, and understanding that success, even if hard-won, is best remembered for how it ends, not how chaotic the middle was.

11. PUT MORE WOOD BEHIND THE ARROW

The phrase "put more wood behind the arrow" is a vivid metaphor that conveys the idea of adding greater substance, energy, or resources to a particular effort in order to increase its chances of success. It encourages a focused commitment, doubling down on something with the belief that the added force will yield a better outcome. In archery, the strength and impact of an arrow depend on both the tension in the bow and the quality of the arrow itself. In this analogy, the "wood" refers to the arrow's material, and putting more wood behind it implies fortifying the effort with something stronger, more forceful, and more deliberate.

I first heard the phrase used in a PE setting during a strategy session about a potential investment opportunity. As the team examined different facets of the opportunity, one colleague pointed out a niche subsegment that hadn't been thoroughly explored but showed early signs of potential. The room grew quiet as people considered the idea. Then another colleague, leaning forward with noticeable energy, said, "This could be very interesting. We should roll up our sleeves and dig deeper. Let's *put more wood behind the arrow*. I think it's worth the time investment."

In that moment, the phrase clicked. The "wood" represented not just time, but investment team hours, subject matter experts, deeper market mapping, and a broader lens on competitive dynamics; all the resources we would need to push forward with more confidence and clarity. It signaled a shift from passive interest to active pursuit.

Although it was the first time I had heard the expression, it struck me as both clever and purposeful. Since then, I've come to appreciate it as a concise way to describe the decision to escalate effort toward a promising path. It's not about being reckless or impulsive, but rather about recognizing when something deserves a stronger push and the willingness to commit the resources to see it through.

12. TRYING TO HOLD A BEACHBALL UNDER WATER

The Covid-19 pandemic had a profound and complex impact on companies in the healthcare and life sciences sectors. While it placed extraordinary stress on nearly every aspect of the healthcare system, the effects on hospitals and the in-vitro diagnostics sector were particularly dramatic, but in starkly different ways.

Clinicians and hospital executives I've spoken with shared first-hand accounts of the chaos and emotional toll inside their institutions. Hospitals were overrun with patients, short on staff and beds, and forced to operate under quarantine protocols with limited access to diagnostics and therapeutics. The resulting financial strain was severe and long-lasting. Hospitals faced early retirements, widespread burn-out, and persistent absenteeism, ultimately leading to an increased reliance on travel nurses and contract clinical staff at premium hourly rates. When word of these inflated rates spread, full-time employees understandably demanded pay parity, adding more pressure to already fragile budgets. For some institutions, the financial burden proved insurmountable.

In contrast, the pandemic created an extraordinary boom for the diagnostics sector. While these companies also faced operational hurdles such as workforce limitations, supply chain disruptions, and sourcing challenges for raw materials, reagents, and consumables, they simultaneously experienced an unprecedented surge in demand for SARS-CoV-2 testing. Fueled by emergency government funding, venture investment, and fast-tracked regulatory approvals, diagnostics companies ramped up R&D, expanded production, and introduced innovative point-of-care and lab-based tests at record speed.

This demand shock opened the door to rapid growth, strategic acquisitions, and sustained investor interest. In a conversation with a partner at another PE firm who had backed a diagnostics company just before the pandemic, he described the experience with amazement: "I've never seen anything like this. The demand is like *trying to hold a beach ball underwater*. It's incredible." He continued, "Our company is flush with cash. We're going to have to figure out how to deploy it. No doubt we'll be on an add-on acquisition spree."

The metaphor of "trying to hold a beach ball underwater" was new to me, but it perfectly captured the intensity of the moment and the sheer force of market demand that simply couldn't be contained. For diagnostic companies supplying critical components like reagents, test kits, and controls, the challenge wasn't creating demand, but scaling fast enough to meet it.

Navigating this surge required swift, agile management and strategic foresight. Companies had to rapidly innovate, scale manufacturing, manage complex logistics, and maintain customer service amid extraordinary operational pressure. The pandemic created a once-in-a-generation business environment; one that rewarded those who could rise to the occasion and execute with speed and precision.

For many diagnostic companies, this period served as a launchpad. By adapting to meet the "rising beach ball" of demand, they not only survived the volatility but positioned themselves for long-term market leadership in a post-pandemic world.

13. SUNDAY NIGHT CULTURE

Much like the role of a corporate CEO or entrepreneur, a career in PE demands an exceptional work ethic and often leaves little room for the notion of work-life balance. Success in this field requires complete immersion, a genuine passion for the chase, and unwavering dedication to surpassing goals. This level of commitment frequently comes at the cost of personal downtime. Being available during vacations, or skipping them altogether, becomes the norm. At various points in my career, my life was fully centered around my CEO responsibilities and the success of the businesses I led, often at the expense of spending valuable time with my family.

Although I thrived in that high-intensity environment and truly enjoyed my work, I now recognize that my work addiction came with a steep opportunity cost. Time with family and friends was sometimes lost to the demands of the job. Fortunately, I had a spouse who understood this compulsion and supported me through it. I regularly worked late into the night, not out of obligation, but because I was energized by the work and eager to return to it the following day. I gravitated toward colleagues with a similar mindset, especially in my CEO roles, where we believed we were on the cusp of transforming healthcare through technologies that had the potential to impact millions of lives. The possibility of significant financial rewards was certainly a motivating factor, but the mission itself often felt just as compelling.

Over time, I came to believe that the health of an organization's culture could be measured by how people felt about Monday mornings on a Sunday night. One of my PE colleagues referred to this as "Sunday night culture." When employees feel anxiety, dread, or emotional fatigue as the weekend draws to a close, it is often a symptom of deeper issues. These may include high stress levels, burnout, lack of growth opportunities, or a toxic work environment. In contrast, when people are working on meaningful projects alongside colleagues they respect—and when the culture encourages learning, challenge, and camaraderie—Sunday night feels different. The anticipation of Monday morning becomes manageable, even exciting.

I can say with confidence that, with few exceptions, I rarely experienced the Sunday night blues when I was working on breakthrough technologies and surrounded by executive teams and Boards I admired. That same positive energy has followed me into private equity, where the intellectual engagement and mission-driven focus have kept Monday mornings from feeling like a burden.

From an organizational behavior standpoint, addressing *Sunday night culture* is essential to building a healthier and more resilient workplace. This is especially important in high-performance environments like private equity and entrepreneurial ventures, where expectations run high and the pace is relentless. The tone is set at the top. CEOs and executive teams have a responsibility to shape a culture that encourages balance, fosters transparency, and invests in employee development. Promoting well-being, offering clear paths for career growth, and ensuring workloads are sustainable can have a profound effect on team morale and long-term performance.

Achieving this balance is not easy. It requires continuous effort, honest reflection, and thoughtful leadership. But in the long run, it is one of the most important investments a leadership team can make.

14. ELEPHANTS DO EAT PEANUTS

I've often encountered the metaphor "elephants do eat peanuts" to describe how large, market-leading companies enter smaller market segments in pursuit of incremental growth. In this analogy, "elephants" represent the big, well-established firms with vast resources and a dominant market presence, while "peanuts" symbolize the smaller, niche markets that are often overlooked or underserved.

The phrase emphasizes a strategic reality: although these larger companies typically focus on high-revenue opportunities, they're not above targeting smaller segments if the return justifies the effort. Even modest wins can help fill gaps in market share or support broader strategic goals. The implication is clear that large companies, once sufficiently motivated, will pursue smaller markets that were once the safe havens of niche players.

I first came across this metaphor while evaluating a potential investment in a technology-enabled healthcare services company. As is often the case in PE, we were assessing a lower middle-market business with differentiated technology and a growing customer base. In healthcare, these companies frequently begin by serving smaller community hospitals or medical centers, eventually working their way into larger academic or tertiary care systems.

As part of our diligence process, we examined the usual mix of risk factors, including what I refer to as the "belief factors" which are the foundational elements that must be in place to justify moving forward with an investment. One recurring concern was the presence of several billion-dollar players in the broader market. These companies had already established dominance among the largest healthcare providers.

But with those relationships often saturated, the natural next move for them would be to look further down market in search of new revenue.

In one internal conversation, after I raised this possibility, a colleague nodded and said, "I agree. I also worry about larger players moving down market. *Elephants do eat peanuts.* Revenue is revenue, and that risk is real. If we're going to move forward, we need to get comfortable with that."

His comment stuck with me. It captured both the threat and the reality of the investment landscape. Larger players may not start out interested in smaller markets, but they are perfectly capable of pivoting if the strategic rationale becomes compelling.

The metaphor serves as an important message: niche businesses can be vulnerable once they gain traction. What looks like a safe space today may become tomorrow's battleground. As investors, we must not only evaluate a company's current position but also anticipate how the competitive landscape could shift and whether the business has what it takes to withstand that pressure.

15. THE SWAN

What binds my colleagues with whom I've interacted in PE is a shared set of qualities: an unrelenting work ethic, a clear drive for success, a pragmatic mindset, and a strong sense of ownership. Before transitioning into PE, I had the good fortune of working in environments where many executives exhibited these same traits. Those who didn't often had short-lived tenures under my leadership.

What stands out most about my PE peers, however, is not just their dedication or intelligence. It's their ability to remain composed under pressure. No matter how intense the workload, how tight the deadline, or how high the stakes, they rarely appear rattled. There's a steadiness to the way they operate that I deeply admire.

One moment that captured this perfectly came during a discussion about closing an investment deal within the narrow timeframe of a Letter of Intent. We were juggling resource constraints and trying to assign responsibilities. One of my colleagues noted that "Sean" would be leading the due diligence and carrying the heaviest load. With a hint of admiration, he said, "Sean never ceases to amaze me. He's a *swan*. You'd never know he's at capacity."

The analogy of the "swan" beautifully captured the essence of this individual's demeanor. Like a swan gliding gracefully above the water's surface, his calm exterior belied the vigorous activity occurring beneath – akin to the swan's feet paddling with great intensity. This clever comparison was not only astute but also served as a perfect portrayal of the individual's contribution within our team.

16. PULL AN INSIDE STRAIGHT

An inside straight draw, also known as a gutshot or belly buster, occurs in poker when a player holds four of the five cards needed for a straight, with one card missing from the middle of the sequence. For example, a hand like 4-5-x-7-8 is just one card short of a straight, needing a 6 to complete it. That 6 could be in any suit—clubs, hearts, diamonds, or spades—giving the player only four possible outs. The objective in "pulling an inside straight" is to draw that one precise card that fills the gap and completes the hand. Because the odds of drawing that exact card are low, the strategy is considered risky and often ill-advised.

In PE investing, I first heard the metaphor "pulling an inside straight" during diligence for an opportunity my colleagues and I had grown unusually attached to early in the process. The market segment was attractive, the founding team was impressive, and many of the operating metrics looked strong. But several major red flags persisted, challenges we couldn't rationalize away, despite our emotional investment.

During a particularly candid discussion, one of my colleagues, a sharp thinker with a healthy dose of skepticism and a talent for cutting through noise, offered a reality check. He said, "Guys, I share your enthusiasm for this deal, but we can't ignore the facts. You're basically trying to *pull an inside straight*. This one's not going to make it past the investment committee."

The metaphor landed. In poker, and in investing, relying on a sequence of improbable events to achieve success rarely ends well. "Pulling an inside straight" may sound bold, even heroic, but more often, it's just a bad bet.

11. WOOD TO CHOP

The acquisition due diligence process in PE involves a deep and methodical examination of nearly every operational aspect of a business. This includes financial analysis, market research, operational reviews, customer diligence, legal and regulatory checks, and assessments of the management team, among other areas. While it's important to stay engaged and optimistic throughout, experienced investors know to keep early enthusiasm in check.

I recall a moment during an internal discussion when a colleague reminded the team just how much remained to be uncovered before reaching a decision. He said, "It's premature to push for a vote or decide whether to proceed with this deal. I'm leaning favorably, but there's still a significant amount of *wood to chop*. We have much more to learn."

The phrase "wood to chop" is often used in our line of work. It represents the tasks, hurdles, or unresolved issues that must be addressed before moving forward, whether that's submitting an Indication of Interest, Letter of Intent, or closing the transaction. It's a lesson that even when things look promising, there is still meaningful work to be done before an investment is ready to proceed.

18. GAMBLING CHIPS DRESSED UP LIKE FINANCIAL ASSETS

Although the topic fell outside of my core investment focus in PE, I fondly recall a dinner with a group of investors in PE funds where the conversation took an unexpected turn. Around the table, we began by discussing the economic climate, various asset classes, and our individual risk tolerance. Eventually, someone brought up cryptocurrency, prompting a wide range of opinions.

Everyone at the table had at least some familiarity with digital currencies, some more than others. I understood the basic premise:

cryptocurrency was designed to function as money and a method of payment, independent of any central authority. It eliminated the need for third-party intermediaries in financial transactions.

Personally, I've always believed that if I can't fully understand an asset and become comfortable with its risks, I have no business investing in it. One individual at the table shared a decidedly bullish perspective, especially on Bitcoin. He spoke enthusiastically about its potential for high returns, the appeal of decentralization, and its role in portfolio diversification. He even mentioned that he had committed a meaningful portion of his personal wealth to it.

Others, however, voiced concerns about its extreme volatility, lack of regulation, cybersecurity risks, and overall speculative nature.

After I shared my own cautious stance, the person seated next to me leaned in, lowered his voice, and said, "Crypto is basically *gambling chips dressed up as financial assets*. I'm with you. I wouldn't go near it."

His description captured my gut instinct perfectly. It reminded me of a Warren Buffett interview I once saw, where he called cryptocurrency "rat poison." Between that image and the caution expressed by others at the table, I had all the confirmation I needed to stay away.

19. SEWAGE LAGOON

Reflecting on the first time I heard the term "sewage lagoon," I'm immediately reminded of a memorable due diligence case in PE. We were evaluating a company that, on paper, seemed like a promising opportunity. It operated in a healthcare subsegment we had been actively targeting and had a track record of consistent revenue growth, even amid internal dysfunction. At first glance, it looked like a hidden gem.

Then we dug deeper.

What we uncovered during due diligence was a parade of red flags: chronic employee turnover, persistent service quality issues, little to no management oversight, and sustained downward pricing pressure. Practically every corner of the business was in disarray. And yet, somehow, the company kept growing. It was as if the business had found a way to succeed despite itself.

The team began to debate whether we could fix the foundation and unlock real value. It would require a total overhaul: new leadership, strong operating controls, tighter financial discipline, and a serious cultural reset. But not everyone was on board.

One colleague didn't hesitate to share his view. During a deal team meeting, he shrugged and said, "I get that it's in a sector we like, but I wouldn't touch this one. It's a *sewage lagoon*. Do we really want to sign up for scrubbing out a cesspool?"

The imagery was blunt—but it stuck.

Another team member chimed in: "Even if we rebuilt the management team and fixed operations, we still couldn't control pricing pressure or fend off better-funded competitors. Too many things are out of our hands."

The group reached consensus. We passed.

20. HAIR ON THE DEAL

I've come to appreciate that in PE, when someone says there's "hair on the deal," they're not talking about a minor cosmetic issue. In our world, "hair" refers to the messy, complicated, or risky elements lurking beneath the surface of a potential acquisition. It's shorthand for anything that could make the deal harder to close, more difficult to manage post-close, or less appealing altogether.

This "hair" can take many forms: customer concentration, pricing pressure, shaky leadership, high employee turnover, suspect growth projections—you name it. If it can cause a headache, it counts.

Importantly, hair on a deal doesn't always mean it's a dealbreaker. But it does mean we need to lean in, do our homework, and sometimes get creative. The diligence process becomes less about checking boxes and more about playing detective: What's the root cause? Can we fix it? How much risk are we really taking on and at what price?

I recall a meeting during which a colleague opened the discussion by stating, "There is *hair on the deal* for sure."

This prompted another to toss out, "There's definitely hair on this one," after which the reaction in the room was telling.

Sometimes it's a knowing nod that indicates, "Let's get to work." Other times, it's more of a grimace, like someone just found a fly floating in their soup.

In the end, every firm has its own tolerance for risk, and every investor has their own definition of acceptable "hair." The seasoned ones get good at spotting it early, knowing which tangles can be trimmed and which ones are better left alone.

21. RACE TO THE BOTTOM

My experience with PE investment metrics has taught me that companies with capable management, a sustainable business model, and significant growth opportunities are highly preferred targets. These companies typically offer differentiated services or products that allow them to command premium pricing. Companies that must solely compete on price to win business typically wouldn't progress beyond the initial diligence stage with the investment firms in which I've been involved.

The phrase "race to the bottom" describes a situation in which companies compete by attempting to offer the lowest prices to gain a competitive advantage. This often involves tactics like cutting corners, implementing short-term cost-cutting measures, overlooking quality, or lowering wages to become the cheapest option in the market.

I first heard this phrase used in a private equity setting while serving on the board of a tech-enabled healthcare company. During a meeting with the CEO, we were reviewing pricing strategy for a major opportunity involving a large potential customer. We found ourselves locked in a bidding contest with a competitor, and the prospect was openly sharing our rival's pricing in an attempt to squeeze more concessions from us.

One of my fellow board members, a seasoned PE investor with little patience for gamesmanship, didn't mince words: "We shouldn't play this pricing game. It's just a *race to the bottom*. At this point, we're basically negotiating against ourselves."

The CEO nodded in agreement. "We offer better performance and better service. The customer needs to understand that you get what you pay for. If we cave on price and erode our margins, we risk setting a lower benchmark in the market and word will get around. We're standing firm with our quote."

After a pause, he smirked and added, "If we lose the deal, I'm betting they'll be back within the year after they experience our competitor's idea of 'value.'"

22. CHOP THE BEAK OFF

In my experience, service-oriented companies in the healthcare sector, whether in contract medical device manufacturing, pharmaceutical services, or tech-enabled platforms, often rely on a mix of full-time employees and independent contractors. In the U.S., these contractors are commonly referred to as "1099s," a nod to IRS Form 1099-NEC used to report non-employee compensation.

Deciding between full-time hires and independent contractors isn't a simple either-or choice. It depends on a range of factors, including company goals, project scope, industry dynamics, and organizational structure. Contractors can offer clear advantages: specialized expertise for short-term initiatives, flexibility in scaling the workforce, cost savings from not having to provide benefits, and access to talent outside the company's geographic footprint. On the flip side, they can also bring challenges, such as lower alignment with company culture, reduced loyalty or accountability, weaker team cohesion, higher hourly rates, and short-term availability.

I remember one board meeting for a portfolio company where we were debating how best to scale the operations team. The management team had proposed a hybrid approach, but some board members leaned more heavily toward the contractor model. One colleague, a firm believer in the 1099 strategy, summed up his view with a line that stuck with me: "We can scale up fast using 1099s, and when the projects wrap, we just *chop the beak off* the expense line. There's no tail."

His vivid, if slightly aggressive, phrasing got a laugh, but it underscored a key advantage of the model: cost control. The ability to ramp resources up or down quickly can be a strategic lever, especially in project-based or growth-phase environments.

Of course, using independent contractors comes with its own set of responsibilities. It's critical to properly classify workers to avoid running afoul of labor laws and to manage the balance between flexibility and continuity. In many cases, the best path forward involves a thoughtful blend of employees and contractors, tailored to the company's needs and stage of growth.

23. SANDPAPERING

Throughout this book, I've emphasized just how deep PE firms dig during the acquisition process. The level of diligence intensifies as the engagement moves from the Indication of Interest (IOI) to the Letter of Intent (LOI), and ultimately to deal close. Every functional area of the business is put under the microscope to evaluate strengths, weaknesses, risks, and opportunities. While this scrutiny is never meant to be personal, it can catch founders and management teams off guard. The sheer volume and depth of the trust-but-verify process can feel relentless.

PE firms must walk a fine line. Pushing too hard can create friction, and if the deal goes through, that friction doesn't magically disappear. It becomes baggage in a long-term partnership. When an investment banker is involved on the sell side, the banker typically helps prepare the founders for what's ahead, setting expectations and offering some emotional insulation. But in proprietary deals sourced directly by the PE firm, that buffer is missing. And in either scenario, things can get tense.

I recall one diligence process for a potential new platform investment where we had developed a strong relationship with the co-founders, signed an exclusive Letter of Intent (LOI), and were deeply into our diligence work. That's when a disagreement emerged over how many customer interviews were needed to complete our commercial assessment.

The co-founders couldn't have been more different. Rick was a charismatic, big-picture thinker, focused on customer relationships and business development. Diane, his counterpart, was a sharp, meticulous operator who was calm, structured, and quietly formidable. Rick had a knack for using humor to cut tension, a skill that came in handy during the diligence process.

As we continued to push for more customer calls, even after already receiving glowing feedback, Rick's patience began to wear thin. He worried that too much outreach might spook their clients or raise unwanted questions about the future of the company under

PE ownership. That fear is not uncommon; diligence can create real anxiety for founders, especially when their customer relationships are at the center of the business.

During one particularly pointed conversation, Rick, visibly frustrated, leaned forward, threw up his hands, and said, "You guys are really *sandpapering* us here. I don't see how talking to five more customers is going to change anything. They'll all say the same thing. It's not going to move the needle."

"Sandpapering" was the perfect word for what the relentless diligence process must have felt like to him. It struck me as both funny and accurate. From the PE side, we were just doing our job. From his side, it probably felt like we were rubbing the same spot over and over, wearing down his patience one grit level at a time.

Ironically, I'd been on Rick's side of the table many times earlier in my career as a seller. I knew what it felt like to be poked, prodded, and questioned into exhaustion, while at the same time trying to run a business. Sandpaper may smooth wood, but too much of it leaves you raw. That moment reminded me that while diligence is essential, empathy is too. Founders are often emotionally invested in what they've built, and it's important to recognize when the process starts to feel less like careful validation and more like abrasion.

24. HARD LANDING

In aviation, landings don't always go as planned. Sometimes, they're smooth and uneventful. Other times, they're anything but—especially in bad weather. Most seasoned business travelers have at least one story involving white-knuckle turbulence, aborted approaches, or bone-jarring touchdowns that make you question your life choices.

I vividly remember one such flight during a fierce rain and windstorm. As we descended, the plane pitched and rolled like a carnival ride. We lurched from side to side and bounced through the air as if riding on potholes. When we finally touched down, it wasn't graceful. The wheels slammed the runway with a bang, and the reverse thrusters roared to life as the aircraft shuddered to a halt.

By chance, I was seated next to an off-duty pilot catching a ride to his next assignment. He turned to me, gave a wry grin, and said, "Captain must've been Navy. That felt like an aircraft carrier landing—hard, but effective."

PE has its own version of this. Deals, negotiations, or exits don't always glide to a clean and gentle close. They can—and often do—end in what we call a *hard landing*. I've heard the "hard landing" phrase plenty over the years, and it means exactly what it sounds like.

Maybe you're negotiating with a seller or their investment banker and the deal takes a turn for the worse. Maybe your bid was used to draw out a better offer from a favored buyer. Or maybe you're on the sell side, and a long-planned exit unravels due to market shifts, buyer retrades, or performance hiccups. Despite the most careful diligence, things can veer off course fast.

A *hard landing* in PE, much like in aviation, isn't just unpleasant, it can leave you rattled. There's no graceful spin or PR gloss that makes it better. You just brace, hold on, and hope the wheels stay on the runway.

25. SELLING PICKS AND SHOVELS TO GOLD MINERS

In my experience with PE, our investment mandate is firmly rooted in avoiding "binary risk." That means steering clear of early-stage pharmaceutical ventures, single-product medical device and diagnostic companies, and similar high-stakes bets where the outcome is essentially all or nothing. Instead, I have focused for example on pharmaceutical services such as bioanalytical labs, contract development and manufacturing organizations, clinical research organizations, and other service-based platforms that support the broader drug development ecosystem.

This strategy doesn't erase all market risk, but it does move us away from the nerve-wracking cliff edge of product success versus failure.

During a meeting, a colleague summed up our approach with a line that stuck with me: "We *sell picks and shovels to the gold miners.*" The metaphor draws from the California Gold Rush of 1848, when more than 300,000 people raced westward in search of fortune after gold was discovered at Sutter's Mill. While most miners never struck it rich, the real wealth often went to those supplying the tools, services, and infrastructure—things the miners couldn't do without.

That's exactly how we view I have come to view investments in pharmaceutical services. By supporting the companies that enable drug and biotechology development, we benefit from the broader industry tailwinds without having to place a single, all-or-nothing bet on a specific therapy making it to market. It's a way to ride the wave without building the surfboard.

We're not chasing gold—we're backing the general store.

26. BEST HOUSE IN A BAD NEIGHBORHOOD

I've found the phrase "best house in a bad neighborhood" to be a highly effective way to describe a situation where something stands out positively despite being surrounded by unfavorable conditions. In business, it captures the contrast between the strong fundamentals of a specific company and the broader challenges of the industry or environment in which it operates.

One memorable example came while evaluating a PE investment opportunity in a Florida-based home healthcare company. At first glance, the deal was appealing. The founder had already lined up several potential add-on acquisitions to pursue after our investment in the core platform. He had negotiated Letters of Intent with these companies at very modest valuations, and they were all eager to join a larger organization. His ability to corral these targets was impressive.

However, we had no prior investments in home healthcare, and there was healthy skepticism among the team. The sector carried a reputation for trouble such as concerns about Medicare fraud, unpredictable reimbursement levels from insurance payers, and persistent difficulty in recruiting and retaining visiting nurses. Despite these headwinds, the opportunity had real appeal: it was proprietary, without an investment banker in the middle, and our relationship with the founder gave us exclusive access. On top of that, the potential for EBITDA multiple arbitrage through the pre-negotiated add-ons was compelling.

We decided to dig deeper, refreshing our understanding of the home healthcare landscape and engaging the founder for more diligence materials. While the business itself had strong fundamentals, one of my colleagues just couldn't get past the industry stigma. In a follow-up meeting to determine whether we'd proceed, he voiced his concerns bluntly:

"I get the appeal and the potential for arbitrage, but this feels like the *best house in a bad neighborhood*. I'm still uncomfortable with the reimbursement risks and the sector's overall reputation."

While I didn't fully share his view, I couldn't help but admire the clarity and humor of the phrase. It perfectly captured the tension between the opportunity's strengths and the environment's weaknesses. In the end, we passed on the investment, but that expression became a keeper in my personal glossary of deal idioms.

27. SNAP THE CHALK LINE

Over time, I've come to interpret the phrase "snap the chalk line" as a useful metaphor for establishing a clear and definitive boundary, much like in construction or carpentry, where a chalk line is snapped to mark a straight reference line across a surface. That initial mark serves as a guide for everything that follows.

When I first heard the phrase used in a PE context, it caught me off guard. I found it oddly amusing, but it also made me think more deeply about its practical meaning. In PE, "snapping the chalk line" generally refers to drawing a firm line around the scope of a project or wrapping up diligence in a particular area. It signals that we've gathered enough information to make a decision and that it's time to stop expanding the inquiry.

I remember a colleague saying during a diligence call, "Let's just *snap the chalk line* here and move on to the next area." It was his way of saying: we've done enough on this front, let's stay focused and avoid chasing tangents.

In the PE setting, the phrase represents discipline. It's about defining what's in scope, sticking to that framework, and knowing when to call it. Especially during due diligence, it's easy to get pulled in by new information and fall into the trap of endless digging. Snapping the chalk line helps ensure the process remains focused, efficient, and aligned with the investment thesis. It's a subtle but powerful cue to keep things moving without losing precision.

28. BAD BOX

Investment diligence runs the gamut from gut instincts to complex quantitative models involving multiple independent variables. The term "bad box" was unfamiliar to me until I entered the world of PE.

I first heard it while on an investment deal team evaluating downside scenarios during the height of the Covid-19 pandemic.

We were evaluating a company in the contract manufacturing space for diagnostics. While customer concentration wasn't a major red flag, there was serious concern about the stability of raw material supply chains, particularly for key inputs sourced from China. Several essential materials were sole-sourced, and any disruption could have serious consequences. Introducing alternate suppliers would involve lengthy revalidation processes and open the door to new risks such as inconsistent performance, higher costs, extended lead times, quality issues, or rigid minimum order quantities.

As we debated the extent of the risk, one of my colleagues voiced concern, saying, "Sole sourcing is a real issue here. There are too many single points of failure. If these supply chain problems continue and this company starts facing price hikes or, worse, long delivery delays, we'll all be in a *bad box*."

Another teammate chimed in: "You can see how this could take the company down. There's a lot here we can't control."

The phrase "bad box" immediately reminded me of the "penalty box" in hockey, where a player is taken off the ice for a set period of time. But in this case, the consequences could last far longer. For this company, a major supply disruption wouldn't just mean a temporary setback but rather could present and existential threat to the business.

29. LANDING LIGHTS

The concept of "landing lights" comes from aviation, where illuminated markers along a runway guide an aircraft to a safe and precise landing. In business, landing lights serve a similar purpose providing clear signals that help steer decisions toward a successful outcome. These markers might include favorable market trends, strong customer feedback, competitive differentiation, or the achievement of key milestones.

I first encountered the phrase during an investment evaluation involving multiple diligence workstreams. We were deep in discussions when a colleague, scanning a whiteboard filled with timelines, metrics, and risk factors, said, "We need *landing lights* here if we're going to land this investment safely."

The metaphor stuck. What he meant was clear. We needed visibility across every critical area of diligence before feeling confident in moving forward. That meant comprehensive workplans covering financial performance, market positioning, customer validation, regulatory risks, competitive landscape, and long-term growth levers. Without those lights in place, we'd be flying blind.

Since then, I've come to appreciate the phrase as a reminder that the strength of any investment thesis depends on how well we illuminate the path. Good data, reliable indicators, and structured analysis function like those runway lights keeping the team aligned and helping us avoid crash landings.

30. LANDING GEAR

In aviation, the landing gear enables an aircraft to taxi, take off, and most importantly land safely. It's more than just wheels; it's the shock absorber that cushions the impact and supports braking, making for a smooth and survivable return to terra firma.

In PE, I've heard the term "landing gear" used plenty of times. But it took on real meaning for me during my time as CEO of a medical device company that had just completed successful human clinical trials. As word of our technology began to spread thanks to peer-reviewed publications and conference presentations by influential surgical key opinion leaders (KOLs), we started getting inbound calls from strategic acquirers. These were the household names of our industry, and their interest came as an unexpected (but welcome) surprise. At the time, our focus had been singular: execute on the technology, navigate regulatory pathways, and scale manufacturing. Exit strategy? That was filed under "someday."

During a board meeting where we discussed the sudden uptick in acquisition interest, one of our directors paused, leaned back in his chair, and said, "Look, we've made a ton of progress... but we're flying the plane with no *landing gear.*"

The room went quiet, and I remember smiling, not because it was funny, but because it was uncomfortably accurate. We were so focused on staying airborne that no one had really thought about how, when, or where we'd eventually land. The assumption seemed to be to build a great company, and the rest will take care of itself.

That comment shifted my mindset. Rather than brushing it off as a future challenge or achievement, we took action. Two board members stepped in to quietly engage with the most serious inbound strategic inquiries. We agreed not to engage a banker just yet but wanted to be ready if the right buyer and the right price came along. It was the first time it felt like we had actual "landing gear" deployed which gave us a clear, intentional approach to the end of our journey.

In hindsight, that moment was a turning point. Because while ambition can get you airborne, and execution can keep you aloft, you still need a plan for coming down, and preferably not nose-first.

31. FIND THE RIGHT ALTITUDE AND CATCH THE TAILWINDS

In aviation, a "tailwind" refers to a wind that pushes the aircraft from behind, increasing its ground speed and allowing for faster arrivals. Frequent flyers appreciate tailwinds for the time savings, although they also know such conditions can bring turbulence, prompting pilots to adjust altitude in search of smoother skies. In many ways, crafting and executing a successful business strategy is about finding those favorable conditions and adjusting course to ride them.

In business, a tailwind refers to external factors that support growth, whether through revenue, market share, or profitability. I've been fortunate to experience a few strong tailwinds, both in my CEO roles and as a PE investor. One particularly memorable example was the diligence and eventual PE investment in BioAgilytix, a founder-led pharmaceutical services company that specialized in bioanalytical lab services for large molecule drugs, also known as biologics.

Large molecule drugs are structurally complex therapies made from proteins or nucleic acids; think monoclonal antibodies, peptides, or RNA- and DNA-based treatments. Unlike small molecule drugs, which have simpler chemical structures and are often taken orally, large molecule drugs are typically injected and used to target specific pathways in diseases like cancer, autoimmune conditions, neurological disorders, and rare genetic diseases.

As we conducted diligence on BioAgilytix, we saw clear signs of a tailwind forming. The pharmaceutical industry was dramatically increasing its investment in biologics, and pipelines at major pharma companies were swelling with these large molecule candidates. Add to that the deep scientific expertise of the founder and his team, and we had every reason to dig in.

After signing a Letter of Intent with the founder, we began final diligence and pushed toward closing. The momentum was palpable. During a team meeting, one of my colleagues nailed the moment with a grin: "This company is at the right place at the right time. Large molecules are only going to gain momentum. We're about to *find the right altitude and catch the tailwinds*. Now we just need to build out the team and execute."

And that's exactly what we did. The investment in BioAgilytix became one of the most successful in Riverside Partners' history. More than just a financial win, it was a mission-driven outcome. We built a thriving business, created hundreds of jobs, and supported the development of breakthrough therapies for cancer, rheumatoid arthritis, lupus, and other serious conditions.

We didn't just catch the tailwind—we soared with it.

32. SKATE TO WHERE THE PUCK IS GOING

While I remain convinced that Bobby Orr is the greatest hockey player of all time, I have to give Wayne Gretzky credit for a quote that continues to resonate with me: "I skate to where the puck is going, not where it has been."

Though rooted in hockey, that mindset applies powerfully in PE investing. Understanding the past is important, but the real edge comes from seeing what's next, predicting where the market is heading and positioning accordingly. I've heard this quote used time and again in my career, especially during diligence discussions, and for good reason: it's a concise lesson that success often depends on anticipation rather than reaction.

In PE investing, analyzing industry trends, competitive positioning, and core value drivers is essential. The goal is to recognize the trajectory of a market segment, build a growth plan that aligns with that direction through hiring the right talent, enhancing technology and product offerings, and refining business development and then execute with confidence. This forward-looking approach has been especially critical in sectors like medical devices, where innovation often reshapes entire markets.

For a medical device technology to be truly disruptive, it must fundamentally change the practice of medicine while delivering meaningful advantages to patients, physicians, and insurance payers alike. The ability to foresee where the clinical and economic incentives are heading and to validate that migration is a skill I've worked hard to cultivate across multiple roles.

One of the most striking examples from my executive career occurred during the early 1990s, when the healthcare industry began a major shift toward minimally invasive surgery (MIS). This movement transformed procedures that once required large incisions, general anesthesia, long hospital stays, and a host of associated risks into safer, faster, and more cost-effective alternatives. Endoscopes, laparoscopes, peripheral catheter systems, and eventually robotic platforms enabled procedures that could be performed under local anesthesia, with patients discharged the same day from hospitals or ambulatory surgery centers.

The benefits were clear. Patients recovered faster, physicians operated with greater precision and less risk, and insurance companies saw lower overall costs. That convergence of value set the stage for explosive growth in MIS technologies.

Savvy venture and PE investors recognized the opportunity early. They focused their capital on emerging companies that were pioneering MIS solutions in cardiology, urology, gastroenterology, and other specialties. Large medtech companies followed suit, forming strategic partnerships, making early investments, and often trying to lock in preemptive acquisition rights. In many cases, they acquired promising MIS start-ups at steep valuations, even before FDA clearance.

Some of these bets paid off handsomely. The early movers reaped the rewards as MIS moved from fringe innovation to standard of care, now used across virtually every surgical subspecialty. They didn't chase the puck—they skated to where it was going. That lesson still holds true. In private equity, as in hockey, knowing where the puck is headed can make all the difference.

33. COIN OPERATED

Throughout my career, I've been closely involved in developing and launching numerous medical devices and diagnostic products. One of the most pivotal aspects of this process is securing reimbursement both from government agencies like the Centers for Medicare and Medicaid Services (CMS) and from private payers such as Blue Cross Blue Shield and UnitedHealthcare. While often arduous, this step is critical for achieving broad market adoption.

I vividly remember one instance from my time as CEO of a company preparing to launch a breakthrough minimally invasive medical device. We had just received clearance from the U.S. Food and Drug Administration (FDA), and excitement was building. The device had the potential to transform treatment for a debilitating condition. It offered a host of clinical advantages: shifting from open to minimally invasive procedures, eliminating the need for general anesthesia, enabling same-day discharge instead of prolonged hospital stays, and more.

Soon after FDA clearance, I met with a prominent surgeon who had participated in our clinical trial. He was a nationally recognized thought leader in the field and practiced at one of the country's top academic institutions. I asked if he would present our trial data at an upcoming national conference, and he agreed without hesitation. But then he asked a question that stopped me in my tracks.

"Have you secured insurance reimbursement for the device? Will Medicare and the private payers cover it?"

At the time, reimbursement was still in progress. We had started down the path, but it was going to take at least another year before coverage would be in place. I explained the timeline, and his expression changed. He leaned forward, rubbed his forehead with the palm of his hand, and squinted at me as if I had just told him we were moving the launch to Mars.

"I didn't realize reimbursement was that far off," he said. Then came the part I'll never forget. With a weary smile and the tone of someone sharing a bitter truth, he added, "Mike, you need to understand, physicians are *coin operated*. We only operate when the coin is inserted. The technology is fantastic, no doubt, but if we can't get paid for using it, it doesn't stand a chance. It doesn't have a snowball's chance in hell."

The phrase "coin operated" wasn't new to me. I'd heard it used before to describe commission-driven salespeople. But hearing it from a respected surgeon, about his own profession, was something else entirely. It forced me to step back and reassess an assumption I had long taken for granted: that medicine was always, first and foremost, about doing what was best for the patient.

To be clear, I've had the privilege of working with many physicians who are selfless, inspiring, and wholly committed to improving lives. But that moment revealed a different, more transactional reality, one that perhaps reflects a broader shift in the healthcare system. It raised a difficult question: in an era where financial incentives increasingly drive behavior, what happens when clinical value alone isn't enough to drive adoption?

34. THE JUICE IS NOT WORTH THE SQUEEZE

Over time, I've come to appreciate the lemon as more than just a fruit. It's a surprisingly apt metaphor in the world of PE investing.

Now, I value efficiency. So, in the morning, rather than buying fresh lemons, slicing them, and squeezing them into my ginger tea, I just grab a bottle of lemon juice from the fridge. It's fast, convenient, and gets the job done. But I have friends who swear by the ritual of squeezing fresh lemons, insisting that the flavor, aroma, and experience make the extra effort worthwhile.

This little breakfast preference actually mirrors a much larger principle in PE. In every potential investment, the time, effort, and opportunity cost of diligence are critical. As the diligence process unfolds, parallel workstreams emerge: market assessments, legal reviews, financial modeling, customer calls, and more. The investment team evaluates all of it in real time while deciding whether to submit an Indication of Interest (IOI), which may lead to a management meeting and, if things look promising, a Letter of Intent (LOI) to purchase the company.

Of course, we're rarely the only ones at the table. Other PE firms and strategic buyers are usually circling the same asset, creating pressure to move quickly and wisely. And sometimes, early red flags start waving: questionable revenue quality, high customer concentration, product or service obsolescence risk, or a management team that's more Houdini than operator.

I vividly remember one internal meeting where a junior team member had just finished presenting a long list of issues on a deal we'd been chasing for two weeks. After a pause, one of the partners leaned back, took a sip of coffee, and said flatly, "I don't know about you guys, but this one feels like *the juice is not worth the squeeze.*"

While I found his comment humorous, the point stuck. In PE, you only have so many hours in the day and so many people to deploy. When an opportunity looks like it's going to take enormous effort without delivering a proportionate return, you have to ask yourself whether the juice is really worth the squeeze. Sometimes it is. Sometimes the complexity hides value, and peeling back the layers reveals a gem. But more often than not, especially when better opportunities are out there, you're better off putting the lemon down and walking away.

35. IT'S NOT WORTH THE SWIRL

A phrases that always brings a chuckle for me in the world of PE comes from a longtime colleague who has a knack for cutting through the noise. Whenever a deal starts to look messy with too many red flags, not enough upside, etc., he'll shake his head and say, "*It's not worth the swirl.*"

It's his version of "the juice is not worth the squeeze," but with a bit more flair. In PE, the "swirl" refers to the flurry of activity that surrounds diligence: endless Zoom calls, data room deep dives, spreadsheet gymnastics, and the collective brainpower spent trying to make a deal make sense when, deep down, you know it probably won't.

The phrase stuck with me because it perfectly captures the reality of modern deal-making. Over the years, I've seen the industry evolve toward a sharper, faster approach to screening opportunities. Time is precious, and I've learned that the best use of it is knowing when not to waste it.

I remember sitting in an early diligence meeting for a healthcare services business that had a decent topline but a lot of noise underneath: customer churn, thin margins, opaque reporting. About twenty minutes into the discussion, someone on the team pointed out that if we had to squint this hard to make the story work, we were probably in the wrong story.

That's when my colleague, without missing a beat, dropped his signature line: "Look, I like a good swirl as much as the next guy, but this one? Not worth it."

We passed on the deal that afternoon.

There's real value in calling it early. The swirl, like the squeeze, only makes sense when the outcome justifies the effort. If it doesn't, it's better to save your time, your team, and your sanity for a deal that actually wants to be done.

36. SQUEEZING THE LEMON AS HARD AS WE CAN

Much like wringing every drop of juice from a lemon for tea or lemonade, business leaders and PE investors often find themselves in situations where the goal is to maximize every possible advantage. In our world, that effort is often referred to as "squeezing the lemon"; putting in the work, pressing for every inch of value, and negotiating until there's nothing left to give.

Whether it's the price on an acquisition, the fine print of a merger agreement, or the scope of a vendor contract, we inevitably go through multiple rounds of back-and-forth, aiming to extract the most favorable terms while also being cognizant of the need to maintain engagement of the founders and management teams. It's a delicate art that can sometimes feel more like an endurance sport.

I remember serving on the Board of a portfolio company during an add-on acquisition negotiation. Things had been dragging on for weeks, and tension was building. The founder on the other side of the table wasn't budging on key deal points. During one particularly exasperated board call, a fellow director sighed and said, "We're *squeezing the lemon as hard as we can*, but this guy's not giving up a single drop more. He's dug in like a tick on a hound."

There was a moment of silence, then a few laughs, and finally a collective nod. We knew exactly what he meant. The team had worked every angle, and the juice just wasn't flowing. Sometimes, squeezing the lemon means knowing when you've hit the rind.

37. YOU CAN'T PUT THE TOOTHPASTE BACK IN THE TUBE

The phrase "you can't put the toothpaste back in the tube" is one of those vivid expressions that perfectly captures the idea of irreversibility. Once something is said or done, especially in a professional setting, there's often no way to undo it. While similar to phrases like "you can't un-ring a bell" or "the genie is out of the bottle," the toothpaste version carries a particularly human, slightly comic visual as something awkward, messy, and undeniably final.

I've heard and used the phrase many times throughout my career, both as an executive and in PE. From an organizational behavior perspective, I've always tried to pause—twice, maybe three times—before speaking, particularly when a topic is contentious. But the real test memorably came with the rise of email. I was there during its earliest adoption, when corporate intranets gave way to full-blown internet connectivity. I learned the hard way that email could be both a tool and a trap.

One especially painful experience stands out. I had just wrapped a grueling transfer pricing negotiation with a European distributor, "Apex GmbH", who had established access to a good deal of the European Market. This CEO was smug and difficult, taking full advantage of his leverage. After finally reaching an agreement, I fired off an email to my VP of Sales, Bryce, and our CFO, Fred, updating them on the deal. Let's just say the message included some colorful language reflecting my less-than-charitable feelings about our European counterpart.

Less than a minute later, my phone rang. It was Bryce. His voice was tight with panic.

"Mike, you cc'd the Apex CEO."

I froze, my head in one hand, the phone in the other. All I could manage was a stunned, "You've got to be kidding me."

There was a long silence on the line. Then Bryce said, with dry resignation, "Well... *you can't put the toothpaste back in the tube.* What's done is done. We have other options."

He was right. The contract never got signed. We had to scrap the deal entirely and start from scratch finding a new distributor. That mistake was mine, born of a momentary lapse in judgment and the early days of email when the "send" button was still a novelty and a hazard. It was a painful lesson, but one that stuck. These days, I triple-check the cc line before sending anything. And I keep a metaphorical cap on the toothpaste.

38. MOVE-THE-NEEDLE

As an Operating Partner in PE, I work closely with the business development executives across our portfolio companies. During my years as a CEO, I was always drawn to business development. There's something addictive about the adrenaline rush of closing a meaningful sale. I also developed a deep respect for field sales professionals who tirelessly advocate for our products and services, often in front of over-worked, skeptical clinicians.

With more than 30 years in healthcare, I've built a broad network of executives across many subsectors. I regularly tap into that network to support business development efforts. Leadership, inside sales teams, and field reps from our portfolio companies often reach out to me directly for counsel and introductions to contacts at key target accounts. I also participate in weekly business development meetings at several of our companies, where the teams review active prospects and pipeline opportunities using Customer Relationship Management (CRM) platforms like Salesforce or HubSpot.

In these CRM systems, target accounts are typically categorized by sales stage—terms like relationship building, evaluation, proposal, contract negotiation, and closing. Each stage reflects a rising likelihood of winning the business. In companies with larger sales teams, it's not uncommon to see more than a hundred target accounts tracked at different points in the sales cycle. Individual deals can range from twenty thousand to over a million dollars, depending on the business and offering.

Early in my time in PE, I sat in on a business development meeting where the team was reviewing dozens of individual opportunities. About halfway through and recognizing a need for efficiency, I suggested, "Let's focus on the *move-the-needle* opportunities in these meetings so we can keep things efficient. Having a big pipeline is a good problem, but we'll never get through all of it otherwise."

One of the team members looked up and asked, "What do you mean by *move-the-needle?*"

I was surprised as it was a phrase I had used for years and assumed everyone understood. But I realized in that moment how subjective it can be. So, I offered a bit more context.

"I mean deals that have the potential to make a material impact on revenue and EBITDA. Think of an analog speedometer. When you press lightly on the gas, the needle might twitch a little. But when you really step on it, the needle jumps. That's what we're looking for—opportunities that push the needle in a meaningful way."

For this particular company, that typically meant opportunities with over two hundred thousand dollars in annual revenue potential.

39. IF WE CAN MEASURE IT, THEN WE CAN IMPROVE IT

How does a management team or Board of Directors measure a company's performance? One of the most common tools I have encountered is the use of Key Performance Indicators, or KPIs. A KPI is a quantifiable measure of performance tracked over time against a specific target. KPIs often appear in employee performance objectives, used not only to evaluate progress but also to guide better decision-making within teams and across an organization. In many cases, achieving certain KPI targets is also required to earn a performance bonus during an employee's annual review. KPIs are unique to each business and, importantly, they are objective and not based on opinion or interpretation.

During my time as an Operating Partner, I served on the Board of a contract medical device manufacturing company. It was there that I witnessed the full potential of KPIs in action. During our investment period, the company went through a necessary CEO transition. The newly appointed CEO, a seasoned industry leader with two decades of experience, was determined to roll out a robust KPI program across the organization, which included four major manufacturing facilities and more than 600 employees.

In a welcomed gesture of transparency and partnership, he invited me to join the weekly staff meetings, where the executive leadership team would review company updates, with a focus on tracking and reporting KPIs.

I still remember his first staff meeting clearly during which he laid out his plan to implement KPIs at every level of the company. This was a high-volume and precision manufacturer, producing medical devices in large batches. Some facilities ran around the clock, churning out hundreds of thousands of parts. The leadership team agreed on a comprehensive set of KPIs: on-time delivery, finished product rework, quality failures, scrap rates, customer returns, and employee safety metrics such as days without injury. To reinforce the importance of transparency and continuous improvement, they also installed large LCD monitors throughout the facilities, displaying real-time graphs comparing actual KPI results to target performance.

The CEO closed the meeting with a line I'll never forget. He said, *"If we can measure it, then we can improve it."*

That simple statement resonated deeply. It was not only refreshing to hear from a new leader but also aligned with my own experiences across various companies throughout my career. He was right. The KPI program created visibility, accountability, and alignment across the organization, and over time, the company saw a dramatic improvement in both operational performance and customer satisfaction. Those gains helped pave the way for a strong financial and strategic exit for both employees and investors.

40. WHAT NEEDS TO BE BELIEVED

In my experience, this statement captures the essence of risk tolerance in PE investment decisions. Like any disciplined investment firm or strategic corporate buyer, PE firms conduct deep diligence when evaluating acquisitions. Throughout this book, I'll revisit the concept of comprehensive diligence, which typically includes analyzing historical financials, management forecasts, team capabilities, customer feedback, market dynamics, SWOT assessments, and many other workstreams. Often, third-party firms are hired to conduct market studies, financial quality of earnings reviews, legal assessments, and more. In some cases I've been involved with, diligence and legal costs have exceeded $1 million.

As part of this process, we develop multiple financial scenarios—base, downside, and upside cases—in addition to reviewing the management team's forecast. All of this is synthesized to inform valuation decisions and guide the ultimate "go or no-go" call on the investment.

As with many firms, my experience is such that the investment team prepares this extensive diligence material for the Investment Committee (IC) at the firm, which makes the final go or no-go decision. There are usually several interim IC touchpoints that serve as checkpoints before the final presentation. I continue to be impressed by the depth and breadth of analysis that goes into these materials. However, despite the hundreds of pages of detail, the final investment decision often distills down to a single slide: "What needs to be believed."

I remember a final IC prep meeting where the deal team was reviewing the opportunity presentation. One colleague had done a fantastic job summarizing key diligence findings: market trends, competitive positioning, customer validation, management strength, sustainability and growth prospects, and the financial outlook under various scenarios.

After walking through the details, he wrapped up by saying, "We've reviewed the positives and the potential concerns, none of which should come as a surprise at this point. Sure, we could dig even deeper, but after all our work, it really comes down to *what needs to be believed* to make this a successful investment.

Another colleague added, "As a deal team, we're aligned. We're comfortable with the assumptions and understand the risks. What has been outlined gives us a clear path to value creation. I have a good deal of peace of mind and confidence going into this investment. We're ready to recommend moving forward."

There is no such thing as a risk-free investment. But in PE, success depends on how deeply and intelligently we investigate every element of risk: internal, external, controllable, and not. The ability to distill all of that work into a clear and cogent summary, especially identifying and articulating what truly needs to be believed for success, is what enables an Investment Committee to make a confident and informed decision.

41. TURN OVER THE NEXT CARD

PE is full of idioms, many borrowed from the world of playing cards. One that has always resonated with me is the idea of "turning over the next card." In games like poker or blackjack, players may be unsure about their current hand but stay in the game, hoping the next card will improve their odds. Similarly, the PE diligence process unfolds in stages, each one revealing more information and requiring a decision on whether to move forward.

Typically, an investment bank representing the seller initiates the process by sending a teaser (an executive summary of the business) to potential buyers. If initial interest is confirmed, the prospective buyer signs a Confidential Disclosure Agreement (CDA) and gains access to the Confidential Information Memorandum (CIM), a detailed document that outlines the company's operations, market, financials, customer base, growth potential, and more. Evaluating the CIM is a critical step in determining whether the opportunity merits deeper exploration and, ultimately, the submission of an Indication of Interest (IOI).

The IOI is a non-binding expression of formal interest, including a proposed valuation range. Once IOIs are submitted, the investment bank and seller select which parties will advance to management pre-sentations. Following those meetings and initial diligence, interested buyers submit a Letter of Intent (LOI), which outlines key deal terms, due diligence expectations, timelines, and parties involved.

Early in my PE career, I quickly learned that the decision to "turn over the next card" is a pivotal one at each step: from teaser to CIM, from CIM to IOI, and from IOI to LOI. Each phase demands time, focus, and financial investment. Still, the desire to keep learning and exploring an opportunity, despite inevitable imperfections, is at the heart of this phrase. The IOI, in particular, marks a critical commitment to continue the process, understanding that challenges will emerge and how management addresses them is often more telling than the issues themselves.

I first heard this phrase during a deal review for a contract manufacturing services company. As the team discussed the CIM, one colleague said, "There's still a lot we don't know, but I like the sector and the apparent differentiation this company brings. I'd vote to submit an IOI and *turn over the next card*. This could be worth digging into."

That mindset stuck with me. Having led businesses through adversity, I know that perfect opportunities rarely exist. I often encourage our teams to look for value in the rough edges and to resist walking away too quickly. Sometimes, the next card is the one that makes all the difference.

42. DOUBLE-CLICK

Anyone who's ever used a computer mouse knows what it means to double-click. A quick tap of the mouse button twice in succession opens a file, launches a program, or reveals more detail beneath the surface. In essence, it's how you dig deeper.

I first heard "double-click" used in a PE setting during an early diligence review. We were examining a potential acquisition, and one red flag jumped out: unusually high employee attrition. This was especially concerning because a large portion of the workforce was based in India, and we weren't sure if the churn was typical for that market or indicative of deeper organizational issues.

As we discussed how to move forward, a colleague said, "We need to *double-click* on the attrition numbers. Is this just the norm for offshore operations in this sector, or is something broken in the company's culture or management practices?"

At first, I blinked at the phrase. Double-click? I was tempted to ask if he wanted a mouse to go with his keyboard of metaphors. But the meaning resonated almost instantly: we needed to dig in, peel back the layers, and understand what was really going on beneath the surface metric.

And so, we did. We pulled benchmark data for similar companies in the region, requested exit interview summaries, and examined how the company onboarded, trained, and managed its teams. What started as a curious blip on a spreadsheet became a full thread we tugged on until the story behind the numbers came into focus.

Since then, I've used "double-click" regularly, and with only mild embarrassment. It's a handy shorthand for "let's go deeper on this issue," and in the high-stakes world of investment diligence, that instinct to dig often separates good deals from costly mistakes.

43. INVESTMENT THESIS

Before I entered PE, the word "thesis" meant only one thing to me: the dense, research-heavy document I wrote and defended during my doctoral studies in chemical engineering. It was an academic rite of passage, a detailed report on original research that consumed years of my life. I had never encountered the term used in a business context until I stepped into the world of PE.

In PE, the "investment thesis" is a central concept. It refers to the core rationale or strategic argument for why a particular investment makes sense. It's not a complicated term, but it's critical to understand the depth and function it serves. The investment thesis is the lens through which the deal team evaluates and communicates the opportunity. It explains how the PE firm believes it can create value and why this company, in this market, at this time, fits the firm's strategy.

More than a hypothesis, an investment thesis lays out a roadmap. It aligns the deal team internally and shapes discussions with the Investment Committee, providing a clear articulation of how the investment could generate attractive returns. It answers the big questions: Why this deal? Why now? How will value be created and ultimately realized?

For example, imagine a company with differentiated technology, a narrow regional footprint, and a modest growth trajectory largely driven by word-of-mouth referrals. A well-formed investment thesis might look like this: strengthen the executive leadership team, build out internal and field sales functions, and pursue strategic acquisitions to expand geographic reach and scale operations. That thesis becomes the backbone of the firm's plan, not just for getting the deal done, but for building the business post-close.

In short, the investment thesis is far more than a buzzword. It's a strategic narrative backed by data, experience, and vision which evolves to one of the most important tools in a PE investor's toolkit.

44. LATEST NEW SNOWFLAKE

As an engineer by training, I appreciate the science behind the formation of a snowflake. It's rooted in physical chemistry and thermodynamics: water vapor crystallizes into a hexagonal lattice as it freezes. While each snowflake may appear different to the naked eye, they all share that same hexagonal chassis at their core. The final structure might look one-of-a-kind, but the underlying geometry is always the same.

The business world is not so different. Many challenges might seem unique at first glance, but more often than not, they're just variations on familiar patterns. Over the years, I've seen investors and board members react strongly to issues that arise during a company's lifecycle, sometimes with a sense of urgency that borders on panic. But from my time on the operational side, I've learned the value of pausing, collecting the facts, staying level-headed, and working a plan. In short, approaching the problem like an engineer.

Many effective CEOs in PE do the same. I remember one board meeting in particular. The CEO was outlining a supplier issue that had caused some disruption. You could feel the tension rise in the room. Board members started tossing out quick fixes and ideas as if we were dealing with a five-alarm fire.

The CEO listened, then calmly said, "I've seen this kind of supplier issue before. We're not chasing the *latest new snowflake* here. We don't need to reinvent the wheel or think outside the box. We'll stick to the fundamentals. We'll fix it."

It was the perfect analogy. Just like a snowflake might appear unique, most business problems have recognizable patterns and proven solutions. The trick is being able to see through the perceived uniqueness and return to the basics. That's what seasoned executives and thoughtful investors come to understand over time: the path forward usually starts with the fundamentals.

45. UNPACK

"Unpack" has always meant one thing to me: arriving at a hotel, opening my suitcase, and hanging my clothes in the closet. So, when I first entered the world of PE and started hearing the term used in a business context, I couldn't help but find it a little funny. Expressions like "Let's *unpack* this trend," "Let me *unpack* what you're saying," or "We need to *unpack* the adjustments to EBITDA" were tossed around with complete seriousness. Apparently, in PE, "unpacking" means breaking down a complex topic into its individual parts to better understand what's really going on.

I came to appreciate the term during diligence on a medical device contract manufacturer we were evaluating. The company's top three customers each made up about a fifth of the revenue, with the three combined accounting for nearly 60 percent. That level of concentration raised some serious concerns about the business's long-term stability. If even one of those customers left, the financial hit would be significant.

In a meeting focused on customer risk, a colleague said, "We need to *unpack* the customer concentration."

At first, I chuckled internally, picturing someone rifling through a suitcase filled with customer contracts. But I had to admit it was an effective way to frame the task. We needed to dig into the specifics of each customer relationship. How many product lines did each represent? What stage were those products in their life cycle? Were there new offerings in the pipeline? Was the revenue growing, stable, or declining?

The goal was to get comfortable with a very real risk. While I tend to be more bullish about our ability to drive post-close growth and diversify the customer base, I've learned that customer concentration is not something you gloss over. It demands focused attention. In other words, it needs to be "unpacked". And if you really want to get clarity, you may need to, as my colleagues like to say, throw in a few well-placed double-clicks.

46. TABLE STAKES

In poker or blackjack, table stakes refer to the money a player puts on the table at the start of a hand. Once the hand begins, players can only bet what's already in play. It's the minimum requirement to participate, and no one can reach into their pocket mid-hand to raise the stakes. In a casino, you'll often see signs: $25 minimum, $50 minimum, or $100 minimum. These are table stakes—the entry fee to sit at the table.

In PE, the phrase carries a similar meaning. Sourcing high-quality investment opportunities is a constant challenge. Many deals come through investment bankers, which makes the process highly competitive. Proprietary deals (those sourced directly through a PE firm's network) without a banker running the process are rare and prized. But whether the opportunity is proprietary or widely shopped, clearing the first major hurdle, the Indication of Interest (IOI), and securing a management meeting is essential.

In these meetings, the management team presents a deeper dive into the business beyond the Confidential Information Memorandum (CIM), and the PE firm gets its turn to pitch. This is more than just asking questions, it's a chance to make a case for why the firm is the right partner to acquire and grow the business. That pitch matters, especially when founders are expected to roll over a portion of their go-forward ownership into the new entity.

For example, if a PE firm acquires a company for $50 million and the founder retains 20 percent of the equity, that "roll-over" can end up being worth more than their take on the initial $50 million payout if the company grows under the PE firm's ownership. That future upside makes the seller's comfort level with the buyer critical. They're not just choosing a buyer, they're choosing a partner for the next leg of the journey.

I first heard the term "table stakes" used in this context during a kickoff meeting with a founder. A colleague, well-respected for his direct style, addressed the founder with calm confidence.

"You're going to have plenty of firms knocking on your door," he said. "They'll all have money to invest. They'll all say they've done a deal in your sector. That's just *table stakes*. It gets us in the room. But what you really need to know is who's going to drive value from here, and how."

That phrase stuck with me. Table stakes are the baseline, essentially the must-haves. Capital, sector experience, a decent track record. Everyone has those. To win, we need to go beyond them. We need to differentiate ourselves by unpacking what truly sets us apart: our healthcare focus, our repeatable value-creation model, our operational resources, cultural synergies, and our specific experience in the seller's niche. Those are the levers that make a founder sit up, take notice, and say, "These are the people I want to go forward with."

41. SECOND BITE OUT OF THE APPLE

When a founder decides to retain an equity stake in their business after a PE acquisition, the outcome can be exceptionally rewarding. Take the earlier example: a founder sells their company for $50 million, receives $40 million in cash at closing, and rolls over $10 million into the new entity, retaining 20 percent ownership going forward. Depending on the circumstances, that founder might continue in an operational role, such as CEO or head of business development, while also serving on the Board, or they might transition entirely to a Board position as a new CEO is brought in.

From there, the PE firm begins executing its value creation plan. Depending on the maturity of the business, this often includes hiring seasoned executives like a professional CFO or COO, strengthening key functions such as HR, marketing, and sales, expanding manufacturing capacity, and investing in core infrastructure systems like CRM and ERP platforms. Add-on acquisitions are frequently pursued to grow the company's geographic footprint, broaden its capabilities, and reduce customer concentration risk. The core idea is to accelerate growth and profitability in a way that the founder, operating independently, likely could not.

Of course, this transformation takes time. The process of building enterprise value can span several years and demands sustained focus and effort. Eventually, the PE firm will look to exit the investment, either through a sale to another PE firm, a strategic corporate buyer, or, less commonly, the public markets. The timing and path of that exit vary, but in my experience, most investments are held for four to six years, sometimes longer, depending on the firm's investment mandate and the specific circumstances of the business.

The goal is that both the PE firm and the founder benefit from the equity growth created during this period. Returning to the earlier example, if the company is sold five years later for $200 million, the founder's original $10 million roll-over investment—representing 20 percent of the company—would now be worth $40 million (before fees). That's a $30 million gain on top of the initial $40 million they received at closing. In PE circles, this is referred to as the *"second bite out of the apple."*

In some cases, I've seen founders stick around long enough to take a third bite. After the business is initially sold to a second PE firm, they retain a portion of their equity and stay on board for the next leg of growth. When that firm exits, the founder participates in yet another liquidity event.

It gives a whole new meaning to the phrase "let it ride."

48. WHAT DOES SUCCESS LOOK LIKE?

I've encountered this phrase in both my operational and PE experiences. From an executive leadership perspective, I've always tied it to the principle behind setting annual performance objectives for both myself and my team. Achieving these stretch goals, while simultaneously improving healthcare outcomes for patients and incentivizing clinicians, was the true measure of success from my point of view.

In the PE world, when engaging with founders during the diligence process, we often ask, "What does success look like if you fast forward two or three years?" The answer gives us valuable insight into areas where the company needs support, potential opportunities for talent acquisition, avenues for growth, and the metrics they deem critical for success. Understanding this helps us build a relationship with the founder and management team, which is key to adding long-term value.

I recall a situation where a PE colleague used a slight variation of the phrase when discussing a potential CFO candidate for one of our portfolio companies. On paper, the candidate looked impressive, but after the interview, it was clear he wasn't a strong contender.

My colleague summed up the situation succinctly: "He doesn't know *what success looks like* for the role."

In this context, the phrase meant that the candidate was unable to clearly articulate how he would optimize the finance function, define measurable objectives for the team, and, most crucially, lacked experience in successfully transforming the finance operations in his previous roles. It was a stark warning that in any role, especially leadership positions, understanding the vision of success is paramount.

49. ORGAN REJECTION

In organ transplantation, rejection occurs when the recipient's immune system identifies the new organ as foreign (like a bacteria or virus) and launches an attack to eliminate it. In PE, I've experienced use of the phrase "organ rejection" as a metaphor when evaluating potential acquisitions that fall below our typical EBITDA threshold. It signals the risk that the business may simply be too small or fragile to withstand the demands placed on it post-acquisition, especially when we intend to potentially layer in debt and scale rapidly.

I remember a particular deal that brought this metaphor to life. We were evaluating a potential platform investment in a company with $3 million in EBITDA, operating in a highly attractive healthcare subsegment. On paper, it checked many boxes. But within the investment team, debate was fierce.

One of my colleagues didn't mince words. "Look," he said, "we're going to need to make significant near-term investments in leadership, systems, and infrastructure. That $3 million is going to vanish almost immediately. This just doesn't fit our mandate." He paused, then delivered the punchline: "I'm worried the size of this company is going to lead to *organ rejection*. I can't get comfortable with it."

That stuck with me. It was a vivid way to summarize the concern that the business might not be robust enough to absorb the changes required to scale. When a platform investment is teetering at the lower edge of our EBITDA threshold, everything else needs to be rock solid: the management team, operational maturity, customer base, market position. If any of those factors are weak, the company could struggle post-close, potentially violating debt covenants and requiring additional capital just to stay afloat.

"Organ rejection" may sound dramatic, but in the world of leveraged buyouts, it's a real risk, and often a costly one. Sometimes the patient just isn't strong enough for the transplant.

50. RUN ALL OF THE TRAPS

The phrase "run all the traps" has its roots in hunting and fishing, dating back centuries. In Maine, where I spend a good amount of time, I've often heard local lobster fishermen use it as part of their daily routine. Each morning, they head out to check their traps, sometimes multiple times a day, to see what they've hauled in. It's a ritual of patience, diligence, and attention to detail.

So, I was a bit surprised the first time I heard the phrase used in a PE context, a couple of years into my tenure. We were in the thick of a diligence process, racing the clock during the exclusivity period. The timeline was tight, and extending it would have meant a delicate dance with the seller and their banker.

During a team call to review the remaining diligence items, one of my colleagues said, "We need to *run all the traps* before we can go to the Investment Committee for final approval. But right now, I don't see any red flags."

In that moment, the metaphor made perfect sense. Just like checking each lobster trap for a catch or a surprise, running all the traps in diligence means combing through every detail. Legal, financial, operational, regulatory. No assumptions, no shortcuts, and certainly no skipped steps.

It was a message that thoroughness is non-negotiable. Because in both fishing and investing, if you fail to check a trap, you might miss something important—or worse, bring back something you wish you hadn't.

51. IT'S ONLY WHEN THE TIDE GOES OUT THAT YOU LEARN WHO HAS BEEN SWIMMING NAKED

Over more than 30 years, I've learned a hard truth: revenue growth can hide a multitude of sins. When a company is growing quickly, cracks in the foundation, whether in leadership, operations, or discipline, can be easily glossed over. The urgency to maintain the growth narrative often trumps the need to fix what's broken. As long as the top line is climbing, no one wants to look too closely under the hood.

It's not unlike what happens during a bull market, where even mediocre investors start looking like geniuses. But when the tide turns: when growth slows, margins tighten, or a macro shock hits, the real story comes to light. That's when you find out who's been coasting, overspending, or simply in over their head.

A PE mentor once summed it up with a sharp idiom: *"It's only when the tide goes out that you learn who's been swimming naked."*

In PE, this moment of truth can be brutal. When things go south, you suddenly discover which members of the portfolio company team were unprepared, ineffective, or just lucky. And at that point, it's often too late to fix the fundamentals without pain.

In my experience, the smarter move is to make changes while the sun is still shining. Growth periods are the best time to optimize, not just celebrate. That means ensuring the right people are in the right roles, building out solid systems and processes, and getting serious about measuring performance. It's about setting KPIs that matter, streamlining expenses, tightening gross profit margins, rightsizing teams, addressing redundancy, and preparing the organization to weather a storm—not just ride the wave.

Because when the tide inevitably goes out, you don't want to be the one running for a towel.

52. HOW THE SAUSAGE IS MADE

The phrase "how the sausage is made" is a metaphor for the often messy and complex inner workings of a system, organization, or production process. It suggests that while the end result may look appealing, the process behind it can be far less glamorous and more complicated than expected. Sometimes, understanding these details exposes hidden challenges, compromises, or unpleasant truths that are not visible from the outside.

Back in the early 1980s, during college, a friend of mine took a summer job at a hot dog manufacturing company. We had always enjoyed Fenway Franks at Red Sox games, but his new job quickly changed his perspective. He claimed, perhaps with some hyperbole, that the ingredients in hot dogs included everything from head meat and feet to liver, fatty tissue, blood, and, jokingly, even floor sweepings. Needless to say, that revelation permanently soured my enjoyment of hot dogs, including the beloved Fenway Franks. It's a clear reminder that sometimes, ignorance truly is bliss.

In a similar vein, in the world of PE, investors often go through the painstaking process of due diligence to uncover the intricate details of a target company's operations; essentially "seeing how the sausage is made." For example, when evaluating a company that provided revenue cycle management services for healthcare facilities, the diligence process involved digging into the nitty-gritty of billing and collections. We had to understand everything from billing code determination to claims submission logistics, payment verification against payer contracts, identifying underpayments, and the algorithms used for denial adjudication.

After we completed the exhaustive diligence and closed the acquisition, the founder of the company turned to me and said, "Well, now you *really know how the sausage is made*." It was a perfect way to sum up how deep we had gone into understanding the business's operations and the challenges that lie beneath the surface. And just like my friend with the hot dogs, I'll never quite look at revenue cycle management companies the same way again.

53. DOG WON'T HUNT

In my younger days, I had the chance to go pheasant hunting with two friends, Steve and Paul, both of whom owned German Shorthaired Pointers. These dogs were a sight to behold: focused, disciplined, and clearly born to hunt. As we walked through fields of knee-deep grass and thick brush, the dogs suddenly froze, heads locked on a bush, front paws lifted in perfect form, tails rigid and straight like arrows. Moments later, they flushed out the pheasants with impressive efficiency. It felt less like hunting and more like participating in a well-rehearsed performance.

On the drive home, still amazed by what I'd seen, I asked Steve how he trained the dogs to be so precise. He smiled and said the instinct was baked into the breed. "You don't teach them to point," he explained. "They just know." Then he added with a grin, "Well, except for one dog I had. No matter what I did, he'd just run around aimlessly, chasing butterflies or his own tail. No interest in birds. Total embarrassment to the family name." He shook his head and chuckled. "That *dog just wouldn't hunt.*"

That phrase stuck with me, and over the years, I've heard it plenty of times, especially in executive leadership and PE settings. In business, "this *dog won't hunt*" typically means an idea or strategy that lacks the support, rationale, or consensus to proceed. It might be a flawed plan, an ill-fitting candidate, or a deal with a fatal flaw. Either way, it's time to move on.

As a CEO, I remember a discussion with my Vice President of Sales and Marketing, Charles, about entering the European market.

He was adamant about building a direct sales force. I, based on experience, preferred a more localized distribution strategy. We went back and forth until I finally said, "Charles, I get where you're coming from, but it's time to let it go. This *dog won't hunt*." He didn't love hearing it, but to his credit, he moved on.

In PE, this phrase surfaces often during investment committee debates. It's easy to develop emotional attachments to a deal: the market is hot, the founder is charismatic, the pitch deck is polished. But sometimes, no matter how much you want it to work, a deal falls apart under the weight of its own flaws.

I recall one deal team meeting where the room had gone quiet after a troubling diligence update. Finally, a colleague spoke up, blunt and to the point: "We know where this ends. We can't do it. *This dog won't hunt*." That single sentence saved us months of wasted effort—and likely a small fortune. Some dogs just won't hunt. And the sooner you figure that out, the better off everyone is.

54. KNOCK-OUT FACTOR

As highlighted earlier, a critical issue uncovered during PE diligence can be the decisive factor that shuts down a deal, much like the proverbial "dog won't hunt." In PE circles, this kind of deal-breaker is often referred to as a "knock-out factor." The phrase borrows from boxing, where one swift punch to the jaw can end the fight instantly. In the same way, a target company might have many appealing qualities, but if a single serious flaw emerges, it can immediately take the deal off the table unless that flaw can somehow be resolved.

Over the years, I've been involved in deal teams that identified knock-out factors ranging from founder-related concerns to structural business issues. These include management teams lacking depth or commitment, key employees refusing to sign non-compete agreements, heavy customer concentration, recent loss of a major client, unsustainable profit margins, or unrealistic seller valuation expectations. In some cases, it's the risk of a well-capitalized competitor poised to move down-market and eat the target's lunch. Other times, it's something more subtle, like a founder refusing to roll equity, which may signal a lack of confidence in the company's future.

I recall one particular investment committee meeting where the room was cautiously optimistic about a target in the healthcare IT sector. The business had recurring revenue, attractive margins, and an expanding customer base. It looked promising. That was until one of the deal team members shared, "I spoke to the banker last night. The founder plans to exit completely after the close and won't participate in an equity rollover. There is nothing we can do to make him change his mind."

The room went silent for a beat. Then one of my colleagues leaned back in his chair and said, "That's it. It's a *knock-out factor* for me. We knew there was key-man risk here. If he's not betting on his own company, why should we?"

And just like that, a deal the team had spent weeks pursuing was off the table.

Of course, different PE firms have varying levels of tolerance for risk. Some may be comfortable with turnarounds or distressed assets, while others, particularly growth-focused investors, view these red flags as non-negotiable. Regardless of the risk appetite, most successful firms build their track records by identifying companies that not only have strong fundamentals but also show promise for growth through talent, systems, process improvements, and strategic guidance.

The goal is not just to win the fight but to make sure you're not stepping into the ring already dazed. Spotting knock-out factors early is critical. It allows you to cut your losses, conserve resources, and focus on deals that position you and the prospective portfolio company for a fighting chance at success.

55. THIRD RAIL ISSUE

Throughout my time in PE, I've often seen the term "third rail issue" used interchangeably with the phrase "knock-out factor." Both serve as shorthand for the kind of problem that can stop a deal in its tracks. The origin of the "third rail" metaphor comes from subway systems, where the third rail carries a high-voltage electrical current. Touch it, and the result can be fatal.

In the world of PE investing, a third rail issue is much the same. It might not be obvious at first glance, but if you get too close without the proper safeguards or ignore it entirely, it can shock the deal to death.

I once heard a colleague describe a target company with a smile that barely masked concern: "On paper, this one checks a lot of boxes. But unless someone figures out how to insulate us from that third rail, we're going to get fried."

He was referring to a founder who insisted on maintaining full operational control post-close, despite having no experience scaling a business and a history of driving away key team members. No amount of customer growth or EBITDA smoothing could cover up that risk. That founder was the third rail.

Whether it's a control-obsessed founder, a toxic corporate culture, or a looming competitive time bomb, these third rail issues are more than red flags, they're often deal-killers. Just like with knock-out factors, unless you can isolate, contain, or remove the threat entirely, you're better off not stepping onto the tracks at all.

In PE, due diligence is not just about validating what's working. It's also about spotting what could kill you. And when someone says, "Careful, that's a *third rail*," it's not a metaphor to take lightly.

56. ELEPHANT HUNTING

I've grown particularly familiar with the term "elephant hunting," especially during my time in executive leadership roles and in PE. The phrase tends to surface most often in sales and marketing discussions, particularly when reviewing a pipeline with a business development team. In nearly every pipeline, you'll find a mix of smaller prospects and a handful of massive, multinational targets. "Elephant hunting" refers to the strategic pursuit of these giants: companies like Johnson & Johnson, Pfizer, or Medtronic in the healthcare sector.

Landing one of these customers can have a dramatic impact. The upside is real: a major boost in revenue and EBITDA, potential Master

Service Agreements, multi-year contracts, and the possibility to expand into additional divisions within the organization after a successful initial engagement. It's the kind of deal that can shift a company's trajectory.

That said, elephant hunting is not for the faint of heart. These deals require persistence, careful orchestration, and typically a long sales cycle. I've always advised teams to complement elephant hunting with a steady pursuit of small to mid-sized accounts. These wins come faster, are less resource-intensive, and provide critical short-term cash flow while the big game remains in your sights.

During a portfolio company board meeting, we were reviewing an underwhelming sales forecast. The head of sales launched into a detailed update about his team's pursuit of a major healthcare system: one of those deals that, if it closed, would dramatically increase the company's annual revenue.

After listening patiently, one of my colleagues raised an eyebrow and said, "I appreciate the ambition, but are we just *elephant hunting* here while the rest of the forest goes ignored?"

There was a pause. The CEO, a veteran operator, smiled and replied, "Yes, we are. But we're also building enough small game traps to stay fed until the elephant shows up."

Everyone laughed, but the point stuck: a smart growth strategy needs both patience for the elephants and urgency with the squirrels. Most seasoned sales executives can recall their biggest elephant hunts with vivid detail: the years-long pursuit, the breakthrough meeting, the nail-biting procurement process. The smaller wins? They blend into the background. But it's the balance between the two that builds sustainable success.

51. LOOK AROUND CORNERS

PE investors constantly face the challenge of staying current on developments within specific healthcare subsegments. Addressing this requires a mix of internal efforts and external collaboration.

My relationship with Riverside Partners began when I joined their Healthcare Advisory Board while serving as CEO of Claros Diagnostics. At the time, the board included about ten senior industry executives with deep expertise across Riverside's target sectors, including pharmaceutical services, medical devices, diagnostics, and tech-enabled healthcare services.

After Claros was acquired, I transitioned into a full-time Operating Partner role at Riverside. In addition, I became Chair of the Healthcare Advisory Board (HCAB). Early on, I began reaching out to physicians I had worked with in prior CEO roles. These were highly respected thought leaders and also C-level executives at major medical institutions. I shared information and invited their perspectives on markets and opportunities we were evaluating during diligence. Their insights offered a valuable complement to the more traditional business viewpoints of the HCAB.

Recognizing the power of this clinical lens, I formalized the effort by launching a Clinical Advisory Board (CAB) composed of these physicians. To foster meaningful interaction and strategic alignment, we began holding annual joint meetings with both boards. These sessions became highly productive forums for deep discussion on investment themes, diligence questions, and emerging trends.

When describing the role of these boards to potential new members or external partners, I often explain that they help us "get smarter" faster.

One colleague put it best: "The insight from our advisory boards helps us *look around corners*. It gives us a real-time view into where healthcare segments are heading and what risks might be coming."

In the world of PE investing, where market trends unfold gradually and margin for error can be thin, having the ability to anticipate shifts is invaluable. This insight, incorporated into our decision-making calculus, plays a crucial role in evaluating investments and associated risks.

58. FROTHY MARKET

Before I ventured into private equity, the word "frothy" referred to the creamy foam atop my cappuccino—a pleasant result of aerated milk and just the right touch of espresso. Back then, it was a word I associated with comfort, not caution.

So I was caught off guard when I first heard it used in the context of investing. In PE, "frothy" had nothing to do with lattes and everything to do with overheated markets. Suddenly, phrases like "the market is frothy" and "we are in a frothy valuation environment" started popping up in deal meetings and investment memos with startling regularity.

In PE, a frothy market describes inflated asset valuations that rise well above what market fundamentals would suggest. This tends to happen when PE firms are flush with capital, debt is cheap and abundant, and competition for deals is intense. In such times, enthusiasm can outpace discipline. Investors, driven by emotion or fear of missing out, may ease up on diligence or overlook potential knock-out factors. Lenders, too, can get swept up in the momentum, offering leverage at increasingly high EBITDA multiples to help get deals over the finish line. But those structures carry more risk, especially if the company stumbles post-close and fails to meet debt covenants.

I have been involved in several acquisitions during market upswings that tested our usual guardrails. Some pushed us outside our traditional diligence thresholds. To justify the price tags, we pointed to broader market conditions, our obligation to deploy capital on behalf of our limited partners, and the reality that, like it or not, these were the table stakes for staying in the game.

One of my partners summed it up well after we stretched to close a particularly pricey deal: "Well, the numbers may be frothy, but so is the competition. Sit it out and someone else grabs the upside."

We understood the risks. But we also understood the cycle. In frothy markets, you do not have the luxury of waiting for perfect conditions. You weigh the trade-offs, manage exposure, and make sure your feet are firmly planted, even if your cappuccino is not.

59. FIXING THE PLANE WHILE FLYING IT

In a perfect world, changes to a product, service, or organization would roll out smoothly, without disruption or risk. But most operating executives know that is rarely how things work. In reality, change does not happen in a vacuum. Managing product development, navigating organizational challenges, and communicating clearly with customers and stakeholders are all essential to minimizing risk.

Early in my career, I was an executive at a company developing a medical device that combined a compact hardware unit, a disposable single-use component, and embedded software that was critical to patient safety. The software had to pass stringent verification and validation protocols required by the U.S. Food and Drug Administration. A cross-functional team spanning research and development, regulatory, manufacturing, sales, and marketing was engaged from the outset. We had clearly defined milestones and timelines, and everyone understood their role. There was real accountability, both individually and as a team.

To make things more intense, we were a public company. The product launch date had already been announced to customers and investors. Delivering on time was not optional.

One of the most important steps in the process was placing the device with lead users, typically influential customers who would provide candid, early feedback. We categorized their suggestions as either "nice to have" or "must have." As we reviewed the feedback, it became clear that several requests were not in the original product specifica-tion. That left us with a difficult decision: do we delay the launch to incorporate changes, or stick to the timeline and push updates later?

Any modification would require a new version of the software, which meant repeating the entire cycle of validation, documentation, and regulatory review. And we knew more requests would come once the product was in full release. Feedback never slows down. If anything, it accelerates after launch.

I remember one post-launch meeting with our cross-functional team, where we were reviewing broader feedback from the field. The sales leader expressed full support for making changes, confident it would strengthen the customer experience. But across the table, Rick, our Director of Software Engineering, was clearly reaching his limit.

Finally, Rick threw up his hands and said, "Do you realize the scope of the software changes we are talking about? We're *fixing the plane while flying it*. You want us to make fundamental changes to a product already in the field, already being used on patients."

That was the first time I heard the phrase "fixing the plane while flying it". And it stuck. It perfectly captured the chaos and intensity of iterative development. You are learning and adapting as you go, hoping the wings stay attached at 30,000 feet.

Since then, I have heard the phrase used often in PE firms and portfolio companies. It is a vivid, shared shorthand for a familiar chal-lenge. In the real world, perfect is rarely possible. The best outcomes come from thoughtful progress, guided by good judgment, strong execution, and calm leadership when things inevitably get turbulent.

60. VOLUNTOLD

At the outset of a competitive sale process for a company I was leading as CEO, a particularly eager suitor made a bold request. They wanted to jump ahead of the pack by visiting our headquarters, meeting with the management team, and touring our manufacturing facilities on a Saturday. This wasn't just any buyer. They were strategically perfect for us and had a reputation for paying up when they saw value.

Given the importance of the opportunity, I huddled with my Chief Operating Officer to figure out how we could make this happen. We would need functional leaders and technical staff on site to run smooth product demos and answer detailed questions. The catch? This particular Saturday was forecast to be a picture-perfect spring day in May. Sunshine, seventy-two degrees, not a cloud in the sky. In other words, a terrible day to ask anyone to come into work.

My COO, ever the optimist, said, "Maybe we should ask for volunteers."

I looked at him and replied, "You can try, but let's be honest, people are going to have to be *volunTOLD*. We don't really have another option."

I first heard the term "volunTOLD" nearly twenty years earlier, during a major product launch that required a string of weekend shifts. It had stuck with me ever since. It means what it sounds like: technically a volunteer, but not really.

To make it more palatable, I told the COO to offer anyone tapped for Saturday duty a four-day weekend the following week. That seemed fair. Amazingly, the plan worked. There was very little grumbling. In fact, some of the team who showed up that Saturday didn't even bother to take their comp days.

That level of commitment said a lot. It reflected the strength of our culture, my team's leadership ability to rally the staff, and the kind of shared purpose that made even a sunny Saturday at work feel—if not exciting—at least worth it.

61. PENCILS DOWN

After more than a decade spent earning multiple degrees, I became very familiar with professors announcing, "Time's up. Pencils down" at the end of exams. It was a phrase that once signaled the end of a test and the beginning of nervous reflection. But in my early years in PE, I discovered it had a second life and a much sharper edge.

PE diligence is not for the faint of heart. The process of evaluating a target company is intense and unpredictable, often filled with unexpected twists. Inflection points arise when negative diligence findings surface, valuations begin to outpace reality, management demands become excessive, or structured earn-outs no longer make financial sense. Throw in a few rounds of difficult negotiations, and tensions can rise quickly.

One of the more charged moments comes when a PE firm attempts to renegotiate terms mid-process, a move known as a "retrade." That word alone can change the temperature of a deal. In these moments, it is common for both sides to step back and reassess.

I remember my first experience with this. During diligence on a potential investment, we uncovered a serious red flag: a major competitor was developing a disruptive technology that directly threatened our target's long-term position. We attempted to restructure the deal around an earn-out to protect against downside risk. The company's banker pushed back hard. They had little interest in revisiting a deal they believed was already fairly negotiated.

In the middle of a tense internal meeting, one of my colleagues finally said, "We are going *pencils down* until we reach an agreement."

That phrase hit with weight. It meant we were not only pausing our internal work but also putting a full stop to all third-party diligence: legal, accounting, market research, the whole package. In effect, it was a way of saying, "We are not spending another dollar or another hour until this gets resolved."

In PE, "pencils down" is not just a phrase from college exams. It is a tactical move, a line in the sand, and a message that the deal is at risk. Sometimes it is a bluff. Other times, it is a genuine breaking point. But either way, when someone says it in the middle of a deal, everyone in the room sits up a little straighter.

62. COLOR OUTSIDE OF THE LINES

Most of us can relate to the coloring books we used as children, carefully staying within the lines with our Crayola crayons. I never expected that this childhood memory would find relevance in PE investing. Yet, I first encountered the idiom "color outside of the lines" during a transaction that brought this metaphor vividly to life.

We were preparing to submit an offer on a company represented by an advisor who was handling the sale on behalf of the founder. It was positioned as a limited process, with the advisor reaching out to a small group of trusted contacts—PE firms with sector experience and interest, committed capital, and the ability to move swiftly through diligence.

Unlike most processes I've been part of, this advisor specified preferred deal terms upfront, including a defined amount of cash at close and an earn-out opportunity based on achieving future milestones. While this level of specificity was unusual, we remained highly interested and decided to engage aggressively.

As diligence progressed and we prepared our Letter of Intent, we began to consider whether we should exceed the terms outlined by the advisor to strengthen our position relative to other bidders. Throughout the process, we had built a strong rapport with the founder, thanks to our industry track record, transparent communication, and long-standing reputation for partnering well with founder-led businesses.

Just before the bid submission deadline, we met with the founder and advisor for a one-on-one discussion. During the conversation, one of my colleagues raised an important question. "We understand the preferred deal structure and target values for both the up-front payment and earn-out," he said. "Rather than simply meeting those expectations, would we be viewed more favorably if we proposed something more compelling overall?"

The advisor smiled and responded, "I would encourage you to *color outside of the lines*. The guidance we provided isn't a floor. It's simply a starting point. Don't be afraid to be creative."

Message received. Our final offer was structured with a significantly more attractive back-end component, tying additional value to specific performance milestones. We included a ratchet mechanism that increased the earn-out as EBITDA grew, delivering both a higher potential valuation and a strong alignment of interests.

63. ONE PLUS ONE EQUALS THREE

I have often encountered the phrase "one plus one equals three." While it is a clear violation of basic math, it is used to describe situations where the combination of two entities creates value greater than the sum of their parts. This idea has surfaced repeatedly throughout my career, both inside and outside of PE. In PE, the phrase is commonly used to describe the strategic benefits of combining companies, such as through an add-on acquisition to an existing portfolio business. These benefits can include financial gains, business development opportunities, customer diversification, and an uplift in future exit valuation.

A classic example is the consolidation of redundant functional areas like accounting, human resources, and IT. After an add-on acquisition, it is not unusual to streamline these operations, which reduces overhead and improves operating margins. That reduction in expenses flows directly to EBITDA. On the revenue side, the newly combined business may be able to cross-sell products or services to a wider customer base, tapping into opportunities that neither company could fully capture on its own.

Geographic expansion is another lever. A company operating only in the United States might gain access to European or Asian markets through its acquisition partner, opening the door to new customers and strengthening its credibility with larger clients and potential future acquirers. Increased purchasing power across the supply chain can also drive down costs, whether through better raw material pricing or faster delivery timelines. These are all tangible examples of the "one plus one equals three" effect in action.

There is another benefit, less talked about but just as powerful. When the combined company exceeds a certain EBITDA threshold, it may enter a new category of buyers or command a higher multiple at exit. This phenomenon is known as multiple arbitrage. For PE investors, this is a prized outcome. It reflects the creation of a more valuable business not just through operational improvements but through strategic positioning and scale.

Of course, none of this happens by accident. Achieving the full benefit of a one plus one equals three scenario requires thoughtful planning, strong execution, and careful integration. When done right, it does not just defy math—it rewards it.

64. CATCH AND CLEAN THE FISH

The phrase "catch and clean the fish" holds a special place in my heart. In fact, my colleagues have heard me say it so many times that most of them now roll their eyes the moment it comes out of my mouth. Still, I stand by it. The idea behind it has proven relevant throughout my executive career and in PE. It perfectly captures the importance of designing an effective business development function that is fully aligned with operations or manufacturing. After all, it is not enough to catch the fish. You also have to clean it before it starts to rot.

I have seen exceptional business development teams land major new accounts and make all the right promises, only for everything to fall apart in delivery. Why? Because operations was not ready. They lacked the systems, the capacity, the people, or the process to execute on what had been sold. That kind of disconnect can damage reputations and burn customer trust.

The solution starts with system alignment. Tools like Customer Relationship Management (CRM) software, such as Salesforce or Hubspot, and Enterprise Resource Planning (ERP) systems, like Net-Suite, are not just digital infrastructure. They are bridges between the commercial side of the business and the operational side. CRM platforms help track the sales pipeline, while ERP systems can trigger the necessary adjustments in production, scheduling, or hiring to support growth. When used well, they make "catching and cleaning the fish" a seamless, integrated process.

One particular example from my own career still stands out. While serving as CEO of a medical device company, I managed to connect with the Chief Medical Officer of one of the largest dialysis clinic chains in the United States. This led to a critical in-person meeting that included my Vice President of Sales and Marketing, Rick, a talented, seasoned, and confident individual.

We came prepared. Our product featured a compact hardware unit that mounted to an IV pole, paired with a disposable cartridge used on every dialysis patient. The opportunity was massive: high volume, recurring revenue, and long-term partnership potential.

During the meeting, we presented extensive clinical data, economic value proposition, and the technology's performance at major academic medical centers. We had a decade of research, strong clinical outcomes, and endorsements from key opinion leaders. As the meeting progressed, the tone shifted from skeptical to enthusiastic.

Then, halfway through the conversation, the CMO paused and asked, "If we decide to move forward, and I am inclined to do so, could you deliver an initial order of one thousand hardware units? Is that something your team can handle?"

Rick and I exchanged a look. Without missing a beat, he replied, "Absolutely. No issue. You would be our top priority."

It caught me a bit off guard, but I nodded and followed up by suggesting a phased rollout. That would give us time to ensure proper staff training across their dialysis centers. The CMO appreciated the approach and said he would present the opportunity to his board.

As Rick and I walked to the elevator, we were elated. We had not expected the meeting to go that well. But the high of the win came with the immediate weight of responsibility. We had caught the fish. Now came the hard part: cleaning it.

65. HE DOESN'T LET GRASS GROW AROUND HIS FEET

Earlier in my career, I had the chance to join UroSurge, a medical device company, as the Chief Technical and Operating Officer. The company was led by David Maupin, a seasoned industry veteran. From our very first meeting, the chemistry was immediate. The opportunity promised meaningful career advancement, a significant equity position, and the chance to work alongside someone from whom I could learn a great deal. I accepted the offer with enthusiasm and full commitment.

In this new role, presenting at quarterly Board of Directors meetings became part of my responsibilities. It was a step up in both visibility and accountability. The first Board meeting came about four months into my tenure, by which point I had relocated my family and made substantial progress across several key initiatives. One of my earliest moves was to recruit a brilliant engineer I had previously managed at another assignment. He hit the ground running, quickly delivering impactful improvements in product design and intellectual property.

As the meeting approached, David gave me wide latitude to prepare most of the presentation materials. While I had met several Board members during the interview process, presenting to them in this formal setting was a new experience. I ran through the presentation several times in advance. I was ready.

David opened the meeting with an agenda overview and a brief financial summary, then introduced me. Placing a hand on my shoulder, he said, "I knew early on that we had made a terrific hire with this young man. You'll understand why in a moment. One thing is clear—*he doesn't let grass grow around his feet.* We've made some real progress in just a few months."

The compliment took me by surprise. I had never heard that phrase before. I smiled at David, expressed my excitement to be part of the team, and launched into the presentation.

After the meeting, I pulled David aside and admitted that I wasn't familiar with the expression "he doesn't let grass grow around his feet." He laughed and explained that it came from his Midwestern upbringing in a farming community. It was a phrase he had used for as long as he could remember, but he reserved it for a select few. It referred to someone who acts decisively, without hesitation. A doer.

Since that day, I have adopted the phrase myself. I have used it in leadership roles and in PE to describe high performers who consistently move things forward and get things done.

That unexpected praise marked the beginning of a great relationship with David, one that evolved into a true mentorship and friendship. For that, I will always be grateful.

66. CARRY THE WATER

While I have heard the phrase "carry the water" many times in PE, my first encounter with it came from my friend and mentor, David Maupin, the CEO at UroSurge. At the time, I was working closely with Steve Preiss, our Vice President of Regulatory and Clinical Affairs, as we prepared for a critical meeting with the U.S. Food and Drug Administration. The purpose of the meeting was to introduce a novel medical device we were developing and to seek guidance on the clinical trial design necessary for FDA submission and approval.

Steve had an exceptional track record with FDA submissions, and he took the lead in preparing all the materials for the meeting. Along with a prominent surgeon who was serving as the principal investigator for our pivotal human clinical trial, Steve and I were scheduled to present our case directly to the FDA.

A few days before the meeting, Steve and I met with David to review the strategy and finalize our materials. The design of the clinical trial carried major implications for both operating expenses and time to market. The number of patients, the selection and number of global clinical sites, and the duration of patient follow-up were all under careful scrutiny. Thanks to Steve's diligence and expertise, every detail had been thoroughly thought through.

At the end of the session, David looked at Steve and said with his usual calm confidence, "Well, Steve, we've got a lot riding on this meeting. You must *carry the water* on this one. I have full faith in you."

Though the phrase sounded simple, I had never heard it used that way before. Coming from David, I assumed it had another of his farm-country origins. To me, it clearly meant that Steve would be the one to shoulder the responsibility and lead us through the moment that mattered most.

And that is exactly what happened. Steve carried the water. He navigated the meeting with poise and clarity. We left the FDA with a well-defined clinical trial path and a strong sense that our technology had made an impression. The FDA team showed genuine interest, recognizing the potential of our product to address a debilitating and underserved condition.

61. UNDERBRUSH

Returning to the topic of thorough PE diligence, another lesser-known term comes to mind: "underbrush." I had previously only encountered the word in its traditional sense, referring to the dense groundcover found in wooded areas: shrubs, ferns, and other low vegetation.

Anyone who has hiked off-trail through thick underbrush knows how cumbersome it can be and how easily one might trip or twist an ankle if not careful.

My first exposure to the term in a PE context came during a deep diligence process on a potential acquisition. We were in a deal team meeting, reviewing a long list of diligence topics. A younger colleague was updating the group on various outstanding items when he said, "There's still some *underbrush* here to get through. It's going to take more time. We can't move to Investment Committee approval on the deal before addressing it."

He was not referring to major red flags or deal-breaking issues. Rather, he was describing a collection of smaller, unresolved matters, details that, while not critical in a go or no-go sense, still needed to be addressed before we could bring the deal to our Investment Committee for final approval.

In that moment, I appreciated the metaphor. Just like in the woods, the underbrush in a diligence process may not block the path entirely, but it can certainly slow you down or cause trouble if ignored. And clearing it is part of doing the work thoroughly.

68. SMOOTH GLIDE PATH

Once again pulling from the world of aviation, I have come across a wide array of flight-inspired phrases in PE. One memorable phrase is "glide path." In its original context, it refers to the descent an airplane takes as it approaches the runway. In personal finance, it often describes an investor nearing retirement who gradually shifts from equities to more conservative, fixed-income holdings, a slow and steady descent meant to reduce risk before touching down into retirement.

A wealth manager might say, "Considering her plan to retire in three years, we've got her portfolio on a *smooth glide path* to retirement," which is a polite way of saying, "We're landing this plane before turbulence breaks the china."

I first encountered "glide path" in a PE setting during the diligence process for an add-on acquisition. In this case, the target company had a very different approach to employee compensation compared to the portfolio company it would be joining. To be blunt, the target's compensation structure was significantly more generous, with open-ended earning potential that looked more like a Silicon Valley startup than a scaled services business.

Given the strategic importance of the deal and the value it would add to our platform, we were highly motivated to work through this issue. A great deal of time and diplomacy went into collaborating with the target's leadership to craft a plan that would align compensation frameworks without triggering a mass exodus of their top talent.

During one key meeting, which included the CEO of our portfolio company, my colleague emphasized the urgency by saying, "At this point, there's a lot riding on this. We need clarity on compensation alignment and timing to ensure a *smooth glide path* to close."

In other words, we needed to land this deal without a bumpy approach while keeping founders and employees calm, coordinated, and onboard. A successful glide path here meant not just closing the deal, but touching down with everyone still smiling, buckled in, and ready for the next leg of the journey.

69. CATCHING A FALLING KNIFE

I was most familiar with the phrase "catching a falling knife" in the context of stock market investing. It refers to the risky act of buying a sharply declining stock in the hope that the price will rebound soon. The danger, of course, is that the stock continues its downward spiral after purchase, leading to painful losses. The metaphor is vivid for a reason: trying to catch a falling knife rarely ends well for your fingers, or your portfolio.

In PE, I have come across situations where this phrase applies just as well. A prime example occurred during the height of the COVID-19 pandemic. Certain acquisition targets experienced rapid, sometimes explosive growth due to pandemic-driven demand, a phenomenon often called the "COVID Bump." Revenue and EBITDA soared, and naturally, some owners viewed this as the ideal time to sell; hoping to exit at a valuation that reflected peak performance. But a buyer paying a full multiple on inflated EBITDA numbers, without factoring in the likelihood of post-pandemic normalization, risked *catching a falling knife*. Once demand subsided, the company's financials might return to earth, leaving the investor holding an overvalued asset.

The phrase also took on relevance in the post-pandemic phase. Many healthcare-related businesses that had thrived during COVID saw their growth stall or even reverse. As the world reopened, management teams of these companies often attributed the downturn to temporary pandemic-related disruptions and presented forecasts showing a strong rebound—sometimes projecting performance levels well beyond pre-pandemic norms. PE firms evaluating these companies faced a tough decision. Move forward with the acquisition and invest in new leadership, ramp up sales and marketing, and increase operating expenses in pursuit of a turnaround or walk away.

If the rebound materialized, it would validate the strategy and create significant value. But if sales remained flat or declined despite the investment, the firm would quickly realize it had misjudged the situation. The rebound was not coming. The knife had already fallen, and they had reached out and grabbed it.

10. THE VACUUM AND THE CLEAN FLOOR

The phrase "the vacuum and the clean floor" may sound a bit obscure, but I first heard it in a PE setting during a Board of Directors meeting for one of our newly acquired portfolio companies. The business provided revenue cycle management services to physician practices, and we were reviewing an early draft of the company's strategic marketing plan.

In that meeting, "Deb," a seasoned marketing executive and consultant serving as a fractional Chief Marketing Officer, led a discussion about how to position the company in a crowded market. She emphasized the importance of identifying what truly set the company apart, particularly its proprietary technology, which had the potential to significantly improve both financial and clinical outcomes for physician-owned practices.

But Deb challenged us to go deeper and focus on what really matters to our clients. She illustrated her point with a simple analogy: "the vacuum and the clean floor."

She said, "Look, we have all this impressive technology embedded in our services. It's important to communicate that so clients know they're getting the best solution—the best vacuum. But at the end of the day, most of them do not care about how the vacuum works. They just want a clean floor. We need to show them results, not overwhelm them with technical detail. Sell them the clean floor, not the specifications of the vacuum."

The analogy landed perfectly. It captured the reality that physicians are, first and foremost, focused on patient care. But the health of their practices depends on getting paid fully and fairly by insurers and government payers. That is where our portfolio company came in. These physicians were not concerned with the algorithms or data science behind underpayment identification or claims adjudication. They wanted to know that their key business metrics: revenue realization, denial rates, aging accounts receivable, and days in A/R were improving. In other words, they wanted the *clean floor*. And it was our job to make sure they got it.

11. SOME OF THE BEST MONEY SPENT IS THE MONEY WE DECIDED NOT TO SPEND

As described previously, before joining Riverside Partners as a full-time Operating Partner in 2012, I spent several years serving on the firm's Healthcare Advisory Board (HCAB). The HCAB is made up of business executives with deep domain expertise across the healthcare sectors where Riverside invests. Our mission was straightforward but impactful: help evaluate deals, support strategic initiatives at portfolio companies, pitch in on functional areas when needed, and occasionally serve on Boards of Directors. I quickly realized that the HCAB was not just a box-checking advisory group, it was a genuine value driver for both the firm and its companies. The commitment level and frequency of engagement from the advisors made it feel more like a hands-on task force than a part-time gig.

During my time on the HCAB, one experience stood out. A colleague reached out to me about an investment opportunity and asked if I could take a look at the technology and clinical rationale behind it. The target company had developed a medical device implant intended for oncology applications. By the time I got involved, my colleague had already spent considerable time on diligence. I could tell right away there was momentum and a touch of "deal fever" involved—as described in another section of this book—but I had to admit, the concept was intriguing.

As part of my diligence, I reached out to physician thought leaders in the field who were trusted experts I had collaborated with over the years. I dug in, and it did not take long to uncover some troubling details. A few key publications I surfaced raised red flags about the core technology, and one respected physician colleague shared serious concerns about the durability of its efficacy and the risk of adverse events. He even ran the issue past a few peers, who unanimously agreed: this was not something they would recommend. His parting advice to me was crystal clear—walk away.

I knew my role in this case was more "confirmatory diligence" than early-stage exploration, so I also knew that delivering this news wouldn't be easy. I met my colleague for coffee and walked him through the clinical feedback and the publications. He listened carefully. Though visibly disappointed, he remained gracious.

"Mike, this is super helpful," he said. "Thanks for sourcing all of this. It's invaluable."

I replied, "I know you had momentum here. Sorry for raining on the parade."

He smiled, shrugged, and said, "Hey, this is the nature of the beast. It's disappointing, sure, but I'm used to it. Comes with the territory. Besides, it's not like this is our only option. *Some of the best money spent is the money we decide not to spend.* We probably just dodged a bullet. Thank you."

That moment stuck with me. In PE, it is easy to get caught up in the excitement of a deal, but sometimes the most valuable contribution you can make is pulling the plug before capital gets committed to the wrong opportunity. This particular experience became one of those quiet victories: no deal, no press release, no closing dinner, but a win nonetheless.

12. TRIALS ON ROMANIANS

An anecdote worth sharing occurred during my tenure as an Entrepreneur in Residence in 2006 at Oxford Bioscience Partners, a life sciences venture capital firm, I came across a promising opportunity involving a novel imaging technology designed to enhance prostate biopsy procedures. The concept was to superimpose MRI and CT images of the prostate in patients suspected of having prostate cancer. At the time, this was cutting-edge. The technology allowed for image-guided biopsies, a significant improvement over the traditional transrectal method, which was essentially a blind multiple-core stab-in-the-dark approach. The goal was to create a more targeted biopsy, improving the likelihood of sampling suspicious areas with greater accuracy.

The company's R&D center and corporate office were based in Israel, led by a CEO and a group of founding scientists. If we were to move forward with an investment, the plan was to relocate the headquarters to the United States while keeping the engineering brainpower rooted in Israel.

After reviewing the materials and being cautiously optimistic, I invited the team to Boston to meet in person and present to the physician advisory board I had assembled at Oxford. The presentation was compelling. Their early data looked promising, and their vision was clearly articulated. At one point, I asked the CEO to walk us through the company's regulatory strategy, particularly their plans for FDA clearance and CE Mark approval in Europe.

The CEO responded confidently, outlining results from successful animal trials and detailing what could only be described as an ambitious regulatory path.

I followed up with, "Have you performed any human trials?"

He paused, then replied, completely straight-faced, "No, not yet. We have only performed *trials on Romanians*."

For a moment, silence.

Then, I burst out laughing. It felt like something straight out of Monty Python. The CEO looked at me, utterly confused, while my colleagues were either laughing with me or staring blankly, trying to confirm whether they'd heard him right.

After some back-and-forth, we realized the misunderstanding was purely linguistic. The CEO had misinterpreted my question to mean, "Have you conducted any trials in the U.S.?" He had meant to say the company had done early-stage clinical work in Romania, not that they had selected Romanians as a distinct experimental group.

The moment quickly became legendary—a perfect mix of language barrier, cultural nuance, and VC absurdity. And nearly two decades later, it still brings a smile when I think about it.

13. SWIM LANES

In a competitive swimming pool, "swim lanes" or "speed lanes" are designed to keep swimmers in their own tracks, allowing them to race without bumping elbows with their neighbors. These lanes are marked by lines on the surface and dividers in the water, and most competitive pools feature between four and eight of them, depending on size and event regulations.

In PE investing, I first encountered the term "swim lanes" in a very different but equally important context: organizational structure and leadership alignment.

In many mid-stage, founder-led companies, the lines of responsibility can be blurry. Founders and early executives often wear multiple hats, sometimes all at once. Post-investment, one of our first priorities as PE investors is to assess the leadership structure and identify gaps. Depending on the stage of the company and its organizational maturity, this often means introducing seasoned professionals into defined roles such as Chief Financial Officer, Vice President of Human Resources, or Head of Business Development.

To support this evolution, we help implement management control processes that include setting annual performance objectives for each executive and sometimes extending those metrics down through middle management and beyond. This practice enhances expectation setting, unity, and overall accountability across the company. Just like in a swimming pool, clearly marked swim lanes help each person know where they're supposed to be and what they're ultimately accountable, without running into someone else's role. Of course, real success also depends on collaboration across lanes, but clarity is the starting point.

I recall a conversation during a post-merger integration planning session for one of our portfolio companies. The team had just completed an add-on acquisition, and we were discussing how to combine two organizations with overlapping functions. A colleague spoke up and said, "As we bring the teams together, we need to define clear *swim lanes* so that everyone knows what they're accountable for."

It was a simple but effective metaphor that highlighted the importance of a structured approach to integration: one that promotes seamless collaboration, avoids functional overlap, and preserves operational efficiency as the organizations come together. Without those swim lanes, the integration could easily devolve into a splashy mess of duplicated effort, missed handoffs, and internal confusion. With them, we could establish structure, promote collaboration, and keep everyone swimming toward the same finish line.

14. STEPPED ON LANDMINES

During the first six months of my role as a C-level executive at a medical device company, we encountered a major challenge: instability in the supply chain for a critical raw material used in our flagship implantable device. Because the device was intended for long-term human implantation, the materials had to meet the highest standards of performance and biocompatibility. One essential component came from a small, specialized materials science company in California called "TCI", founded and run by an eccentric and deeply introverted engineer named Bob.

When I joined the company, I was quickly brought up to speed on the fraught relationship between our CEO ("Dan"), and Bob. Dan approached the relationship without being deferential, as if he had leverage over price, delivery, and data transfer. Not long after, I received an alarming notice from TCI: they were cutting us off. Not only would they no longer supply the implantable component, but they were also refusing to share critical data needed for our FDA submission, including biocompatibility and toxicology results.

I brought the issue to Dan, hoping to strategize a path forward. Dan tried to reassure me. "Listen," he said, "I've *stepped on plenty of landmines* in my career. We'll get through this. We've got a world-class team, and with you at the helm, that's all we need. We can reengineer this material and component ourselves."

While Dan meant well, I could see this was a blind spot. Reengineering the material in-house would be costly, time-consuming, and uncertain. We risked derailing our regulatory timeline and possibly the company's future. I decided to take a different approach. I reached out to Bob directly and arranged a trip to San Francisco to meet him and his wife (co-founder) for dinner. My goal was simple: build a relationship, rebuild trust, and see if we could find common ground.

My background as a Ph.D. scientist turned out to be an invaluable asset. It gave me the technical fluency to connect with Bob and the credibility to earn his respect. Just as important was the emotional intelligence to navigate around the softer issues that had caused the previous breakdown in communication.

Bob and I had more in common than I expected. He also had a doctorate, and we discovered a shared passion for motorcycles and cars. Over the next two months, I made several visits to TCI. We reviewed technical data, shared a few meals, and even rode motorcycles together along the Pacific Coast Highway. A genuine friendship formed, and from that point forward, I handled all communication with Bob.

The result was a breakthrough. We signed a long-term exclusive supply agreement, and Bob provided all the necessary data to support our FDA filing. Crisis averted.

Since moving into PE, I've often borrowed Dan's phrase, "I've *stepped on many landmines* in my career", although not appropriate at the time it was conveyed to me, as a way to defuse tense moments and reassure teams during difficult situations. Looking back on the episode with Bob, I realize just how lucky we were to recover after that near-explosion. It took a lot of effort, a bit of improvisation, and more than a few sleepless nights, but ultimately, it taught me the value of meeting people where they are—sometimes literally, on a motorcycle.

15. YOU CAN'T BREAK THE BIRD'S WINGS AND EXPECT IT TO FLY

I first heard the phrase "You can't break the bird's wings and expect it to fly" early in my career at a medical device company. It came after a contentious cross-functional meeting focused on strategy and timelines for a new product launch. Leaders from every area of the business were present.

After I outlined key deliverables for my team, the executive running the meeting: Jared, a C-level leader known for his insecurity and bullying, turned to the regulatory affairs team and asked for an update on our FDA strategy.

Tom, the regulatory lead, responded with a cautious but clear plan for achieving FDA clearance. The timeline, however, extended far beyond what Jared had hoped for.

Visibly irritated, Jared launched into a tirade. He called the strategy ridiculous, questioned the competence of the team, and openly referred to Tom as a "moron." The room fell into an awkward silence. Tom, clearly shaken, kept his composure and agreed to revisit the plan and timeline.

Jared's behavior was not an anomaly. It was part of a broader company culture where arrogance was tolerated, sometimes even rewarded. His rise to power had come too quickly, without enough operational experience or guidance, and his need to assert control was thinly veiled insecurity. People who challenged him often paid the price. At that company, compensation packages were engineered to attract top talent: above-market salaries, six-figure sign-on bonuses (forgiven over time and functioning like golden handcuffs), generous stock options, company cars, and more. Speaking out or getting fired often meant forfeiting life-changing compensation. That fear kept most people quiet.

After the meeting, Greg, a senior R&D colleague who had been with the company since its founding, pulled me aside. He was someone I respected deeply, a steady presence who had seen the company evolve from an entrepreneurial startup into something much less inspiring.

He was angry.

"We won't hit the original timeline," he said, shaking his head. "Jared thinks pushing unrealistic deadlines is motivational."

He wasn't wrong. I had yet to see a timeline at that company that wasn't wildly unrealistic.

Greg continued, "Does anyone stop to think what happens if Tom leaves? Is this going to change the outcome? *You can't break the bird's wings and expect it to fly.* Do you think anyone left that meeting more motivated? Do you think it brought the team closer? I'm sick of it. I might just quit."

His words stuck with me. The imagery of the broken bird was unforgettable and painfully accurate. Over time, the company struggled to recruit and retain top talent. Its culture had become toxic, and despite the generous compensation, people left. Eventually, change came. The company ousted the misfits, including the CEO. Greg, true to his nature, stayed through the storm and saw the company return to a healthier culture.

That experience taught me valuable lessons I carried into future CEO roles and, later, into PE. During my time as an advisor to River-side Partners, long before I joined full time as an Operating Partner, I observed something very different. The partners treated one another, and the leadership teams of our portfolio companies, with deep respect. I never saw disrespect. I never saw bullying. And I certainly never saw anyone trying to motivate a team by breaking its wings.

Riverside's approach was about honoring the vision of founders, building high-functioning leadership teams, and fostering sustainable, mission-driven businesses. We work side by side with our management teams to achieve growth that, in many cases, founders once dreamed of but didn't know how to reach. And we do it without breaking the bird.

16. IF WE HAVE LEARNED FROM GETTING OUTBID, THEN IT REALLY ISN'T A LOSS

This idiom is somewhat analogous to a phrase I've shared before: "Some of the best money spent is the money we decided not to spend." In PE, there is a learning curve that deserves respect, even when the outcome is disappointing. The diligence process is often rigorous, time-consuming, and expensive. As it unfolds, it is easy to become emotionally invested, which can cloud judgment and make it harder than it should be to walk away.

After Indications of Interest (IOIs) are submitted by PE firms and strategic buyers, the investment bank representing the seller may advance a group of suitors, sometimes ten or more, for management meetings. These sessions prepare investors for the next phase: submission of Letters of Intent (LOIs). LOIs mark the final step before entering confirmatory diligence and, ultimately, deal closure.

Occasionally, especially in high-valuation deals, the investment bank does not grant exclusivity to just one party after receiving LOIs. Instead, they may allow two or three finalists to proceed in parallel before selecting a winner.

I recall one particularly memorable situation in which, after a long and intense diligence process, we found ourselves in exactly that scenario. We advanced to the final stage but were ultimately outbid by another PE firm. Their winning edge came not only from offering a higher price but also from already owning a platform investment into which they planned to integrate the target company. They had momentum in the sector and a compelling story. We did not.

I was disappointed. I had become fully immersed in the opportunity and was eager to begin working with the founders post-close. I had already envisioned the value-creation plan and felt we were ready to execute. Sensing my frustration, one of my colleagues pulled me aside and offered some perspective: "This happens. You just have to get used to it. Remember, *if we have learned from getting outbid, then it really isn't a loss.* We're better for having gone through the process."

It was wise advice, and it stayed with me. While the outcome still stung, we came away with meaningful insight into the subsector, built relationships with domain experts, and gained a strong understanding of pricing benchmarks. There is no denying that losing out on a deal hurts. But in the end, the learning gained along the way can make the next opportunity even stronger.

11. NOT ALL CUSTOMERS ARE CREATED EQUAL

The phrase "Not all customers are created equal" can be controversial, but I have embraced it throughout my career. In PE, it became especially relevant during our investment in a bioanalytical laboratory services company serving pharmaceutical and biotech clients. I was deeply involved with this company: serving on the investment team, stepping in as interim CEO for the first six months post-close, and continuing on the Board of Directors. Originally a founder-led business, the company evolved into one of the most successful investments in Riverside Partners' history, generating the largest cash-on-cash return the firm had ever realized.

Throughout our investment period, we took a strategic and comprehensive approach to building the business. We filled key executive leadership and Board positions, stood up a world-class business development and marketing team, strengthened the scientific organization, and made critical investments in infrastructure. We implemented new enterprise resource planning and laboratory management systems, expanded laboratory capacity, and completed a transformative international acquisition. These efforts fueled significant growth in both revenue and EBITDA.

But with that growth came new challenges. As demand surged, the organization faced real constraints in capacity and service delivery. The company had matured past the stage of accepting any and all business. We needed to become more selective, disciplined in pricing, realistic about timelines, and clear on project scope.

I vividly recall a pivotal moment during a Board meeting when tensions flared between the operations and business development teams over deliverables and sales performance. A colleague, "Jen", spoke up. *"Not all customers are created equal,"* she said.

There was a mix of reactions around the table. Some nodded immediately. Others looked unsure.

Jen continued, "We need a near-term strategy to classify and prioritize both our existing clients and those in the business development pipeline. We should establish client tiers using clear metrics: revenue opportunity, client tenure, and likelihood of future work."

The CEO leaned forward, listening carefully, as Jen expanded her point. "For each customer, we should also consider the product pipeline in development, pricing dynamics and elasticity, margin contribution, and the client's financial health. If we're constrained, let's prioritize Tier 1 clients and assign dedicated account managers to ensure successful delivery and continued growth."

It was a decisive shift in thinking. We were no longer simply chasing growth—we were managing it strategically. Jen's framework helped balance the tension between service quality and financial performance, aligning the team around smarter resource allocation.

Implementing this approach was not easy. It required a cultural shift and tighter coordination across functions. But over time, the organization became more aligned, more disciplined, and ultimately delivered on both service excellence and aggressive growth expectations. The phrase may still raise eyebrows in some circles, but in this case, it helped successfully guide a high-growth company through the transition to maturity.

18. VENTURE CAPITAL REQUIRES PRAYER

After serving as CEO of Claros through a successful sale transaction, I received a steady stream of inbound interest and offers for CEO roles at both venture capital and private equity-backed companies. At the same time, opportunities emerged to join VC and PE firms directly. The idea of transitioning into a full-time investing role was intriguing. My background was somewhat unconventional compared to typical partners at those firms, and I believed it might offer a valuable complement.

To gain perspective, I reached out to several trusted friends and colleagues. One of them was Tony Crisman, Managing Director and Head of Healthcare Investment Banking at Stout. I had known Tony for many years, and his advice was both candid and insightful.

"You would make an excellent partner at a VC or PE firm," he said. "But there's a fundamental difference between the two. In PE, investment diligence is mostly about looking in the rearview mirror. You analyze where a company has been and why. In venture capital, it's more about foresight and betting on what could happen. PE is about 75 percent hindsight, while VC is 75 percent foresight."

I asked him to elaborate.

Tony continued, "In PE, you're looking at companies that already have revenue, EBITDA, and customers. You need to understand the details behind those numbers, drill into customer trends, and forecast what's ahead. But in venture, you don't usually have that luxury. Most of the time, you're betting on a core technology. It's promising, but most often unproven. *Venture capital requires prayer.* You're hoping the technology performs as expected. Trust me, there's a lot of praying."

I understood exactly what he meant. At that stage in my career, I was drawn to the adrenaline of driving operational growth, especially through business development. The idea of partnering with founders on their growth journeys, while shifting from being a player to more of a coach, was deeply appealing.

Since transitioning to PE full-time, the experience has been everything I hoped for. I've never second-guessed the decision. There is certainly execution risk in PE, and some situations may still call for prayer, but the level of uncertainty is far lower than what comes with early-stage venture investing.

19. SOFT-CIRCLED

I have encountered the term "soft-circled" frequently in both venture capital and private equity healthcare investing. In the VC context, it typically refers to conditional investment interest. A company may receive preliminary commitments from VC investors, but these are contingent on meeting specific criteria. Most often, that includes iden-tifying a lead investor who will set the terms, price, and valuation for the entire round of financing. Sometimes, the commitment may also be tied to achieving a performance milestone, such as filing a patent, completing a clinical trial, or securing regulatory approval.

For example, if a company is raising a $10 million venture round and has $3 million in conditional commitments, the CEO might say, "We have $3 million *soft-circled*, waiting to close once we secure a lead investor for $7 million who will set the terms for the round." The term is also used to indicate proximity to a fundraising goal, as in, "We have $8 million *soft-circled*, and we're seeking an additional $2 million to complete our $10 million target raise."

Beyond company financing rounds, "soft-circled" is also common in fundraising for VC and PE firms. Limited Partners (LPs) who invest in these funds may include institutional investors such as banks, insurance companies, university endowments, hedge funds, and pension funds, as well as family offices and high-net-worth individuals. During a fundraise, capital pledged by an LP is described as either "soft-circled" or "committed." A soft-circle in this case indicates that the investor has expressed interest and specified an amount they are willing to invest, though the commitment is not yet finalized.

80. PULLED THROUGH MANY KNOTHOLES

Anyone with a few years on an executive leadership team, especially those of us with decades of operating experience, knows that crises are not rare events. They are regular guests at the leadership table. Organizational dysfunction and operational meltdowns may take different forms, but they often follow familiar patterns. What truly sets apart effective leaders is not the absence of crises, but how they respond. Over time, I've learned to replace panic with perspective and knee-jerk reactions with calm deliberation.

One phrase that has stuck with me like duct tape on a leaky pipe is "pulled through many knotholes." It's one of my all-time favorites, and it has served as a guiding mantra in both my operating roles and later in private equity.

I first heard it from a mentor early in my career. We were dealing with a potential fiasco involving the FDA. The agency had provided preliminary feedback on a critical product in development, and it was not encouraging. The clinical trial design would need a major overhaul, complete with a tripled budget and a much longer timeline. Tension was rising, and members of the Board were circling like storm clouds, their concern shifting toward pessimism and, frankly, alarm.

During one especially tense Board meeting, the CEO, to whom I reported, calmly folded his arms across his chest and said, "Listen, I've been *pulled through many knotholes* in my career, especially with the FDA. We need to gather more data, study the predicate devices, and return to them with a plan. Until we do that, we're just speculating. Let's stop throwing darts in the dark."

That moment stuck with me, not just the colorful phrase, but the poise, clarity, and refusal to let urgency turn into chaos.

In the years that followed, I found myself repeating that phrase more times than I can count. I've been pulled through more than a few knotholes myself. Each time, the experience has been intense, transformative, and, frankly, humbling. You never come out the same on the other side. You emerge tougher, smarter, and occasionally, with just enough perspective and wisdom to smile at the absurdity of how tight the squeeze was.

81. SALT ON THE STEAK

I was first introduced to the idiom "salt on the steak" in 2000, during my recruitment to serve as CEO of a private equity-backed company called In-Line Diagnostics (ILD), later rebranded as HemaMetrics and ultimately acquired by Fresenius Medical Care.

As part of the interview process, I was scheduled to have dinner with Dr. Constantine "Gus" Hampers, Chairman of ILD and a member of the investor syndicate. Gus, a trained nephrologist, had developed a reputation as an aggressive business pioneer who helped revolutionize the delivery of high-quality, low-cost dialysis care. He had founded National Medical Care, Inc. (NMC), and grown it from a single outpatient clinic in Massachusetts into more than a thousand worldwide. Over time, NMC was acquired first by W.R. Grace & Company and later sold to Fresenius.

Naturally, before meeting Gus, I did my homework—and I wasn't quite sure what to expect. His business track record was undeniable, but he had been mired in personal and professional controversy. From an ethical standpoint, I was aware of his legal troubles involving the illegal import of animal skins from endangered big game cats. According to a multi-count indictment, he had participated in a scheme to hunt endangered species in Mexico between 1985 and 1988. After a hung jury in his first trial, he pled guilty in 1990 to a lesser charge and contributed $180,000 to a wildlife preservation fund.

His time at NMC also seemed anything but smooth. According to a New York Times article by Kenneth Gilpin titled "A Tough Grace Insider Gets Even Tougher" (May 8, 1995), Gus had continued to manage NMC as if it were his personal empire even after Grace acquired it. When he was passed over for the top job at Grace, he launched a $3.5 billion hostile takeover attempt to win back control of the company he had founded in 1969. This offer conveniently aligned with the news that NMC was under investigation by two federal grand juries. One, in Virginia, was looking into contracts related to medical directorships and third-party services. The other, in New Jersey, was investigating whether NMC had sold defective products and mishandled customer complaints.

Sources quoted in the article painted a vivid picture: "Gus is not a team player. It's his team or no team." "He is very much a Machiavellian." "He is an overwhelming study of striving."

By the time NMC was spun out and acquired by Fresenius, it was clear Gus had a voracious appetite for power and control which, I admit, made him even more intriguing as I prepared for our dinner.

We met at a private country club outside Boston. Gus was polished, reserved, and surprisingly welcoming. As we talked, we discovered common ground in our immigrant roots and blue-collar upbringings. As he grew more comfortable, he opened up, shared his views on ILD's strategy, his need for a CEO "soldier" to execute it, and his very specific opinions about the senior leadership team. Some, he believed, needed to go. Others could stay. His plan included relocating much of ILD's operations from Salt Lake City to Boston. The Board, he explained, was divided, some aligned with him, others loyal to the company's founder in Utah.

It was a lot to digest over one meal. But one thing was crystal clear: the Machiavellian traits described in Gilpin's article were on full display.

When Gus asked for my reaction to his strategic vision, I gave a measured response. I acknowledged the complexity, said I'd need time to evaluate the team and revisit the strategy once I was in the role, and emphasized the importance of earning employees' trust. After all, the company had ambitious clinical and commercial goals.

Gus paused, holding eye contact for a few beats longer than was comfortable.

"I understand," he said. "I wouldn't expect you to parachute in and do anything draconian from day one. But now you know where I stand. That will be important for you to remember."

Then he added, with a slight smile, "I liked your answer. I'm not afraid to debate decisions, but you'll need to be very... very prepared to debate me."

I could see why some might run for the hills, but I was energized by the challenge. Plus, the compensation package pitched was meaningfully above market and the opportunity to move my family from the Midwest back to Boston where we had family was very compelling. Even with the apparent volatility of the Board and the intensity of its Chairman, I was hooked.

And then came the moment I'll never forget.

Dinner had wrapped. I had a salad to start, filet mignon for the main course, and a cappuccino with a scoop of chocolate ice cream for dessert. As we sipped coffee, Gus leaned in.

"I'm quite impressed with you," he said. "I don't want to waste time. I'll recommend to the Board that you be hired. I'll have you meet each of them, and we'll put together an offer."

He stirred his coffee thoughtfully. "Your background is very unusual—science and business. It's rare. I consider myself bilingual in that sense too."

Then he added, "Do you know what else convinced me?"

I paused, unsure. Playing to his ego a bit, I offered, "I think you and I would work well together. I like your straightforward, pull-no-punches style."

He grinned. "That's true. But I noticed how you ate your steak."

I froze. What the hell is he talking about?

"You took a few bites. Then, you added *salt*," he said. "That told me everything I needed to know. I want someone who tries something first before assuming it needs to be changed. I could've told you the steak needed salt, but you figured it out for yourself."

I was blown away.

I accepted the CEO role, moved my family back to Massachusetts, and spent the next several years working to transform the company while navigating ongoing Board drama, frequent clashes with Gus, and a deeply divided leadership team. Eventually, I left to lead RMH, a company in the orthopedic sector.

Despite the turbulence, HemaMetrics was built on a brilliant scientific foundation. Its founder and technical team had developed groundbreaking technology that truly improved patient outcomes. The company was ultimately acquired by Fresenius, and I'm proud to have played a part in that journey. My signature is on the company's story, and I continue to hold deep respect for the talented functional leaders who helped make the eventual exit a success.

82. GIVEN THE HEISMAN

The Heisman Memorial Trophy is awarded annually to the most out-standing player in college football. It features a classic figure in vintage gear (leather helmet, baggy pants) twisted mid-stride with a football tucked under his left arm and his right arm fully extended to fend off tacklers. That extended arm, known as a "stiff arm," is used to abruptly and forcefully push defenders away.

I never imagined I would hear the Heisman Trophy referenced in the world of private equity. But then came Kate.

Kate was the founder of a growing company in a sector we were actively targeting. She was hard to reach, but after some persistence, I got her on the phone. Cautious at first, she gradually warmed up. We hit it off quickly, probably helped by the fact that we were both engineers by training. She appreciated that I had walked in similar shoes and conveyed she was happy that I "wasn't just another suit with a spreadsheet".

During one of our calls, Kate mentioned she would be exhibiting at an upcoming industry conference. I couldn't attend due to a sched-uling conflict, but she offered to meet a colleague of mine who would be there. He was bright, eager, and well-intentioned—but young, not too far removed from business school, and lacking any real operating experience. His EQ was still a work in progress, especially when it came to connecting with skeptical founders. I had a gut feeling this might backfire, but against my better judgment, I let him handle the meeting.

When I followed up after the conference, I asked how it went.

He shrugged, "She was kind of non-committal. I was, uh… *given the Heisman.*"

I knew immediately what had happened. The stiff arm. Classic.

It took almost four months to get Kate to return my call. When she finally did, she was fired up.

"I'm not going to have some freshly minted MBA telling me how to run my business," she said bluntly. "Believe me, I know the type. These PE guys are all clones. I'm not going to let it happen to my company."

I let her vent. She needed to. Then I calmly explained how we were different: our operating backgrounds, our collaborative approach, and our long-term vision. Slowly, she eased back into the conversation.

The whole episode was a masterclass in founder psychology. And it gave new meaning to "getting the Heisman." It is the perfect metaphor for the kind of stiff-arm we often get in proprietary deal origination, especially from founders who aren't actively looking to sell and assume we are just another financial suitor with polished pitch decks and no substance. Sometimes in PE, you've got to eat a few stiff arms before you find your opening.

83. GODFATHER OFFER

You don't need to be a film buff to guess what a "Godfather Offer" means. But until it happened to me, I'd never actually heard the phrase used in a business setting.

My familiarity with the term, of course, came from the iconic Paramount Pictures film The Godfather. In one of its most unforgettable scenes, Vito Corleone uses the phrase when helping his godson, Johnny Fontane, land a crucial movie role. The studio head, Jack Woltz, refused to cast Johnny. Vito assured Johnny that he would make Jack an offer "he couldn't refuse."

The next morning, Jack woke up screaming, covered in blood, with the severed head of his prized racehorse lying next to him in bed. Not exactly subtle. Johnny got the role.

My brush with a "Godfather Offer" was much less gruesome, but the implication was the same: resistance was futile.

At the time, I was CEO of a company backed by a family office investor. We were actively searching for a strategic distribution partner in Europe. I reached out to an old colleague, Steve, who was based there and working as an independent investment banker. Steve was a force of nature: a former semi-pro hockey player, a hard drinker, and a straight-shooter with a killer global network. Think "gladiator in a suit," just without the suit.

Steve didn't do small talk. His negotiation style was blunt, sometimes to the point of discomfort, but it got results. We engaged him to find a partner, and after some hunting, he identified a company in an adjacent sector that looked like a perfect fit.

Steve took point on diligence and led several meetings, including product demos and time in the field with our business development team. Everything seemed to be progressing smoothly.

Then came a Board meeting, where Steve joined by phone to give an update. His tone was calm but definitive.

"Guys, they're not interested in a strategic distribution agreement for all of Europe."

I was caught off guard. "What do you mean? They've been with our team, done pricing analysis, market diligence. There hasn't been a single red flag."

Steve didn't miss a beat. "No, Mike. They don't want to be a partner. They want to buy the company."

The Chairman responded instinctively, "The company's not for sale."

Steve laughed. "Well, I think that's about to change. They're going to make a *Godfather Offer*. And they're dead serious."

No horses were harmed, thankfully, but the offer that followed was indeed too compelling to ignore. After discussions with the Board, we entered negotiations and ultimately sold the company. The outcome was outstanding—for our investors, the leadership team, and, yes, for me.

The term might come from Hollywood, but in business, a real "Godfather Offer" is one that politely clubs you over the head with logic, value, and timing. And, like Vito said, it's one you just can't refuse.

84. THE OPPORTUNITY IN EVERY DIFFICULTY

The phrase "seeing the opportunity in every difficulty" speaks to optimism, resilience, and the ability to find upside in the face of obstacles. In business, it's a mindset that turns problems into catalysts for innovation, growth, and value creation. That perspective has served me well in both executive leadership and private equity.

In 2011, I had the privilege of meeting Dr. Phillip Frost, the legendary healthcare entrepreneur, investor, and CEO of OPKO Health, during the sale of Claros Diagnostics, where I was serving as CEO. After the acquisition, I joined OPKO and developed a strong working relationship with Dr. Frost. Leaving OPKO a year later to transition to PE remains the hardest career decision I've ever made, given the deep respect I had for him.

While leading Claros, I had formed a Clinical Advisory Board made up of top urology thought leaders. Among them was Dr. Peter Scardino, Chief of Urology and Chief Clinical Officer at Memorial Sloan Kettering in New York. A brilliant surgeon and researcher, Peter eventually became a close friend.

During my time at Claros, I became aware of an innovative diagnostic tool developed by Peter and his colleagues Hans Lilja, Ph.D. and Andrew Vickers, Ph.D. at MSKCC. Their research had produced a new blood test for prostate cancer that combined four biomarkers with a proprietary algorithm, refined over more than a decade and thousands of patients. The goal was to improve decision-making for patients with elevated PSA results before proceeding to a biopsy. It would later be branded as the 4KScore®.

The test produced a risk score that could predict long-term likelihood of aggressive cancer, metastasis, or prostate cancer–related death. It was a leap forward from traditional PSA testing. I saw its potential immediately, despite obvious regulatory and reimbursement hurdles.

I arranged a breakfast meeting at the Pierre Hotel in New York with Drs. Frost and Scardino to explore the opportunity. As expected, Peter came armed with data and conviction. Within minutes, Dr. Frost recognized the strategic importance of incorporating this technology into OPKO's portfolio, aligning seamlessly with the diagnostic continuum of products and services we were building for prostate cancer. Our conversation transitioned to exploring licensing strategies, logistical considerations, and we mutually agreed to reconvene at the end of the week.

"This is a great find, Mike," he said. "We need to collaborate with Peter and get this into our portfolio. What do you see as the risks?"

"Rarely do I come across technology that can truly change how medicine is practiced," I said. "This is one of those times. It's a win for patients, doctors, and insurers. Same with Claros. They complement each other."

"But what are the risks?" he pressed.

"Two main ones: regulatory and reimbursement. The FDA will be skeptical of a test designed to prevent biopsies. They'll worry about false negatives."

"And reimbursement?"

"I think we have a good case to make. Avoiding unnecessary procedures saves money. If we build the right economic model, payers should come around."

He nodded thoughtfully. "Would you move forward with the deal?"

"Absolutely," I said.

Dr. Frost pulled at his chin and looked at me intently. "I agree with your assessment. The opportunity here is bigger than urology. Think about general practitioners. They're often the first to order PSA tests. This could be a reflex test before referral. The market is huge. Yes, there are hurdles. But like you said, this is about changing how medicine is practiced. And remember: *look for the opportunity in every difficulty, not the difficulty in every opportunity*. I know you would not have brought this forward unless you saw that."

That phrase stuck with me. It wasn't just encouragement—it was a challenge to lead boldly. We ultimately licensed the technology, addressed the regulatory and reimbursement challenges, and launched the 4KScore® with OPKO.

Years later, in PE, that mindset continues to shape how I approach diligence and decision-making. Every deal has flaws. Perfection is a myth. But if you're only looking for red flags, you'll miss the real opportunity. And often, it's buried right there in the difficulty.

85. ENTROPY

My understanding of the term "entropy" comes from my background in chemical engineering, specifically from studying thermodynamics. In theory, entropy is a measure of thermal energy per unit of temperature. I learned to think of it as an indicator of disorder within a system. As molecular randomness increases, so does entropy.

Consider an ice cube, for example. Its water molecules are tightly ordered in a crystalline structure. When it melts, the molecules begin to move more freely and become less organized, increasing entropy. Once the water evaporates into vapor, the molecular movement becomes even more chaotic, and entropy rises further.

So, when a colleague in PE casually dropped the term "entropy" in a diligence meeting, it immediately caught my attention and, I admit, brought me a bit of joy.

We were evaluating a technology-enabled healthcare services business. The company offered valuable, specialized services and had demonstrated steady average growth. But its revenue was lumpy, driven by short-term, project-specific engagements. That made it difficult to predict future performance.

During a meeting to decide whether we would move to the next phase of diligence, I shared my hesitation.

"I'm struggling with how we forecast this business beyond a quarter or two," I said. "I just don't see how we can get comfortable."

My colleague nodded. "I agree. There's too much *entropy* here. It's too unpredictable. Hard to get our arms around it."

His use of the word was perfect. He had captured the essence of the problem in one word. The disorder and unpredictability of service demand. The uneven flow of projects. The lack of visibility into what the next few quarters would look like.

But entropy in a business can show up in more ways than just unpredictable revenue. It can surface as organizational chaos, poor communication, inefficient systems, low productivity, or weak operational data. And while too much entropy can make a business unmanageable, a controlled amount can actually be useful. It can spur innovation, adaptability, and creative problem-solving in a dynamic environment.

Managing entropy is about finding the right balance between order and flexibility. You cannot eliminate all disorder. Nor should you try. But you do need to understand it, contain it, and occasionally embrace it.

That moment in diligence reminded me how science and business thinking can intersect in unexpected ways, and how a single word, borrowed from thermodynamics, can neatly capture the messiness of real-world operations.

86. FLYING SUBMARINE

Fresh out of graduate school with a doctorate in chemical engineering, I accepted a role as Senior Scientist at Delta Surprenant (DS), a company specializing in polymer compounding for proprietary formulations and extrusion. Our work supported specialty wire and cable manufacturing for industries such as healthcare, electronics, defense, and aerospace. I was quickly immersed in complex material science challenges, working across multiple projects to develop next-generation polymer compounds for electrical insulation.

One project in particular stands out as a legacy moment in my career. The goal was to create a polymer compound that was both flame retardant and emitted minimal smoke with zero halogens when ignited. For context, Group 7A of the periodic table includes the halogens: fluorine, chlorine, bromine, iodine, and astatine. Polyvinyl chloride, or PVC, is commonly used in wire insulation due to its performance characteristics. But when PVC burns, it releases toxic byproducts, including hydrogen chloride, a severe irritant, and carbon monoxide, a lethal asphyxiant. My task was to eliminate PVC while meeting strict military-grade flame retardance and low-smoke emission standards—particularly for use in naval ships and submarines.

When I was assigned the project, the CEO described it as the "Holy Grail" of electrical cable insulation. No one had solved it.

Over the course of several months, I worked side by side with my technician, Dave, running dozens of designed experiments and enduring countless rounds of trial and error. The final compound contained nearly a dozen distinct chemical components and required a highly specialized standard operating procedure for compounding and extrusion. Dave, with his tireless work ethic and practical ingenuity, was the ideal partner. After multiple manufacturing validation runs, we confirmed that the formulation met all product release criteria.

I will never forget the moment Dave walked into my office, grinning, raised his hand for a high-five, and said, "Damn! You created the *flying submarine*. This is it."

The term "flying submarine" was new to me, but I instantly understood the meaning: something thought to be impossible. Fittingly, our compound was ultimately used in submarines.

Over the years, I've been involved in some record-setting cash-on-cash returns as both a CEO and a PE investor, some of which might earn the same nickname. But none have matched the personal significance of that early-career chemistry breakthrough. It was a moment where science, perseverance, and purpose came together in a way I will never forget.

87. UNDER-THE-TENT

Growing up in the city just outside of Boston, my exposure to camping was limited to a handful of Boy Scout trips more than 50 years ago. But I had a chance to get a different perspective of what it means to be "under the tent" during my time on the Board of Directors of a private equity-backed, technology-enabled revenue cycle management company serving the hospital market. After building a world-class organization and achieving several years of consistent revenue growth post-investment, the company had become a leader in its sector. With that success in hand, we began to explore a potential sale and initiated conversations with investment bankers.

Early in the investment, we had completed a transformative add-on acquisition and made the critical decision to hire a new CEO to lead the combined business. We brought on Mark Talley, a seasoned revenue cycle management executive, and it turned out to be one of the best decisions we made. Mark brought a mix of southern charm, sharp leadership instincts, and a great sense of humor. He handled the organizational challenges that come with rapid growth and integration with skill and humility. His competence and the open communication between us set the stage for continued growth.

By 2021, the market was primed with low capital costs and high valuations, making it an ideal time to consider a sale. Mark was actively involved in conversations with investment bankers to evaluate options and represent the company through the process. The response was overwhelmingly positive, and the Board decided to formally engage a banker.

As part of the sale preparation, the team began developing a Confidential Information Memorandum (CIM): a detailed document outlining the company's market position, operations, financials, customer base, and future growth opportunities. The CIM would be shared with potential acquirers under strict confidentiality.

In a meeting with the Board to review the CIM, Mark raised a critical point about confidentiality, both outside the company and within it. "I don't want our employees catching wind of a possible sale and panicking," he said. "We could see unnecessary attrition. But to get this done right, I'm going to need some of my team involved."

He paused, rubbed his forehead, and added, "I have no choice. I'm going to have to bring them *under the tent* as we move forward."

The phrase made me smile. Mark's use of "under the tent" perfectly captured what was needed; a careful, selective disclosure to a trusted few on a need-to-know basis. He understood that assembling the sale materials, managing the data room, and participating in management presentations required the cooperation of his top team. Yet he also understood the human side of the equation: if word got out and the deal fell through, the resulting disappointment and disruption could be costly. His thoughtful, strategic approach to bringing key staff "under the tent" reflected both business savvy and emotional intelligence.

88. ROCK STAR

I have always found the use of the term "rock star" to describe a high-performing executive, both in and outside of PE, mildly amusing. Throughout my career, before and during my time in PE, the need to recruit top-tier talent has been a constant. As a CEO, I was always on the hunt for individuals with serious chops, a track record of success, and the ability to work well with others. In short, the kind of people you could trust to build and lead real businesses.

In PE, the pattern is familiar. Shortly after closing an acquisition, we often sit down with the founder to assess the executive team and identify gaps. When we decide to bring in new C-level talent, the next step is usually to engage a professional search firm.

And this is where the comedy starts.

Without fail, someone will say, "We're looking for a *rock star*." Or, "This person has to be a total *rock star*." Or my personal favorite, "You need to find us a *rock star* for this role." At this point, I usually can't help but smile, or snicker, depending on the delivery.

Why? Because when you take the term literally, the image it conjures is not exactly what you want running your business. Are we truly looking for someone who stays up all night, trashes hotel rooms, indulges in substances of questionable legality, and has a string of lawsuits in their wake?

The irony always cracks me up. The stereotypical "rock star" persona is about as far from the buttoned-up, emotionally intelligent, metrics-driven executive we actually need as you can get. Yet the phrase persists. It has become shorthand for a game-changing leader, someone who can walk in, light up a room, and deliver results under pressure.

So, yes—we all want a "rock star." Just maybe not the kind with a backstage rider and a tour bus.

89. ACQUI-HIRE

Although our investment thesis for new platform acquisitions in private equity almost never depends on executing add-on acquisitions, we've employed this strategy opportunistically in every portfolio company I've been involved with over the past decade. Add-ons can take many forms: expanding into new geographies, acquiring complementary technologies, diversifying the client base, and more. In my experience, the financial thresholds for add-ons, particularly minimum EBITDA requirements, tend to be more flexible than those for platforms. Strategic fit often outweighs strict financial criteria.

It was during diligence on an add-on for one of our pharmaceutical services portfolio companies that I first encountered the term "acqui-hire."

In an early meeting, a colleague remarked, "This is basically an *acqui-hire* deal. It's just the founder and a couple of consultants. Over 90 percent of their work is in toxicology consulting. It's a valuable niche that complements what we already do."

The term caught my attention. "Acqui-hire", a blend of "acquisition" and "hire", refers to a small, often talent-driven transaction. The goal isn't to acquire revenue or infrastructure but to bring in the people, their expertise, and their client relationships.

While my introduction to the concept was in pharma services, acqui-hires are far more common in tech. Large companies like Microsoft and Google often acquire smaller firms to gain access to specialized talent, optimize their products, enhance expertise in a specific area, and more. For example, the development of the Touch ID and iPhone fingerprint scanner resulted from Apple's 2012 acquisition of AuthenTec, effectively an acqui-hire deal.

Since that first encounter, I've come to appreciate acqui-hires as a strategic tool in the M&A toolkit. Sometimes the most valuable asset isn't the company itself—it's the people behind it.

90. SHOTGUN MARRIAGE

Most people understand the term "shotgun marriage" as referring to a rushed or pressured union, typically resulting from an unplanned pregnancy. The origin of the phrase suggests the bride's father metaphorically standing behind the groom with a shotgun, encouraging him to do the honorable thing. The couple may not be ready, but social pressure or perceived responsibility forces their hand. I've always found the metaphor amusingly fitting in the context of PE.

In foundational platform investments, we rigorously evaluate acquisition targets based on defined financial performance metrics. However, when it comes to add-on acquisitions, those metrics are often more flexible. Strategic considerations like geographic expansion, customer diversification, or access to new technologies can outweigh pure financial performance.

I vividly recall evaluating one such add-on, "Project APEX," for a portfolio company in our healthcare services group. APEX was not the typical high-growth bolt-on. In fact, it was quite the opposite. Over the prior four years, both revenue and EBITDA had remained flat, with projections suggesting more of the same under current leadership. Although the company consistently brought in new customers, its overall revenue was declining. Seven of its top ten clients had meaningfully reduced their business, indicating a troubling pattern: strong sales but poor retention.

To complicate matters, APEX was backed by a PE firm that had held the company longer than usual. Their window was closing. The investment banker representing the company, someone we had worked with previously, hinted that the deal would likely trade at a below-market EBITDA multiple.

During a deal team meeting to review the opportunity, one of my colleagues leaned back in his chair and said dryly, "This is clearly a *shotgun marriage*. The investors are long in the tooth and probably forcing the exit."

That line stuck with me. It captured the entire dynamic perfectly. The sellers, like the metaphorical father, were pressuring a sale, and anyone stepping into the deal had to accept that it came with baggage. My take was that the company had a solid business development engine given the rate of new client acquisition and a brand that still resonated in the market. However, the execution of delivering the service had faltered, leading to consistent customer attrition. Clients came in the front door but quickly found the back one.

In this case, "shotgun marriage" wasn't just a clever analogy. It was a fair assessment of a deal shaped more by urgency and fatigue than mutual readiness.

91. YOU CAN'T GET THE BOAT TO SHORE BY THROWING AWAY THE OARS

While I began using this phrase more frequently later in my PE career, I was first introduced to it around 2002 by a dear friend and colleague, Paul Volpini. Paul passed away far too soon in 2010 at the age of 53. I met him almost 20 years prior when he served as a Senior Development

Engineer on my team. I was immediately impressed by both his talent and his integrity, and I later recruited him into senior project management roles at several of my subsequent companies.

Paul was an intense project manager. Outspoken, blunt, sometimes abrasive, but hands down the best I ever worked with. He led by example with an unmatched work ethic and total commitment to the success of any project under his care. He was equally tough on vendors who made rosy promises about delivery times and pricing. Never disrespectful, but never one to let things slide. He held peers and subordinates accountable and expected no less than full ownership from everyone involved. He focused relentlessly on building realistic project timelines. Once they were set, he made sure deliverables landed on time and on budget. With his background in high-stakes medical device programs, Paul had a sixth sense for spotting the landmines that could derail progress. People either loved Paul or hated him, there wasn't much middle ground.

Years later, as the CEO of a PE-backed medical device company, I walked into a minefield of leadership dysfunction. Two factions dominated the executive ranks: one loyal to the Chairman of the Board, the other to the physician founder and Chief Medical Officer. Their objectives were often at odds. I spent too much time playing peacemaker, trying to build bridges where perhaps fences would have served better. In hindsight, that effort diluted my focus on what really mattered: scaling a company built on groundbreaking technology for hemodialysis patients.

As we ramped up the business development team to drive our core commercial product, we also had multiple new product development initiatives underway. Most were late and over budget. It was clear we needed a professional project manager. I called Paul.

Hiring him was a turning point. As expected, he delivered. He broke down the project timelines, line by line, grilling the engineering teams and challenging their assumptions. If a timeline passed through Paul's gauntlet and emerged intact, I could sign off and take it to the Board with confidence.

In one of his first project meetings, frustration mounted as Paul dissected every line item. It quickly became evident that the issues weren't just with process—they were with people. Some members of the engineering team lacked either the skill or the discipline the job required.

After the meeting, Paul and I debriefed in my office. I shook my head and said, "Paul, I should've trusted my gut and brought you in sooner to scrub this team."

He cracked a wry smile. "They've never had a seasoned project manager lead them through a real commercialization effort. Great tech, but they're operating like it's a university research lab. If you want to turn this into a high-performance team, it starts with leadership."

We talked candidly about the Chief Technology Officer, whose shortcomings were becoming harder to ignore. I began listing the team members I thought needed to go immediately.

Paul, tugging at his goatee, leaned back and said, "It's basically day one for me. *You can't get the boat to shore by throwing away the oars.* Think of this like Marine Corps boot camp. I just smacked them upside the head. They needed it. I'm not here to win popularity contests, you know that. I've seen you set expectations and hold the line. As long as I've got your backing, we're fine. But let's give it a little time before you start tossing people overboard."

True to form, Paul didn't make friends on that assignment. But he did exactly what I brought him in to do. Accountability spiked.

Performance improved. He respected the "oars"—but only if they rowed in the right direction. He didn't use kid gloves, but he led the team toward success.

In every CEO role I've had since, I've thought about how Paul could have made a difference. I've never found anyone quite like him. I still miss him, both as a colleague and as a friend.

92. DEATH BY A THOUSAND CUTS

While I had long understood the phrase "death by a thousand cuts" in a business context, some cursory research led me to its unsettling origin. The term comes from Imperial China and refers to a form of torture in which a criminal was slowly sliced in small increments until death. Gruesome, yes—but oddly fitting when describing how slow, incremental damage can quietly unravel a company.

In operations and PE, this concept often plays out in the form of drawn-out headcount reductions. I have seen it many times: a few lay-offs here, a trimmed department there, then another round a quarter later. The strategy is often rationalized as "managing to the numbers" or "preserving flexibility," but it rarely works out that way. Instead, the drip-drip-drip of uncertainty steadily erodes morale, productivity drops, and the rumor mill kicks into overdrive. Pretty soon, no one is focused on the work anymore, but rather they're too busy updating their résumés or watching for the next axe to fall.

In one company I led, I remember raising this concern with a colleague who was championing a gradual approach. I said, "If we keep nibbling like this, we're going to kill the company's culture before we fix the P&L."

He replied, with a sheepish grin, "I know what you're saying. This is a *death by a thousand cuts.*"

"Exactly," I said. "Only nobody dies. They just disengage and quit in place."

The truth is, when a reduction in force becomes necessary, it is almost always better to make a clean, decisive move. Get ahead of it. Rip the Band-Aid off. The best managers I have worked with take the painful step once, and then move quickly to rebuild confidence and momentum. Ironically, going a little deeper than what seems strictly necessary often results in better outcomes, not worse. It minimizes repeated trauma and allows the organization to begin healing and refocusing sooner.

What separates merely competent managers from great leaders in these moments is communication. The best executives over-communicate. They are honest about what is happening and why. They give people the facts and resist the temptation to spin. When employees understand the rationale behind a tough decision, and believe it was made thoughtfully and fairly, they are more likely to stay engaged. Even those affected often walk away with a surprising degree of respect for the leadership team.

It is not easy, and it is never pleasant. But in my experience, one clear message delivered directly, backed by integrity, and followed by real support, beats a thousand small, quiet decisions that slowly bleed a company dry.

93. WEAKNESS INVITES THE WOLVES

The phrase "weakness invites the wolves" has echoed throughout my career, particularly in the worlds of politics and venture-backed businesses. In every case, invoking it served as a precautionary warning: sometimes strategic, sometimes simply a classic "cover-your-ass" maneuver.

Without getting too deep into politics, I grew up in a neighborhood where physical confrontations were a fact of life. I was taught early on never to start a fight, but never to show weakness either. "Turn the other cheek" was not part of the curriculum. Instead, I learned to defend myself fiercely and to never tolerate a bully. That mindset came from my father, and his father before him, and made the idea of "strength as deterrence" feel not just familiar but essential. It's no surprise that, later in life, the phrase "weakness invites the wolves" resonated so strongly with me whenever foreign policy debates emerged on the evening news. Whether you are negotiating with foreign adversaries or navigating a corporate boardroom, people tend to test boundaries when they sense vulnerability.

By nature, I have always supported the military, not out of romanticism, but because I believe strength keeps the peace. While the United States possesses the most capable armed forces in history, adversaries still test the waters when they sense indecision or disunity in leadership. Strength, whether real or perceived, is often what keeps potential threats at bay.

The same principle applies in business, especially in the venture-backed world. During my time as CEO of a VC-funded medical device company, we were preparing for a major European launch and had not yet reached cash-flow breakeven. On paper, we had plenty of runway. In reality, we all knew that venture-backed companies live or die by their ability to secure the next round of funding.

As strategic interest, both for investment and potential acquisition, poured in as a result of our scientific publications and media coverage, the Board of Directors, considering the inflated valuation figures for comparable companies and inbound interest, began discussing whether it made sense to explore a potential sale, especially since comparable companies were trading at eye-popping valuations. That discussion came to a head at a pivotal board meeting.

"John," an independent board member, was bullish. He believed in our team, our plan, and our technology. "Let's get the product launched in Europe, hit profitability, and then we'll talk about exit options. The company's value will double, maybe triple, if we're patient."

"Matt," a venture investor, was less sanguine. "We're still pre-revenue," he reminded everyone. "Let's not pretend the funding risk is behind us. We have no control over macro trends, and markets turn quickly."

"Emily," another VC on the board, chimed in with a middle-ground proposal. "Let's take the calls. Explore the inbound interest. No need to hire a banker just yet, but let's see what's out there."

I remember leaning in. "I have been on the receiving end of the interest, which is significant. But let's not create a circus. We need to have controlled discussions. I'll entertain conversations, but we need a tight process. Otherwise, we risk distracting the team and derailing execution."

John eventually agreed, but not before offering a parting observation. "Let's also be careful," he said, looking around the room. "*Weakness invites the wolves.* If the market thinks we're running out of cash, we're going to get low-balled by every bottom feeder in the industry."

He was right.

To counter that perception, I suggested a bridge financing round from our existing investors—enough to beef up the balance sheet and send the message that we were not desperate.

The board agreed. We raised the bridge. And less than four months later, we closed a strategic sale without compromising our negotiating position. Of course, the real punchline came in the fine print. That bridge financing? It came with a 2.5 times participating preferred return and a 9 percent interest rate.

In hindsight, the wolves weren't at the gates—they were already seated around the boardroom table, dressed in sport coats and holding term sheets.

94. EAT WHAT YOU KILL

I have encountered and used the phrase "eat what you kill" countless times throughout my career in business and PE. But my first exposure to the term came in a very different setting.

Aside from tagging along with friends on the occasional duck or pheasant hunting trip in my youth, I had never hunted large game. That changed in 1984 when a friend invited me on a three-day deer hunting trip near the Berkshires in western Massachusetts. At the time, I was mostly there for the beer, cigars, poker, and camaraderie.

I still vividly remember the first day. It was cold and snowy. My friend and I headed east into the woods, while the other two guys in our group went south. We saw little more than the occasional squirrel. At dusk, we reconvened to grill, drink, play cards, and eventually collapse into sleeping bags in the camper. Day two was much the same.

On the third and final day, sleep-deprived and slightly hungover, I decided to take things more seriously. Armed with my Mossberg 12-gauge shotgun, I set out alone, heading west into the woods. I came to a wide brook, about thirty yards across, and carefully made my way over the scattered stones to the other side without getting wet.

There, I found a winding trail leading up a hill. At the base, I noticed spots of deer scat. Encouraged, I began my climb, moving slowly and quietly, stopping now and then to rest, drink water, and listen to the forest.

Around midday, I stepped off the trail about fifteen yards and sat at the base of a tree to eat my sandwich. Snow was falling gently. The tall pines above swayed with the wind, but down on the trail, it was quiet, the canopy muffling most of the breeze. As I stood up and took a few steps, I heard a rustling ahead and froze.

Off to my right, about forty yards up the hill, I spotted two large deer. One stood alert, acting as lookout, while the other grazed in the underbrush. I slowly raised my shotgun, clicked off the safety, and took a deep breath. Looking closer, I realized they were does. I had no special permit, and taking a doe would be illegal.

I clicked the safety back on and lowered the gun. To my surprise, I felt more relieved than disappointed.

I stood still for several minutes, quietly watching as the deer continued to forage, then slowly trotted off into the woods. As I made my way back to camp, I found myself reflecting. Even if I had a permit—or if they had been bucks—could I have pulled the trigger? I had grown up in the city. I had never been that close to such beautiful animals in the wild. Watching them disappear into the snowy woods, I felt certain I could not have taken their lives.

Later, on the drive home, I shared the story with my friend.

"If I'd had a doe permit, I'd have taken the shot," he said without hesitation. "Wouldn't have thought twice."

"I couldn't do it," I admitted.

"I get it. But I don't hunt for sport. You have to *eat what can kill*, man. That deer would've fed me all winter. I don't waste anything."

"It's not for me," I replied. "I'll stick to the grocery store and save my conscience."

That was the first time I had ever heard the phrase "eat what you kill." I had to admit, there was a certain logic to it. Still, I never hunted again.

Years later, the phrase resurfaced in a different context—one that would prove far more relevant to my career. In CEO roles and PE, I learned the "eat what you kill" expression was especially relevant in the business development function. Sales professionals are typically compensated with a base salary and sales commission, the latter of which is a percentage of the revenue generated from their wins. Although not a pun based on my earlier anecdote, companies will often seek out sales "hunters" whose mission is to source and drive new client wins. Their compensation can be heavily weighted on the commission component, hence the applicability of the "eat what you kill" analogy. The more customer wins or kills they generate, the more they can earn or eat.

However, due to the scarcity of available talent and the pressure companies face to expand their field sales teams, I've noticed a gradual increase in the base salary component. This shift is designed to attract top performers with a proven track record, essentially serving as a hedge against future success. As these professionals close larger deals and drive greater sales, their total compensation, or, metaphorically, what they "eat", rises accordingly.

95. HERDING CATS IS EASIER IF YOU USE A PITCHFORK

Chances are you've heard the sarcastic phrase, "It's like herding cats," or its equally exasperated cousin, "It's as easy as herding cats." Anyone who has ever tried to coax a cat into doing anything it didn't already plan on doing understands the futility. Now imagine trying to corral several cats toward a common goal. Welcome to cross-functional collaboration in business.

The analogy gets tossed around often in organizational discussions, especially when you're dealing with departments that have conflicting priorities, competing performance metrics, or long-standing turf wars. Coordinating efforts across such silos can feel less like leading a team and more like trying to get six cats into a canoe.

I remember a particularly vivid moment from a Board of Directors meeting at a PE-backed medical device company. A serious product quality issue had surfaced, one with the potential to sink the entire business if not addressed immediately and comprehensively. The CEO laid out his remediation plan, which would require flawless cooperation from every functional group: sales, engineering, manufacturing, quality, you name it. Unfortunately, the company had a history of internal fiefdoms, and we were already in the middle of trying to reshape the culture into something a little less, well, feline.

The CEO walked the Board through his action plan: "Our field sales team will handle damage control with customers. Engineering is accelerating validation of a second source for the faulty component. Manufacturing needs to clear time on the line for the new part. Quality will prioritize testing as the updated units come off production."

Enter the CFO, a man who treated optimism as a personal affront. He sighed and muttered, "This is going to be like herding cats."

Sitting next to me was one of my PE colleagues who had heard the CFO's comment. I leaned over and said quietly, referring to the CEO, "He needs full cooperation. No side agendas. He has to put the hammer down. There's no bigger priority in the company today."

My colleague nodded, then looked directly at the CEO. "This takes precedence over everything else. Revenue goals are secondary until this is fixed." He glanced at the CFO and added dryly, "*Herding cats is easier with a pitchfork.*"

The image was mildly horrifying, but the point landed. The message to the CEO was crystal clear: he had full Board backing to do whatever was necessary, including firing anyone who did not fall in line with the recovery plan.

That moment was a turning point. The CEO got the air cover he needed, the organizational lines got blurred in the right ways, and everyone understood that this wasn't just another operational fire drill. This was the fire.

96. NICE DOGGY...NICE DOGGY

Throughout my career, I've been fascinated by how staff behavior shifts when a key employee decides to resign. Of course, there are legitimate, unavoidable reasons: spouse relocation, a desire to change industries, health issues. In those cases, people are showered with gratitude, farewell cake, and good-luck emails.

But things get more complicated when someone leaves for a competitor. That situation is usually driven by financial incentives, and it becomes even trickier when the employee uses the offer to squeeze their current employer for more money, threatening to walk if their demands aren't met.

Early in my career, I saw how this can play out—and how it can backfire.

I had been working on a new product project with "Barry," a key member of the Sales and Marketing team at a medical device company. Barry and I had traveled together several times, and a solid camaraderie developed. He was a classic type-A: serious, competitive, and laser-focused on results. Like many in sales, his primary goal was to maximize his earnings, which, to be fair, often aligned nicely with company success.

After about six months working side by side, Barry confided in me during a trip to a clinical site using our product. He had been approached by a competitor and had accepted a verbal offer: a more senior title, a 50 percent salary bump, and a generous package of stock options. He planned to resign when we got back to the office that Friday.

I was disappointed. Not just because I genuinely liked Barry, but because I knew his contributions could be critical to the commercial success of the product I was overseeing.

That Friday evening, I called him.

"How did it go?" I asked.

He chuckled. "They were surprised. Said they didn't see it coming. Asked if there was anything they could do to keep me."

"And what did you say?"

"I told them I'd consider a counteroffer, but I had already given my word to the other company. I even shared the offer details. They asked for the weekend to think about it. I said okay."

On Monday, our company matched the offer. Barry stayed. We went back to work like nothing had happened.

Six months after the project wrapped, Barry was abruptly let go. No cause, no warning. We were both blindsided.

A week or so later, I had lunch with "Gerry," a seasoned executive and someone I considered a mentor. I brought up Barry.

"I was shocked they let him go," I said.

"You knew he pushed for more money and threatened to leave, right?" Gerry asked.

I played dumb. "I knew he had another offer, but he stayed. That was months ago."

Gerry leaned back, arms folded. "You haven't been here long enough to know how things work. Ever heard the phrase *Nice Doggie... Nice Doggie?*"

I looked at him blankly. "Nope. Never heard it."

He smirked. "It's what you say while petting a dog you know is going to bite you. You stroke it with one hand saying 'Nice Doggie...

Nice Doggie,' while the other hand is quietly looking for a rock to smash it over the head."

I stared at him, half amused, half horrified.

Gerry continued. "That's how it goes here. No one holds the company hostage. Not you, not me, not Barry. If you threaten to leave for more money, we'll do what it takes to keep you—for a while. We'll match the offer to buy time. Let the competitor cool off. By the time they realize you're not joining, they see you as unreliable. You've burned the bridge. And once you're no longer useful to us, your time's up. Game over."

I was stunned. This wasn't in any business school curriculum.

"That's cold," I muttered.

Gerry leaned in. "It is. But entertaining another offer is seen as disloyal. Using it as leverage? That's betrayal. Emotions take over. Vengeance drives the outcome." He smiled, just barely. "Pretty twisted, huh?"

Looking back, it was my first real lesson in Machiavellian corporate behavior. A masterclass in passive-aggressive retaliation dressed in professionalism. I've had similar feelings of betrayal in later roles as CEO, as an investor; especially after pouring time and energy into someone's growth, only for them to walk away.

But I never once reached for the "Nice Doggie" rock. It's not my style.

I've learned that while unexpected departures can disrupt operations on various levels, one must persevere, dust oneself off, and move forward. People leave. It hurts. It disrupts. But you regroup and reset. Because no one, no matter how talented, is irreplaceable.

97. WITHOUT TRUST THERE CAN BE NO BETRAYAL

I thought it fitting to include the idiom "Without trust, there can be no betrayal" as a follow-up to the "Nice Doggie… Nice Doggie" anecdote. It perfectly aligns with the dysfunction Gerry was describing. As our lunch conversation continued, he offered more insight into the organizational behavior that had festered over his twenty years with the company.

"As long as Justin is CEO, tread carefully," he warned. "This mindset is baked into the culture. Watch who you trust. I keep my head down, focus on advancing the technology, and make sure my team hits our objectives. That's what keeps me here. The work matters. The patients matter. The rest? These characters come and go."

"I find this hard to believe," I said, shaking my head.

Gerry leaned in. "Let me tell you something even crazier. We've actually used recruiters to dangle fake job offers in front of employees, just to test their loyalty."

I blinked. "Wait, what? That's straight out of *The Firm*," I said, referencing the Tom Cruise thriller.

He nodded. "Exactly. You're not wrong. Trust no one. *Without trust, there can be no betrayal*. Trust no one."

That phrase hit me like a riddle. At the time, it felt like cynical wisdom from someone who'd been burned too many times. But over the years, I kept returning to it: *Without trust, there can be no betrayal*.

It took time to unpack its meaning. Eventually, I realized trust and betrayal are not opposites. They're intertwined. To trust someone, you have to be vulnerable. You have to take the risk. And that very risk creates the possibility of betrayal. It is a profound and deeply unsettling truth.

Years later, I came across the book *Underboss: Sammy the Bull Gravano's Story of Life in the Mafia* by Peter Maas. It chronicles the rise of Sammy the Bull, who became underboss to John Gotti, head of the Gambino crime family. Sammy was notorious for his role in at least 19 murders during the 1970s and 1980s and ultimately became the highest-ranking Mafia member in U.S. history to flip and testify for the government.

Somewhere in those pages, I noted a familiar quote from The Bull himself: "Without trust, there can be no betrayal."

That stopped me cold.

To see that same sentiment echoed by a Mafia enforcer and a seasoned corporate executive was a striking reminder that human nature plays out in remarkably similar ways—from the underworld of organized crime to the glass towers of corporate America. Even in that narrow chapter of my own career, the truth held up. The players might change. The stakes might differ. But the game? The game stays the same.

98. NORTH STAR

Although I didn't first encounter the term "North Star" during my time in PE, its meaning has followed me throughout my career and life. It originated much earlier and has proven especially relevant in PE when building relationships with founders and management teams.

Understanding their journey, and identifying their "North Star", offers critical insight into what drives them. It fosters trust and strengthens collaboration.

The concept of a North Star has both spiritual and scientific roots. In the biblical account from the Gospel of Matthew, the Star of Bethlehem guides the Magi from the East toward Jerusalem. That star served as their unwavering point of orientation. Astronomically, the North Star (Polaris) occupies a fixed position in the night sky, unlike the other stars that shift over time. It offers a reliable, constant reference point for navigation.

To explain how the idea of a "North Star" became personally meaningful to me, I have to go back to high school. At Malden Catholic High School, I gravitated toward math and science. While my parents emphasized the value of hard work, they had little guidance to offer about career planning. Early on, I thought I wanted to be a surgeon and planned to major in pre-med. But my high school guidance counselor, Brother Kevin Kenney, C.F.X., encouraged me to take a step back and think more broadly. He saw my strength in calculus, chemistry, and physics and recommended I consider chemical engineering. "It's a solid foundation," he said, "whether or not you continue on to med school."

I followed his advice and enrolled in Northeastern University's Chemical Engineering program. Through the university's Cooperative Education Program, I spent time working at the U.S. Army Materials Research Command. Mentors there, along with professors at Northeastern, influenced my decision to pursue a Ph.D. in Chemical Engineering at UMass Amherst. My doctoral research focused on materials science for aerospace and defense, but my passion ultimately shifted toward healthcare. I saw a chance to work on technologies that could change or even save lives. That possibility inspired me far more than anything else.

Years later, during an interview for a senior executive role at a public medical device company, I found myself in a rather unexpected meeting with the company's consulting psychiatrist, "Dr. Stephens." As we conversed in his office overlooking the ocean and sipping tea, Dr. Stephens posed a profound question, "What has been your *North Star* throughout your career thus far?"

No one had ever asked me that question before, at least not in those words. I paused, thought carefully, and answered with conviction: "I want to have a meaningful, positive impact on patients' lives through innovative medical technologies. That's what drives me, more than any financial outcome."

That response, in many ways, summarized a lifetime of decisions to date. It captured what had pulled me through uncertainty and steered me toward a life of purpose. Like Polaris in the night sky, it was the steady point that kept me oriented.

Through the twists and turns of my career, from R&D to the C-suite to private equity, that North Star has remained constant. In my current role, it helps me stay focused when challenges arise. It reminds me that success is not just measured by financial return, but by the lives we touch. It is possible to deliver strong outcomes for investors while also creating jobs, building enduring companies, and improving the lives of patients and caregivers. The *North Star* makes both ambitions possible, and meaningful.

99. LAND AND EXPAND

In private equity circles, the phrase "Land and Expand" is commonly used in the context of business development, especially within account management strategies. A typical business development pipeline can be segmented into three categories: (i) potential new clients (NC), (ii) existing clients (EC), and (iii) new relationships within existing clients (NR). NCs refer to clients the company has not previously engaged, often called "new logos." ECs are clients with whom the company is currently working or has worked in the past.

I regularly emphasize to portfolio companies that some of the most promising and overlooked growth opportunities lie within ECs, specifically through the cultivation of new relationships (NRs) within these accounts. When a company has delivered value and built credibility with a client, those established relationships often present the path of least resistance for expanding business. NRs involve broadening the company's reach across different departments, business units, or geographies within the same client organization.

Over time, effective business development and account management teams gain insight into the broader needs of their clients. When performance has been strong and trust has been earned, it becomes both logical and productive for a business development executive to seek introductions to additional stakeholders who may benefit from the company's offerings.

This strategy, widely known as "Land and Expand," applies far beyond PE-backed companies. At its core, it is about recognizing the power of satisfied clients as ambassadors. Asking for a referral within an existing client organization, when done at the right time and in the right way, is a low-friction, high-upside move. It leverages goodwill and past performance to unlock new revenue opportunities with relatively little resistance.

I have implemented this approach successfully in my own experience as a CEO and have consistently advocated for it across my PE portfolio companies. It is a proven, repeatable strategy to deepen client relationships and drive sustainable growth.

100. PEOPLE QUIT PEOPLE BEFORE THEY QUIT A COMPANY

I first encountered the phrase "People quit people before they quit a company" during one of my earliest assignments, and its relevance has stayed with me—particularly in the world of private equity investing.

My introduction to the phrase came through a colleague named "Jack," who was the Engineering Manager reporting to "Shelly," the Vice President of Operations. Shelly fit the classic profile of an insecure egotist; quick to claim credit, never willing to accept blame. He was difficult to work for, but Jack, who was deeply passionate about technology and manufacturing engineering, stuck it out for years. He did his best to manage up and stay focused on the work. Eventually, though, he reached his limit. Jack resigned and accepted a more senior role at a competitor, along with a higher salary.

Shortly afterward, I had lunch with my friend "Bob," the company's Vice President of Human Resources. I mentioned Jack's departure and said, "I really hated to see Jack leave. He was sharp and dependable. Great guy. It's definitely a loss."

Bob nodded. He understood the situation all too well. "No question," he replied. "But you know, *people quit people before they quit a company.* I've had multiple complaints about Shelly. His behavior is a real problem. I'm working on getting ahead of this with the CEO before we lose more good people."

That was the first time I heard the phrase, and it resonated immediately. It captured what we had both witnessed. But over time, I've come to see that the deeper truth is more complex. While toxic managers like Shelly can absolutely drive people away, the reasons people leave are often broader and more systemic.

Some of the most talented individuals I've worked with have departed not because of one bad boss, but because they felt they were no longer growing. They were underutilized, stuck in roles that didn't match their strengths, or operating in cultures that prioritized output over development. A lack of learning opportunities, poor leadership alignment, and a disregard for work-life balance all contribute to attrition. And none of these issues happen in isolation. They reflect gaps in leadership, broken feedback loops, and weak management systems.

There is no substitute for strong leadership that builds a culture of accountability, professional growth, collaboration, and purpose. In organizations where leadership actively invests in people and fosters cross-functional teamwork, employees stay engaged and energized. They are not distracted by recruiter calls, internal politics, or low-trust environments. They are focused on doing great work and building great teams.

Throughout my own career and through observing others, I have seen that when a company creates the right culture, talent retention follows. Employees are not just motivated by compensation or titles: they stay because they feel valued, challenged, and supported.

So, while the phrase "People quit people before they quit a company" still holds weight, a more complete version might be: "People quit cultures before they quit a company."

101. LET THE MISSION DICTATE YOUR ACTIONS

Successful executives operating within the venture capital and private equity ecosystems understand that mastering the art of managing up is essential. Investors vary significantly in their level of involvement. Some appear only at quarterly board meetings, while others feel the need to check in with the CEO and executive team multiple times a week. I have worked with both types throughout my career, and learning to navigate these dynamics has been especially valuable during my transition into PE.

In my experience, more hands-on investors often display knee-jerk reactions during moments of crisis. Early in my career, managing this behavior created substantial stress. However, I was fortunate to work with a PE investor I'll call Elliot, who served on my board and offered a perspective that proved invaluable. Elliot was a seasoned executive before becoming an investor, and his approach was consistently thoughtful and measured. He had an ability to cut through noise and focus on what truly mattered. I came to rely on his insights and often sought his counsel between meetings.

One particular episode stands out. During a challenging period involving unexpected FDA feedback on a clinical trial, I was faced with difficult decisions related to forecasting, operating expenses, and personnel. Elliot remained calm and focused on the long-term strategy. In contrast, another investor, whom I'll call Joe, reacted with relentless anxiety. Joe called daily, escalating tension and creating unnecessary chaos. He embodied the Chicken Little mindset, treating every setback as catastrophic.

Looking for steadier ground, I turned to Elliot. He advised me to resist reacting impulsively and instead to anchor decisions in the company's broader purpose. He said, "Think about it, Mike. Step back and refresh your understanding of the long-term mission you helped build. *Let the mission dictate your actions.* Everything else is noise."

His words brought clarity. In the midst of confusion and pressure, Elliot's guidance helped me reset, refocus on our mission, and lead with intention. Reconnecting with our strategic purpose became the compass that guided our response to the FDA situation.

I have been fortunate to work with investors who take this kind of long-view approach: those who remain committed to the company's mission even in turbulent times. Their steadiness has been both grounding and instructive.

In summary, mastering the art of managing up is essential in navigating the diverse dynamics of VC and PE investments. Drawing upon the wisdom of experienced mentors like Elliot equipped me with invaluable insights and strategies to confront challenges and stay focused on our collective mission. Ultimately, managing up is not just about communication, it is about alignment. Drawing on the wisdom of mentors like Elliot has equipped me to stay calm in crisis, maintain perspective, and make decisions that support the company's long-term success.

102. FOG A MIRROR

Talent acquisition, both in the investment and corporate worlds, can be a significant challenge, particularly in competitive labor markets. Fast-growing companies often struggle to keep pace with hiring needs and may settle for candidates who fall short of expectations.

I vividly recall one experience when I was invited as a consultant by Dillan, a General Partner at a venture capital firm, to attend a management presentation for a potential investment. The firm had recently closed a new fund and brought on several junior associates, two of whom joined us for the meeting.

Dillan had a forceful and highly self-assured presence. In meetings with management teams, he adopted a sharp, probing style of questioning that sometimes bordered on condescending. This approach was consistent, even when it would have been strategically wiser to present a more collegial tone. Companies exploring investment options often evaluate not just the capital but the people behind it. First impressions matter, and I had little doubt that Dillan's demeanor made a lasting impact, though probably not a favorable one.

During the session, Dillan led the questioning, frequently interrupting the presenter with a rapid series of detailed inquiries. I chimed in occasionally, sticking to a set of thoughtful, prepared questions. The associates, however, remained completely silent, focused on taking notes.

After the meeting, Dillan and I debriefed in a nearby conference room.

"Have you interacted with these new associates at all?" he asked, shutting the door behind him.

Caught off guard by the shift in topic, I replied, "I briefly met them in the kitchen this morning when I grabbed coffee, but I haven't worked with them on a deal until today."

Clearly frustrated, Dillan shook his head. "They sat in that meeting for two hours and just took up space. Hiring can't be about checking boxes. We should not bring someone on board just because they can *fog a mirror*. I could have invited my admin to take notes if that's all I needed."

I found it odd that his focus had shifted so quickly from evaluating the deal to critiquing the associates. Internally, I chuckled at the "fog a mirror" expression, imagining holding a small mirror under associates' noses to confirm they were alive. It was a humorous image, but also a distraction from the conversation we should have been having.

103. FOG BANK

Most of us have encountered fog during travel, whether by car, boat, or airplane. A fog bank, often referenced in maritime settings, is a dense patch of fog that can dramatically limit visibility, much like driving through a whiteout in a snowstorm. I vividly recall being caught in one while on a tuna fishing boat miles from shore. For the uninitiated, it is a disorienting and unsettling experience.

That moment came to mind during an investment evaluation that felt eerily similar. The situation involved a medical device company seeking PE backing. The company manufactured and sold capital equipment to hospitals, and as we emerged from the pandemic, my colleagues and I wrestled with how to assess market demand.

Specifically, we were trying to understand whether hospitals were ready to resume capital spending, particularly for a type of equipment that, while helpful to clinical workflow and management, was not considered mission-critical. In the post-pandemic environment, these purchases were increasingly viewed as discretionary.

Hospitals were under immense financial pressure. Labor costs were surging, staff shortages were widespread, and patient volumes remained high. Many healthcare workers had left the field altogether, burned out from the demands of the pandemic. To keep operations running, hospitals were canceling surgeries, turning to expensive contract labor, and facing internal tension as full-time staff pushed for higher wages in response.

Amid this strain, many hospitals had frozen or significantly reduced capital spending, prioritizing only the most essential needs. While we understood these constraints might be cyclical, we struggled to determine whether the slowdown in equipment purchasing was temporary or indicative of a deeper, longer-term shift.

To gain additional perspective, I reached out to a hospital executive who was also a practicing physician. His assessment was blunt. Hospitals, he explained, were delaying or canceling equipment purchases across the board, unable to justify the expense in the face of staffing shortages and shrinking budgets.

When I shared this insight with my PE colleagues, one of them offered a fitting metaphor. He described the situation as a *fog bank*—thick, uncertain, and impossible to see through.

"I have no doubt the product holds clinical value," he said. "But I just can't get comfortable with the market uncertainty. There's no way we can see our way through this *fog bank*."

The analogy captured our challenge perfectly. It was not the quality of the product that was in question, but rather the lack of visibility into when, or even if, the market would recover. And in PE, making investments without market line of sight is a risk few are willing to take.

104. ALL HAT AND NO COWBOY

You have likely come across phrases like "all sizzle and no steak," "all icing and no cake," and "an inch deep and a mile wide." But one that stuck with me and that I had never heard until my first C-level role, is "all hat and no cowboy." All these expressions capture a common reality: individuals who portray themselves as experts, leaders, or visionaries, but whose lack of real substance becomes apparent over time. In my experience across executive leadership, venture capital, and private equity, I have met more than a few people who fit these descriptions: often overpromising, underdelivering, and ultimately failing to live up to the image they project.

One such example came during my time at UroSurge, a medical device company focused on novel urology technologies. A few years after I joined as Chief Technical and Operations Officer, we began receiving acquisition interest due to the clinical promise of our innovations and the attention they were generating at conferences and in medical literature.

Among the interested parties was George, a CEO who lead a small public company in our sector, "JGYN". At that time, the market allowed pre-commercial, pre-FDA approval companies to go public successfully, something that would be almost unthinkable today. George had managed to take JGYN public, raise significant capital, and achieve a high market capitalization despite a lack of regulatory approval or clinical validation.

Though George had an impressive academic background, he lacked any meaningful technical or scientific expertise. He was also known for his powerful connections in finance, particularly a well-respected family member who had helped him generate investor excitement before and after the IPO. I had heard him speak at industry conferences and gathered feedback from physicians familiar with JGYN's product. My impression of him was that of someone entitled and self-important. More importantly, I had reason to believe there was a fundamental flaw in JGYN's core technology: an issue that could ultimately be fatal to the business. Despite this, the buzz around the company was strong enough that David, our CEO, and I agreed to take a meeting with George.

We met informally for drinks during an industry conference. George launched into a polished monologue about JGYN's supposed revolution in gynecology and urology, dripping with self-assurance. I could not help but imagine a silver spoon dangling from his mouth as he spoke. I thought of the eager financial analysts who had likely fallen for this same speech, mistaking slick delivery for substance.

As I provided George with an overview of UroSurge's technologies, he seemed impressed, asking technical questions that belied his lack of understanding. When I had the chance, I asked him about the flaw I had identified in JGYN's product. His demeanor shifted. He brushed his hair nervously to the side with his hands several times, repeated himself, and stumbled through a vague response. I nodded politely, offering a look of false affirmation. By the end of the meeting, George floated a proposal: a modest cash offer combined with a large portion of JGYN stock, hoping to leverage their inflated valuation. David responded that we would socialize the proposal with our board for review and follow up.

On the drive to the airport afterward, David, as he often did, asked for my take before sharing his own.

I replied bluntly. "The technology is fundamentally flawed. The valuation he's offering is tempting, but this would essentially be a reverse merger. They are sitting on a war chest of cash. We'd be taking UroSurge public through JGYN, whose underlying business is a house of cards."

David nodded. "That question you asked exposed a real issue. It's only a matter of time before the clinical community calls them out."

I continued, "George knows. You can see it in his reaction. It's like watching a train crash. We just have to decide if that's the train we want to be on—because there's no long-term value there."

David agreed. "Yes, I'm with you."

I asked, "If we even considered this, what would your role be after the transaction?"

He answered, "No role operationally. I'd most likely stay on the board. You'd move laterally and report directly to George."

I shook my head, clearly displeased. David noticed, laughed, squinted out the window, and said, "I know what you're thinking. This guy is a piece of work. He's *all hat and no cowboy.* Thank God the father came before the son."

Until that moment, I had never heard the phrase "all hat and no cowboy." I immediately added it to my repertoire.

In the end, we passed on the offer and stayed focused on building value at UroSurge. Several years later, we executed a sale transaction. JGYN, as we predicted, eventually collapsed under the weight of its flawed technology and hollow leadership. In hindsight, my only regret is that I was not savvy enough at the time to short their stock.

105. THROW A TOWEL OVER THE WARNING LIGHTS

There are many clever idioms associated with air travel, but one in particular struck me as especially relevant during a private equity experience. While serving on the Board of Directors of Tegra Medical, a medical device contract manufacturer, I witnessed firsthand how a well-placed metaphor can cut through complexity and drive accountability.

Tegra specialized in precision manufacturing, including metals fabrication, plastic injection molding, and over-molding. We acquired the business from its founders and launched an ambitious strategy for organic and acquisition-driven growth. Over time, the company expanded to four facilities: two in Massachusetts, one in Mississippi, and one in Costa Rica, growing to more than 600 employees.

As the company scaled, we recruited and hired a world-class Chief Operating Officer, Mark King, who was later promoted to CEO. One of Mark's early priorities was uniting the company culturally and operationally. Prior to his arrival, each facility operated in relative isolation, led by separate General Managers with little alignment across sites. Mark implemented a system of visible reporting, regular cross-facility meetings, and shared performance objectives to build cohesion across the organization.

Given the company's rapid growth, fueled by add-on acquisitions, investments in a dedicated business development team, and strategic partnerships, Mark recognized the need for rigorous performance management. With an engineering background and deep operational instincts rooted in his own early career on the factory floor, Mark understood that revenue alone often conceals underlying problems. He emphasized a disciplined focus on Key Performance Indicators (KPIs) at each facility, including material scrap, product rework, on-time delivery, and out-of-box quality.

To reinforce accountability, he installed large LCD displays throughout the plants that showed real-time KPI performance. These dashboards were updated daily, and a consolidated monthly report was distributed company-wide to highlight performance trends by facility.

During one particularly memorable executive meeting, each General Manager presented their facility's KPIs. It quickly became clear that one site was struggling. The GM, "Ken," explained that demand had spiked to record levels, pushing the facility beyond its production capacity. Increased overtime and strained resources had led to declining performance metrics and higher costs.

Mark listened carefully, then responded with clarity and resolve. "Ken, this decline in performance didn't happen overnight. I need you to get in front of it now before it really spins out of control. You can't *throw a towel over the warning lights* and expect the plane not to lose altitude."

Ken nodded, acknowledging the message and agreeing to take action.

Mark followed up, "Our margins are already showing signs of pressure. This cannot continue. I need your full attention on this. Involve me directly if you need support."

Mark's use of the phrase "throw a towel over the warning lights" captured the heart of the issue with precision. It evoked the futility of ignoring visible risks, akin to surrendering on quality and cost control just to keep up with production targets. It also suggested the false comfort of appearances, when what is really needed is intervention.

That moment landed powerfully with the team. It was a clear example of how strong leadership, delivered with clarity and urgency, can reinforce culture and accountability. Under Mark's oversight, Ken course-corrected, and the facility's performance stabilized.

This experience left a lasting impression on me. A well-timed metaphor, grounded in operational reality, can be a powerful tool for driving alignment and action, especially when the stakes are high.

106. DOING THE WRONG THING HARDER

I was first introduced to this idiom over 20 years ago when I hired a former colleague, "Paul," to help streamline the R&D function at a PE–backed company where I was serving as CEO. Paul had little tolerance for team members who couldn't multitask or manage their time effectively, and he brought a no-nonsense approach to organizational improvement.

I vividly recall a conversation we had early on, as he was assessing the department.

"I know you've heard the definition of insanity," he said, looking at me pointedly.

"Yes, I'm well aware of it," I replied.

Naturally, Paul pressed on, undeterred. "Insanity is doing the same thing over and over and expecting a different result," he repeated.

I nodded, and he continued, "These folks are hardworking, no question. But you can't fix time management by just working longer hours. *Doing the wrong thing harder* isn't going to get us where we need to be. There's no accountability, no clear project prioritization, and frankly, a lack of competent management."

I smiled because it captured the situation perfectly. His observation was blunt but accurate, and it stuck with me. That lesson has proven invaluable in my PE experience, where we routinely work to strengthen management processes and implement systems that align with growth goals. Creating accountability, improving prioritization, and building effective leadership are critical levers for driving productivity and efficiency across our portfolio companies. Paul's insight served as an early message that effort alone is not enough: it has to be directed, measured, and led.

107. FAIL FAST

Nobody likes to fail, but the opportunity cost of failure increases the further along you are in a process or project. Failing early is painful, but failing late after significant investment of time, resources, and energy can be far more costly. Throughout my career, both prior to and within PE, I've had the privilege of working with outstanding manufacturing executives across medical device and diagnostics companies. One of the most valuable lessons I've learned is the importance of inspecting for quality at critical points throughout the manufacturing process.

Waiting until final inspection to discover a product defect is a costly mistake. By then, not only are the materials lost, but also the labor and overhead that have been invested up to that point. This simple truth reinforces the value of measuring quality and monitoring key performance indicators throughout the entire production cycle.

The stakes are even higher in the pharmaceutical and biotechnology industries, particularly when it comes to product development. The lifecycle, from discovery and preclinical work through multi-phase clinical trials, can easily cost billions of dollars. While every company hopes to deliver the next breakthrough therapy, the reality is that most molecules will not make it to market. That is why significant effort is placed early in each phase to identify red flags and determine whether a program should move forward, be restructured, or halted altogether.

The concept of "failing fast" is especially relevant in this context. If failure is unavoidable, then discovering it early saves time, money, and organizational energy. In my work across the pharmaceutical services sector in PE, I've heard the term "fail fast" countless times, and I've come to deeply appreciate its importance. It is not a mindset of pessimism, but one of discipline and an acknowledgment that smart resource allocation often requires difficult decisions, made early and made well.

108. SUCCESS HAS MANY FATHERS... FAILURE IS AN ORPHAN

Many years ago, a mentor in PE shared a phrase that has stayed with me: "Success has many fathers, but failure is an orphan." It remains one of my favorite expressions, resonating across both my personal life and professional experiences. The quote's origin is debated. I've heard it attributed to Mussolini's son-in-law and later popularized by JFK after the Bay of Pigs fiasco, but regardless of its source, its truth is timeless.

While I could offer countless examples that illustrate this concept, I'll take the high road and focus on a few that are more ironic and, frankly, a bit humorous.

One recurring scenario in PE that never fails to amuse me happens during interviews with candidates for C-level positions, particularly for CFO roles. As both a former CEO and a current investor, I've noticed a consistent pattern: some candidates tend to attribute a company's success almost exclusively to themselves. This tendency is especially pronounced among CFO candidates, who often position themselves as the primary driver of the organization's accomplishments.

Let me be clear—I have worked with outstanding CFOs and have great respect for the role. A talented CFO adds tremendous value in areas like financial planning, performance measurement, reporting, and strategic analysis. But the bravado that sometimes surfaces in interviews can be ironically overblown.

I have heard CFO candidates claim, "I grew the business 40 percent annually over five years," "I led three successful add-on acquisitions," or "I expanded the company internationally." These statements often prompt a simple follow-up: "To whom did you report?"

The answer is almost always, "I reported to the CEO."

Which leads to my next question: "And what were the CEO's responsibilities?"

Of course, the CFO contributed meaningfully to the business's growth. But the casual self-attribution of success, often framed as if they singlehandedly fathered it, is usually a stretch, and sometimes outright comical.

The dynamic flips entirely when I interview CFO candidates from underperforming companies. Suddenly, the tone changes. "I wasn't responsible for business development or sales," or "I didn't have a role in the international acquisition strategy," are common refrains. The once-proud parent of growth now distances themselves from the shortcomings, as if poor results arrived unannounced and unparented.

No one enjoys discussing failure, and it's human nature to highlight strengths. But I've always found it ironic how crowded the room becomes when credit is being handed out, and how empty it gets when accountability is required.

Over time, I've learned to pay close attention to how candidates describe both wins and losses. I try to give credit where it's due and take blame when it's deserved. Still, I'm never surprised by the familiar pattern: the many fathers of success, and the lonely orphan that is failure.

109. PATTERN RECOGNITION

The concept of "pattern recognition," often discussed by my colleagues in PE, did not fully resonate with me until several years into my role as an Operating Partner. In my experience, the companies we invest in, typically founder-owned or majority management-owned, are already successful businesses. These companies, which fall into what we refer to as the "lower middle market," usually demonstrate sustainability and generate enough revenue to produce more than $3 million in EBITDA and are not distressed situations.

We recognize that these businesses would continue to succeed without our involvement. The founders have poured immense sweat equity into building them, often tying up a significant portion of their personal net worth in the process. At some point, they reach an inflection point and begin to consider liquidity. In our case, that often means partnering with a PE firm, taking some chips off the table, retaining a minority equity stake, and launching the next chapter with a partner who brings the experience and resources to pursue meaningful growth.

Although these companies are successful when we engage with them, they often share a set of common deficiencies. A colleague once described this observation in a way that stuck with me: "You'll find there's a *pattern recognition* with these companies. You'll notice it early in diligence. While no two companies are identical, there is a recurring set of gaps or areas where we can plug in and add value."

This idea became clearer the more I worked with founder-led businesses. At this stage, founders are often wearing multiple hats: handling finance, operations, sales, HR, and more. One of the most consistent gaps is in finance. Many of these businesses lack a professional CFO who can implement formal budgeting, establish reporting processes, track key performance indicators that reflect the health of the business, and manage the debt that often accompanies a PE investment. I recall one target company that was generating $5 million in annual cash flow but relied on a relative of the founder to manage finances using QuickBooks, with no metrics or structured reporting in place.

Another common shortfall is in human resources. These companies frequently lack formal HR leadership to address day-to-day organizational issues, design effective talent acquisition strategies, reduce attrition through career laddering, and shape corporate culture. The need for a Chief People Officer is often immediate.

Sales and marketing gaps also tend to emerge. Many of these companies are growing at impressive rates, sometimes in the double digits, but rely entirely on word-of-mouth referrals. They often have no dedicated business development leadership, no inside or field sales function, and no Customer Relationship Management (CRM) tools to build and manage a robust sales pipeline. Despite their momentum, these businesses are frequently operating without the infrastructure to sustain or scale that growth.

Each company brings a unique story and set of circumstances, but over time we have learned to recognize consistent patterns. These insights help us craft a tailored but familiar growth playbook, with necessary adjustments to fit the specific context of each business.

Addressing these gaps typically increases the company's expense base in the early years. We may need to invest in new leadership roles, enterprise systems, and operational processes to support scalable growth. As a result, it is not unusual for EBITDA to decline during the first couple of years post-investment. But this short-term dip is a strategic investment. It positions the company with the right people, systems, and processes to drive the aggressive organic and acquisition-based growth we target as part of our investment thesis.

110. STUPID GAMES...STUPID PRIZES

As I've noted several times throughout this book, some of the most persistent challenges in any business, whether it is an early-stage venture or a Fortune 500 company, stem from organizational behavior. These issues typically involve a lack of accountability, gossip, employee infighting, weak leadership communication, poor feedback loops, and the absence of a cohesive team dynamic.

In my experience, gossip and the individuals who perpetuate it can be especially damaging. It undermines trust, erodes morale, increases anxiety, and leads to a loss in productivity. Rumors can fracture teams, harm reputations, and create a toxic work environment. As I reflect on my career, a few anecdotes stand out that have shaped my zero-tolerance stance toward workplace gossip, each one reinforcing the phrase "stupid games win stupid prizes."

The first story involves "Jorge," a Vice President of Manufacturing at a PE-backed company where I served as CEO. Jorge was an exemplary leader. He set a positive tone, led by example, and was deeply committed to fostering a healthy workplace culture. His team included both full-time employees and part-time hourly staff. The latter group was often the source of discontent, gossip, and rumors, and Jorge had little patience for such behavior.

As the company scaled and product demand increased, Jorge would often promote high-performing part-time employees into full-time roles. These decisions sometimes triggered resentment among those who were not selected. Two notable sources of that discontent were a mother and daughter, "Kathy" and "Samantha", who both worked as part-time hourly employees on the manufacturing floor. Kathy had been hired first, followed by Samantha about six months later.

Roughly a year after Samantha joined, we began preparing for a sale of the company. Only the senior executive leadership team was aware of this process. As part of the diligence, potential acquirers would tour our manufacturing facilities. During one such tour, Kathy overheard visitors discussing details that hinted at a potential transaction. She began speculating, which ignited the company rumor mill.

Shortly afterward, a key manufacturing manager named "Rick" resigned to take a role elsewhere. During his exit interview, Rick shared that Kathy had told him the company was being sold and that manufacturing operations would be relocated to a facility 500 miles away. Rick, acting on this rumor and without confirming it with Jorge, panicked and accepted a lateral position at another company.

After Rick's departure, Jorge conducted an internal review and confirmed that Kathy was the original source of the rumor. She was terminated immediately. Samantha resigned the following month.

Another story that stands out involved a more unconventional tactic used by a former colleague named "Henry," a Senior Vice President at a medical device company. Henry had a sardonic personality and absolutely no tolerance for gossip. He shared with me his unique approach to rooting out rumor-mongers: he would intentionally "plant" an outrageous story with an employee he suspected of having loose lips and swear them to secrecy. If he later heard that story repeated by someone else, he would promptly terminate the original recipient.

While I understood Henry's rationale, I would not personally employ such a strategy. The risk of the rumor spreading and creating broader disruption would outweigh any short-term gain. When I asked him about the potential fallout, Henry replied, "I love weeding these people out of my organization. Hey, *you play stupid games, you win stupid prizes*. We are better off without these people."

While extreme, Henry's sentiment speaks to a truth I have come to respect: culture is fragile, and allowing corrosive behavior like gossip to fester can quietly undermine even the most promising businesses. In PE, where time horizons are compressed and organizational performance is paramount, addressing these issues swiftly and directly is not optional, it is essential.

III. EXCEL SPREADSHEET JOCKEY

The career path for venture capital and private equity professionals often bypasses any time spent working in an operating company. It typically begins right after college, with a few grueling years in investment banking or management consulting. Some take a detour through business development or product management roles at private or public companies, while others jump straight into a VC or PE firm as an Analyst or Associate. These early-stage professionals usually bring a relentless work ethic: some firms expect 80-hour weeks without blinking.

Their days are packed with due diligence, financial modeling, and building pitch decks, investment memos, and presentations for both internal teams and external stakeholders. They also coordinate with legal, financial, and other third-party advisors to help close deals. After a few years in the trenches, many leave to earn an MBA, then return and ascend the hierarchy: Senior Associate, Vice President, Principal, Partner, and eventually, General Partner.

I first heard the term "Excel spreadsheet jockey" during my time at a venture-backed company. Though I encountered it in a VC setting, the phrase is just as applicable in PE. At the time, our company was pre-commercial and raising a Series B financing round. A well-respected independent board member, "Scott," introduced me to "Derek," a General Partner at a venture firm who seemed genuinely interested in the opportunity. Scott had known Derek for years and had great respect for both him and his firm. He joined me for the meeting.

Scott and I got along well. He had a long career running operating companies, including one in our space that sold for a huge multiple. A former Marine, he appreciated straight talk and did not hesitate to speak his mind.

Derek arrived with two associates from his firm, Eve and Pat. Derek was sharp and engaged. He asked thoughtful questions about the technology, preclinical results, regulatory pathway, and manufacturing readiness. Eve remained silent but typed furiously on her laptop, documenting every word. Pat, on the other hand, seemed determined to assert his value by grilling us on our financial model.

Now, to be fair, the model was basic. This was a breakthrough technology play, and our plan was to sell the company before meaningful commercial scale-up. We hadn't spent much time refining five-year forecasts. Still, Pat fixated on them. He questioned every assumption, challenged our go-to-market plan, wanted details on salesforce compensation, global distribution, marketing partnerships—you name it. All valid questions. Just wildly premature.

I kept my cool, answering as best I could and offering some context on the total addressable market and our initial sales strategy. But the rhythm of the meeting was off. Scott, increasingly annoyed, began sighing audibly every time Pat spoke. Derek glanced down at his PDA more than once during Pat's tangents.

On the drive back to Boston, Scott let loose.

"You want to learn how to run a business with Excel? That guy will teach you," he muttered.

"I'm sure," I said, trying not to laugh.

"He's never run anything. Never made a payroll. Never built or scaled a team. How does someone like that add value?"

I shrugged. "I've seen it before. He was just asking questions to ask questions. You have to stay calm and deferential."

Scott rolled his eyes. "You gotta love these *Excel spreadsheet jockeys*. No idea how to run a business. They're at every firm. They're like clones."

Scott may have been a little over the top, but I have to admit, I've used the phrase ever since. And it always gets a knowing laugh from operating executives and PE colleagues. No explanation needed. Most can spot one from a mile away.

112. THE AIRPLANE TEST

VC and PE-backed companies typically maintain a formal Board of Directors composed of representatives from the investment firms, key executives, founders, and often independent members. The independent directors I have worked with are usually seasoned industry experts or current and former executives who bring real operational insight. They can add significant value in areas such as strategic planning, talent acquisition, fundraising, exit readiness, and nearly every functional vertical.

While serving on the Board of a PE-backed company prior to my full-time role, we began the process of recruiting a new independent Board member. The CEO asked me to lead the effort, including sourcing, screening, and interviewing candidates. I kicked off the process by drafting a role specification and aligning with the rest of the Board on the key criteria.

In a meeting with the CEO to review the spec, I walked him through the profile I had assembled.

He nodded with a relaxed confidence and said, "I've no doubt you'll find us candidates with great pedigrees. You know what we need…you know what it takes."

I appreciated the trust. He then added, "Just make sure they can pass the *airplane test*."

I paused. "The airplane test?"

He leaned back, smiled, and explained, "We've got a great Board. No egos. No assholes. So yeah, find someone qualified, but ask yourself—could you survive a cross-country flight sitting next to this person?"

Ah. The *airplane test*. It landed perfectly. And years later, I still reflect on that phrase. It has become a surprisingly effective litmus test, not just for Board members, but for anyone you're inviting into a leadership team. It speaks to culture, group dynamics, and the importance of surrounding yourself with people who bring both competence and cohesion to the table.

113. THE PRICE OF SUCCESS IS NEVER TOO HIGH COMPARED TO THE COST OF REGRET

Throughout my career, I have encountered many moments where the path forward involved risk and required stepping outside my comfort zone. Sometimes it meant pursuing a role that felt just beyond my perceived capabilities. Other times, it meant making investments in venture or private equity with uncertain outcomes, where success or failure could be binary. One particular experience from my early CEO days stands out: not only for the challenge it presented, but for the sage advice I received about the "cost of regret."

I was approached to lead a medical device company in need of an operational turnaround. It was a very different opportunity from any of my past roles. The company was generating meaningful revenue, but years of operational mismanagement had led to high employee turnover, shrinking margins, and sustained negative EBITDA. The business was privately funded by a family office with no sector expertise, and they were in the process of replacing the CEO. The Board Chairman reached out and asked me to consider taking the helm.

After reviewing the business plan and speaking with several team members, it became clear that while the company had a solid product portfolio and competitive pricing, it lacked strategic direction and operational discipline. Success would require a full-scale transformation: restructuring the business development and clinical services teams, rationalizing the product portfolio, outsourcing select manufacturing functions, and putting in place clear performance metrics and accountability systems.

It was a big lift, but also a tremendous opportunity. If executed well, the turnaround could be achieved in a relatively short period, with meaningful upside in both compensation and equity. I had to make a decision quickly, so I reached out to a trusted former colleague, "Bill," a private equity investor with a background in operating roles and a reputation for wise, no-nonsense advice.

After I laid out the opportunity and my plan, I admitted my apprehensions about the scope and complexity of the challenge.

Bill was direct: "You're not going to know until you get in there, roll up your sleeves, and dig in. But you have to get a read on the people first. The Board. The investors. Are they serious about the turnaround? Are they willing to back real change?"

He continued, drawing from his own experience: "Look, Mike, these kinds of chances don't come around often. You've still got plenty of career runway if it doesn't go as planned. You'll be well-compensated, and you'll know soon enough if your plan is gaining traction."

He emphasized the value of operational focus and sound execution, but then paused and added something I'll never forget.

"No doubt you're at a crossroad. With this sort of decision, either you're all in or you're out to lunch. You can stand on the sidelines and watch this thing pass, or you can grab it and make a real difference. I'll tell you this—you won't regret taking the shot. *The price of success is never too high compared to the cost of regret.*"

His words hit home. I took the job.

With a supportive Board and a committed team, we executed the turnaround over the next few years. The business stabilized, grew, and was eventually acquired at a premium valuation.

Looking back, I am grateful for Bill's advice and for taking the leap. That decision became a defining moment in my career: a reminder that calculated risk, when matched with focus and discipline, can create lasting impact. And most importantly, I have never second-guessed it.

114. N OF ONE

One of the most rewarding experiences during my tenure in private equity to date was an investment in BioAgilytix (BAL) and my active involvement in the company's journey. BAL was founded by Afshin Safavi, Ph.D., whose visionary perspective on the growing market for large molecule biologics positioned the company at the forefront of next-generation therapeutics spanning oncology, rheumatology, central nervous system disorders, and beyond. As a bioanalytical contract research organization, BAL specialized in large molecule bioanalysis for preclinical and clinical studies, supporting the development and release testing of biologic drugs.

While it is difficult to fully capture Afshin's leadership, the evolution of the company, and the contributions of my colleagues in a single reflection, I want to share a glimpse into that experience and an idiom that has stayed with me ever since: "N of One."

After our investment, I stepped in as Interim CEO to help launch key strategic initiatives alongside Afshin and lay the groundwork for operational improvements until we appointed a permanent CEO. Afshin was an outstanding partner: visionary, collaborative, and fully aligned with our goals. We later recruited a terrific CEO, a pivotal decision that helped shape BAL's next phase of growth.

Over the following years, we executed a comprehensive strategy: building a seasoned management team across all functions, strengthening business development, improving operational efficiency, upgrading lab infrastructure, expanding U.S. facilities, and completing a transformational European acquisition giving BAL a global footprint.

Like any fast-growing organization, BAL faced its share of challenges. But it emerged as a market leader, known for its scientific integrity, quality standards, remarkable client service, and execution. Despite competing against much larger industry players, BAL consistently won new business and demonstrated its distinctive value proposition.

After five years, we initiated a sale process, engaging Wells Fargo and Lincoln International as our banking partners. Tony Crisman, then Managing Director and Co-Head of Healthcare at Lincoln, played a central role. He has since become Head of Healthcare Investment Banking at Stout.

As offers began rolling in, many far exceeding our expectations, I remember having a private conversation with Tony. I shared my amazement at the valuations we were seeing.

Tony, a straight-talking Midwesterner known for his integrity and insight, nodded and said, "Mike, you have to understand. BAL is an *N of One*. There's no one else in the market delivering this level of scientific depth and personalized service. They're an island, man."

His words stuck with me. BAL truly was an "N of One"; a singular company with no real peer in the market. That unique positioning translated into extraordinary strategic value.

BAL was ultimately acquired by Cobepa, a PE firm, delivering the highest cash-on-cash return in my firm's 30-year history. I remain immensely proud of my role in helping build BAL. It was a rare and meaningful opportunity to contribute to the creation of a truly distinctive organization, a living example of what can be achieved when vision, discipline, and collaboration come together.

115. OUR PEOPLE ARE OUR IP

Reflecting on the BioAgilytix (BAL) experience, one pivotal moment during the early diligence phase stands out as especially formative. It occurred during our first management meeting with BAL's founder, Afshin Safavi, Ph.D. As I listened to his presentation, I found myself grappling with a concern that I could not easily dismiss: the absence of proprietary technologies or products. Coming from a background where my CEO roles often centered around differentiated, IP-driven businesses, the lack of clear protectability in a service-based model like a clinical research organization (CRO) gave me pause.

At the conclusion of the meeting, I asked Afshin a direct question: "What is proprietary about the business? There's no intellectual property, correct? What is protectable?"

His answer was immediate and sincere: "*Our people are our IP.*" He went on to explain that the company's true value lay in the depth of expertise, experience, and commitment of its staff, the very people who delivered BAL's scientific excellence every day.

That moment reshaped my thinking. Afshin's response helped me understand that in service-oriented businesses within the pharmaceutical sector, differentiation often stems not from patents or platforms, but from people. Talent acquisition, retention, and the cultivation of an entrepreneurial culture become the critical assets. It is this culture, anchored in ownership, pride, and accountability, that clients experience and value most.

Afshin's perspective stayed with me and proved true throughout our journey with BAL. Since then, we have continued to invest successfully in the pharmaceutical services space, guided by a deeper appreciation for what truly drives value in these companies: the caliber, character, and commitment of their people.

116. BREADLINES ARE A GREAT PLACE TO MEET PEOPLE

My mother, who lived through the Great Depression, often shared stories about the hardships her family endured during those unimaginable times. Having never finished high school, she began working at a young age alongside her father and siblings, selling fruit at Boston's Faneuil Hall Marketplace, just outside the North End.

During the Depression, thousands of unemployed people faced eviction and were forced to rely on public assistance and charity. Breadlines, long queues of individuals waiting for food, were common, typically organized by government agencies or charitable groups like the Red Cross. For many, standing in those lines carried a sense of shame and personal failure.

Early in my career, I found myself in a high-visibility, high-accountability role where I was performing extremely well. Buoyed by that success, I began to feel overconfident. I considered making compensation demands, despite not having another opportunity lined up if those demands were rejected.

At the time, my wife and I had just welcomed our first child, which added another layer of risk. During a Christmas visit with my parents, I shared my plan. My mother, never one to hold back, made her disapproval clear.

"Why would you want to leave this job? I thought you were doing well," she asked, clearly puzzled.

"I am. That's why I want to ask for more money," I replied confidently.

"It doesn't sound like you're asking," she said. "It sounds like you're trying to force their hand and you're coming off as disrespectful."

"I deserve a higher salary for the value I've created," I argued. "The company is making a fortune from the products I developed."

"Isn't that what they hired you to do?" she countered.

Frustrated, I snapped, "You don't understand. I'm being paid less than people who are making half the contribution."

She paused, then said calmly, "That might be true. But do yourself a favor—don't worry about other people. There will be a time and place to have a fair conversation about your salary. I'm sure your boss, and his bosses, recognize what you're doing. Wait until your annual review. Have a rational discussion. You've told me he's treated you well. He hired you, he brings you into meetings with the CEO. Clearly, he values your contributions."

Then she looked at me with quiet intensity and said, "Nothing good comes from acting like a bully. And what if he says, 'Take a hike,' and fires you? What then? You have a house. A mortgage. A new baby."

Her words hit me. And then, in the way only she could, she added, "Michael, it's your decision. Do what you think is right. Just remember—*breadlines are a great place to meet people.*"

Her advice, shaped by the lens of the Great Depression, may have sounded dramatic at the time. But she was absolutely right in calling out the flaws in my thinking and my approach to organizational behavior. It had nothing to do with education. I was simply too young, too confident, and too inexperienced to see it clearly.

I took her advice, stayed the course, and was ultimately promoted several times and compensated generously. That conversation taught me a lasting lesson, one I would return to many times throughout my executive career and even today in PE. It shaped how I've approached difficult conversations, power dynamics, and long-term thinking ever since.

117. PRICED TO PERFECTION

In my experience with financial modeling during due diligence for potential PE investments, we create base, downside, and upside forecast models. While I don't usually handle the Excel grunt work that involves incorporating all the independent variables and calculating the financial returns, I often weigh in on the assumptions behind each case.

In competitive processes, we sometimes find ourselves stretching the upper bounds of enterprise value for a target, based on our return models, to the point where it starts to feel a little uncomfortable. One such memorable moment occurred during a competitive process for an acquisition target. As we were assessing the growing price tag in a team meeting, one of my colleagues remarked, "Our offer is essentially *priced to perfection* for this company."

He explained further, noting that as the valuation continued to rise, the margin for error on performance assumptions became increasingly tight.

"We're at a point where everything has to go right for us to hit our base-case financial model, especially the customer attrition assumption," he said. "I think we're hitting our head on the ceiling here."

The phrase "priced to perfection" may sound like a beautiful thing, but in this context, it carried significant execution risk. Essentially, if everything didn't go according to plan. If anything went wrong, then it would be a tough climb to meet our targets. The company's success would be too reliant on external factors outside of management's control, leaving us highly exposed to downside risk.

It was a sharp reminder that in investing, even the most perfect scenarios are still filled with uncertainty.

118. WHAT MAKES A GREAT EXECUTIVE IS NOT WHAT ONE CAN MAKE, BUT RATHER WHAT ONE CAN FIX

I've come to view the process of hiring C-level executives as more of an art form than simply checking boxes. While past performance and relevant experience are certainly important, I also consider factors like leadership style, cultural fit, the ability to implement management control processes, execution of growth strategies, and long-term vision. After all, almost any competent executive can run a company smoothly when conditions are ideal: during times of market tailwinds, stellar product performance, limited competition, and minimal customer attrition.

However, my experience in executive leadership and PE has taught me to seek out leaders who have not only succeeded in stable environments but have also weathered the storms when things get tough.

I remember a conversation early in a CEO search for a PE portfolio company with an independent board member. As we discussed specific criteria like sector experience and founder dynamics, one quote from our conversation particularly resonated with me.

I said, "The company is doing well. We don't need a babysitter here. We need someone to take the wheel and drive growth. Experience in managing significant growth will be a key factor for me."

My colleague responded, "I agree. Challenges will inevitably come with growth. We may get some things right and some things wrong, but hopefully fewer of the latter. *What makes a great executive is not what they can build, but what they can fix.* I want to see real experience in navigating a company through growing pains."

Growth is undeniably rewarding, but it often comes with its own set of challenges: talent acquisition, maintaining quality, managing lead times, and enhancing customer service, just to name a few. During times of aggressive expansion, it's crucial to have a proactive leader who can draw on their experience to identify problems early and address them effectively. It's this ability to steer the ship through turbulent waters that distinguishes great executives from good ones.

119. WE DON'T HAVE A BIG ELEPHANT IN THE ROOM...WE HAVE A HERD OF LITTLE ONES

The phrase "elephant in the room" is a widely used idiom to describe a significant issue or problem that everyone is aware of but chooses to ignore or avoid discussing. It refers to a matter so obvious and prominent that it becomes difficult to overlook or pretend it doesn't exist. Much like a large elephant standing in the middle of a room, this issue draws attention and creates a sense of discomfort or unease among those present. The metaphorical "elephant" represents a sensitive topic that people tend to tiptoe around, often due to fear, social norms, or the potential tension it may cause. Addressing the elephant in the room means openly acknowledging the issue, discussing it, and working toward a resolution or a deeper understanding of its implications.

When it comes to organizational behavior challenges, there is often a "elephant in the room": an issue that executive leadership and staff avoid confronting because it may be awkward, disrupt the status quo, or create tension. These situations can take various forms. In my experience, they have ranged from toxic CEOs, board members, or dysfunctional executive teams to employees who are family members of the founder and receive preferential treatment. While these individuals can sometimes be resistant to constructive feedback, I've found that once these issues are brought to light, they are usually straightforward for Board leadership to address.

At Riverside Partners, we've adopted the practice of holding an annual CEO conference, during which we discuss general topics of interest, share ideas, and foster camaraderie. It's always an opportunity for cross-pollination of experiences and a sense of unity among the leadership. During one particularly memorable conference, we invited Pat Richie, a Principal Consultant from The Table Group, to speak. Pat has been a regular guest at several CEO conferences I've attended. He's an engaging speaker who connects with his audience and uses real-world case examples to illustrate key points, especially when discussing organizational behavior.

Pat frequently uses corporate and sports team examples to demonstrate how "elephant in the room" situations have been addressed. However, describing a consulting assignment during which he was engaged with an executive leadership team about organizational cohesion, he made a point that stuck with me. Rather than identifying a single "elephant in the room," Pat told the leadership, *We don't have one big elephant in the room. We have a herd of little ones.*"

This idea resonated with me because I've seen firsthand how a collection of small organizational behavior issues, when accumulated, can dramatically hinder a company's performance. These "small elephants" can be more challenging to tackle than a single large issue, but they can lead to the same negative outcomes. In either case, it is essential for executive and Board leadership to be proactive, decisive, and address these issues swiftly. The sooner these concerns are addressed, the less likely they are to escalate and disrupt the organization's success.

120. DEAL FATIGUE

Considering company sale processes, PE diligence often demands substantial resources and attention from the selling company's management team. To help navigate this process, companies typically engage an investment banking firm to lead the sale. Occasionally, the banker will describe their client, the business seller, as experiencing "deal fatigue" when the PE acquisition diligence process is prolonged. "Deal fatigue" refers to the exhaustion and weariness felt by the target company's management team and employees during an acquisition process that can be rigorous and drawn out. It occurs when the process stretches on too long, draining the founders and executive team who are involved in managing the company being acquired.

Diligence can feel like a full-time job for an executive leadership team, making it challenging to balance with the daily responsibilities of running a business. The acquisition process often disrupts normal operations, as management finds themselves dedicating significant time and resources to acquisition-related activities, diverting their attention from core business operations. The additional workload, combined with the pressure of compiling information, attending meetings, and responding to due diligence requests, can create stress that impacts morale, productivity, and job satisfaction. Moreover, it can also strain the relationship between the management team and the PE firm, who must collaborate effectively after the transaction is completed.

As the acquisition diligence timeline extends, founders and management inevitably face increasing uncertainty and ambiguity. Stress and anxiety around the deal's closure certainty, the opportunity costs involved, and the potential changes in ownership, organizational structure, or strategic direction begin to build. These factors generate tension about management roles, job security, and the future direction of the company.

To combat "deal fatigue," I've found that clear communication, support, and transparent expectations from the PE acquirer are essential throughout the diligence process. At the same time, founders and management need to be well-prepared, ensuring the data room is comprehensive, financials are audited, earnings analysis is robust, and customer data is thorough. Often, investment banking firms can help companies prepare for this intense diligence process well in advance of soliciting interest from potential buyers.

PE firms must take the lead early in establishing open communication, transparency, and clear timelines to mitigate the impact of "deal fatigue" on the target company's management team and employees. By doing so, they can facilitate a smoother transition and a more collaborative post-acquisition environment.

121. FIRST LOSER

The term "first loser" is often used to describe a participant or entity that finishes in second place or narrowly misses out on achieving a desired outcome or winning a competition. It refers to the individual or organization that, despite performing exceptionally well and surpassing many competitors, falls just short of securing the top spot.

I first encountered the phrase "first loser" during my time as CEO of a company, and it has since proven to be a useful concept in my subsequent CEO roles and current position in PE, where I've heard it used more than once.

My introduction to the idea came during a competitive business development bidding process for a request for proposal (RFP) issued by a potential new customer. Despite our company being the underdog due to its size, we put considerable effort into the proposal, met with the customer, and quickly responded to all diligence requests. Unfortunately, we were not chosen.

During the process, our VP of Sales had built a strong rapport with one of the decision-makers, who later informed us that we had finished as the runner-up among five bidders. While the news was disappointing, it helped raise our company's profile with the prospective customer, ultimately working in our favor for a future project.

When I shared the disappointing outcome with one of my investors, a member of the Board, his response was blunt: "It doesn't matter where we finished. We're the *first loser*. We might as well have come in last place. If you're not first, then you're last."

Though his statement reflected his critical nature, I couldn't resist replying with a quote from a past mentor: "You miss every shot you don't take."

That moment highlighted why this particular individual had never successfully run a company. In times like these, I've learned that the most productive approach is to pick yourself up, dust yourself off, and keep moving forward. This mindset has been a cornerstone of the culture I've fostered in every management team I've led and in my role as Operating Partner with PE portfolio companies.

122. TAKE-OFF VELOCITY

During a conversation with "Francine," a General Partner at a large private equity firm whom I met at a conference, she expressed a strong interest in our investment mandate at Riverside Partners and the metrics we use to evaluate potential opportunities. Her firm primarily invests in companies that are more mature in terms of revenue size and market penetration, with financial performance metrics typically requiring EBITDA greater than $50 million. In contrast, Riverside Partners focuses on the lower middle market, where the typical EBITDA at the time of investment ranges from $3 million to $12 million. Our goal is to help these companies execute growth strategies that increase EBITDA to levels similar to those targeted by Francine's firm.

As our conversation progressed, Francine shared that she was feeling bored in her role and even expressed some envy towards me, which took me by surprise.

Curious, I asked, "I would've thought just the opposite. You're investing in some incredible businesses. How can you get bored?"

She responded, "You're involved with these companies at such a pivotal point in their journey. The impact you make in each functional area has a real influence on their success. You're helping them achieve *take-off velocity*. That's real excitement. I envy that. Our objectives are very different."

"Take-off velocity," in this context, refers to the initial momentum required for a company to successfully launch and experience substantial growth. It describes the rate at which a business gains traction, accelerates forward, and begins to achieve meaningful progress. This mirrors the concept of an aircraft's take-off velocity, the speed needed for it to lift off the runway and become airborne.

Reflecting on Francine's remarks, I realized she was absolutely right. Her insight perfectly encapsulated the reason I transitioned from CEO roles to PE. I often describe the "adrenaline rush" I get from managing the breadth of responsibilities involved: from deal origination to engaging with portfolio companies, each with its unique challenges. Being part of a team that helps scale companies to achieve *take-off velocity* is incredibly rewarding. It sets the stage for increased market presence, greater profitability, and potential opportunities for future investments or acquisitions.

123. DEAL IN THE CURRENCY OF THE TRUTH

During my tenure in private equity, I first heard the phrase "deal in the currency of the truth" during a conversation with a colleague about organizational behavior at one of our portfolio companies. We were discussing the importance of CEOs effectively managing relationships in both directions—upward with their investors and downward with their executive leadership teams. The idea resonated deeply with me, both in light of my prior experience as a CEO and in my current role as an Operating Partner. Whether I was leading a company myself or advising portfolio company leaders, I have consistently found that strong organizational behavior is rooted in honesty, both with superiors and with subordinates.

My colleague, referring to a CEO who had failed to be forthcoming with critical information, remarked, "Our CEOs have to remember to be truthful not only with themselves and their teams but also with us as investors. There must be full transparency. No surprises. They have to *deal in the currency of the truth*. Otherwise, it inevitably comes back to bite you."

That phrase stuck with me, because it captures the essence of effective leadership and healthy culture. Dealing in the currency of the truth involves more than just factual accuracy. It requires transparent communication about financial performance, operational challenges, and strategic opportunities. It means recognizing and celebrating wins, giving credit where it is due, owning mistakes, and seeking input with genuine openness. It also means setting realistic expectations, clearly communicating timelines and goals, and delivering difficult news with honesty and empathy.

To *deal in the currency of the truth* is to lead with integrity, even when the truth is uncomfortable. It is about prioritizing honesty over spin, substance over optics. Leaders who embrace this principle create organizations grounded in trust and accountability. They foster a culture where feedback is valued, learning is continuous, and team members feel respected and included. In my experience, this approach is not only essential for long-term performance, but also the foundation of a resilient and aligned leadership team.

124. VISION WITHOUT EXECUTION IS HALLUCINATION

During my time working with Dr. Phillip Frost, the billionaire entrepreneur, following his acquisition of Claros Diagnostics where I served as CEO, nearly every interaction proved to be a master class in business. I had the privilege of presenting alongside Dr. Frost at major investment banking conferences and occasionally participate in meetings related to OPKO Health and some of his other ventures.

Following a highly attended investment banking meeting at the Waldorf Astoria in New York City, during which Dr. Frost and I presented on OPKO to a large audience, he invited me to join him for a meeting with "Paul", an executive from another business in which Dr. Frost was involved. The discussion centered around go-to-market strategies for the company's consumer-related product. Despite this being far from my expertise, Dr. Frost graciously welcomed my contributions to the conversation, a gesture I truly appreciated and enjoyed during my time with him.

After the meeting, as we rode the elevator down, Dr. Frost turned to me and asked, "What did you think of Paul?"

I replied, "Nice guy. He seems sharp and genuinely committed. His vision for the brand sounds exciting."

Dr. Frost nodded thoughtfully and said, "He's an idea man, Mike. But there's a lot more to it. *Vision without execution is hallucination.* The company has to go deeper than ideas. If we don't execute, then they're just stories we tell ourselves over lunch."

That line stuck with me. "Vision without execution is hallucination." It has echoed in my mind ever since and continues to guide my work in PE and with portfolio company leadership teams.

No matter your functional area, vision is important. It sets the direction and can be genuinely inspiring. But execution is what turns aspiration into outcome. Execution requires accountability. It means following through, taking ownership, tracking progress, adapting when things go sideways, and occasionally making hard choices that no one's lining up to make.

Dr. Frost's comment was a reminder that visionary thinking is only as good as the grit behind it. Without action, effort, and discipline, vision becomes little more than a motivational poster waiting to be ignored. The most effective leaders I've worked with are not just dreamers. They're doers. They can see the mountaintop and then lace up their boots and start the climb.

125. NON-COMPETE BURN OFF

Non-compete agreements are legal contracts between an employee and an employer that restrict the individual from joining or starting a competing business for a defined period after leaving the company. This timeframe, typically one to three years, is often referred to as the "burn-off" period. During this time, the individual is bound by the terms of the non-compete and must refrain from engaging in competitive activities.

Once the burn-off period expires, the non-compete is considered "burned off," and the former employee is no longer subject to its restrictions. At that point, they are free to pursue opportunities in competing businesses without legal or contractual risk.

Throughout both my CEO roles and my time in PE, I have repeatedly encountered situations where highly attractive candidates were in the middle of a non-compete burn-off period. In many of these cases, particularly in industries with intense competition, the only path to secure that individual was to enter into a "garden leave" arrangement. This allowed the candidate to resign from their current role and remain professionally inactive until the non-compete expired, after which they could join our organization.

In some cases, candidates have been able to negotiate a reduced non-compete duration by offering their employer a longer transition period. This often helped facilitate a smoother handoff of responsibilities while demonstrating goodwill.

I recall a situation pertaining to recruiting a Chief Commercial Officer at one of my portfolio companies during which a PE colleague and I had a discussion with the CEO, "Bob".

Bob shared, "I spoke with the candidate last night. She's a slam dunk for the Chief Commercial Officer role. Deep therapeutic experience, direct market knowledge, super high energy, and she's scaled commercial teams before."

I responded, "Agreed. I had the same reaction. But there's a wrinkle, she's still under a non-compete from her last role. It has another six months before burn-off. That's going to slow things down. Did she offer a workaround?"

Bob seemed optimistic, "Yes, she's open to a garden leave setup. She'll formally resign and sit tight until the burn-off is complete. We'll need to plan for a six-month delay, but if we're serious about getting A-level talent, it's worth it."

My colleague offered, "Let's loop in legal to confirm exposure is minimal. We don't want any surprises from her prior employer. But if it checks out, I say we lock her in and start the onboarding prep now."

Bob agreed, "I'm with you. If we can time her onboarding right after the non-compete burns off, we'll hit the ground running."

In PE, where timing and talent are both critical, understanding and managing around non-compete burn-off periods is often essential. The best firms proactively structure creative solutions to secure top-tier executives without triggering legal issues, while keeping portfolio companies on track for growth.

126. HIRE ATTITUDE...TRAIN SKILL

The phrase "hire attitude and train skill" refers to a hiring philosophy that emphasizes a candidate's mindset, character, and cultural fit over their specific technical experience or qualifications. The idea is rooted in the belief that skills can be taught through training and experience, but core attitudes such as drive, resilience, adaptability, and emotional intelligence are far more difficult to instill. A resume may showcase credentials and experience, but those attributes alone don't guarantee effectiveness, especially in roles that require high emotional IQ, self-motivation, and collaboration.

Throughout my time as a CEO and now in PE, I have seen this principle in action, particularly when hiring for sales and business development roles. Some of the most successful individuals I've hired did not come from the same subsegment of the industry, or even the same industry at all. I've watched high performers make seamless transitions from medical device to healthcare services, or from pharmaceutical services to technology. Their success was largely independent of the specific products or markets they sold into.

What set them apart was a must-win, adaptable attitude. These individuals dove into new sectors with energy and humility. They quickly learned the nuances of the business, developed strong relationships with physicians and healthcare professionals, intuitively grasped client pain points, and presented compelling value propositions that resonated. Their attitude was the common denominator across every success.

I first encountered this idiom during a conversation with "Nancy," the Chief Commercial Officer at one of our portfolio companies. I had questioned her decision to hire inside sales representatives straight out of college, many with no industry experience.

"Nancy," I asked, "what's the thinking behind hiring people this green?"

She replied without hesitation, "I see someone who is going to charge through walls for us and relentlessly hunt for new business. For this role, I *hire attitude and train skill*. We put them through an intense onboarding program. By the time they're in front of prospects, they'll know the service offering cold."

She paused, then added, "Honestly, I prefer they don't come in with old habits. I want to mold them into exactly what we need. And I can usually tell within the first fifteen seconds whether someone has that spark."

Her logic made sense. While technical proficiency matters, it is often the intangible traits such as hustle, grit, coachability, and cultural alignment that determine whether a new hire becomes a top performer.

This principle remains one of the most reliable filters I've seen for building high-performing teams across any industry.

127. IT'S NEVER A STRAIGHT LINE UP TO THE RIGHT

The phrase "straight line up to the right" typically refers to a graphical depiction of continuous positive momentum. On a chart, it describes a line with a consistently upward and rightward slope—often used to represent growth over time, such as revenue, customer acquisition, or sales performance. In this context, it implies a smooth, uninterrupted trajectory of improvement, suggesting success without setbacks.

In business, this phrase is commonly used to describe idealized outcomes, such as month-over-month sales growth with no dips or volatility. Colloquially, it symbolizes sustained progress, upward momentum, and overall achievement.

However, in PE, this phrase is often used with a degree of skepticism or irony. A "straight line up to the right" can reflect selective memory more than reality. Human nature tends to remember successes and smooth over the struggles. We recall the victories, financial returns, and market wins more vividly than the long nights spent solving problems, navigating operational challenges, or managing interpersonal dynamics within leadership teams.

In my experience, both as a CEO and now in PE, I have been part of operating teams that built companies into success stories and investment teams that backed winners. Yet even in those standout cases where we generated strong financial outcomes, expanded clinical impact, or created significant job growth, the journey was far from flawless. There were fierce competitors, internal friction, execution missteps, and plenty of moments that kept us awake at night. The path to success was rarely linear.

I first heard this phrase used in a portfolio review meeting when a colleague reflected on one of the firm's most successful exits. We had just reviewed the extraordinary return metrics and strong market position the company had achieved. But rather than basking in a picture-perfect narrative, my colleague grounded the moment with a dose of reality.

He said, "The company's ultimate valuation blew past even our most optimistic projections. But let's be honest, *it's never a straight line up to the right.* We hit some real bumps. We had to earn it."

That moment stuck with me. It was a lesson that true success is never effortless. Behind every impressive chart lies a more complex, messy, and very human story.

128. HOCKEY-STICK FORECAST

In keeping with the earlier discussion of the "straight line up to the right," it feels only right to bring up its close cousin: the "hockey-stick forecast." This term refers to a financial projection shaped like a hockey stick: flat or modest growth for a while, followed by a sharp upward curve that signals a sudden surge in revenue or performance. The spike is usually attributed to factors like market expansion, product launches, or newfound customer adoption. Sometimes, it is attributed to pure hope.

In PE circles, the *hockey-stick forecast* has become something of a running joke. It is a favorite feature in investment banker pitch decks, where the miraculous growth always seems to occur just after the sale closes. Timing is everything.

I have heard my PE colleagues sigh and mutter with seasoned cynicism, "Here we go again. Another *hockey-stick forecast* with zero evidence to support it."

To me, the inclusion of a dramatic hockey-stick projection is often a red flag. At best, it signals wishful thinking. At worst, it hints at a seller trying to manufacture excitement without the data to back it up. I often find myself asking: If the founder truly believes this surge is imminent, why sell now? Would they not want to hold on a bit longer and ride the blade of the stick to a much higher valuation?

This is precisely why, in PE, we tend to take management forecasts with a grain of salt, or perhaps a whole salt shaker. Instead of blindly accepting the projections in a pitch deck, we build our own financial models. We construct downside, base, and upside cases informed by detailed diligence, market analysis, and a healthy sense of realism.

In short, we believe in *skating to where the puck is going*. But we also make sure we know how fast it is moving and whether anyone actually has control of it.

129. THE MOST SENSITIVE NERVE IN THE BODY IS THE ONE THAT TOUCHES YOUR WALLET

The phrase "the most sensitive nerve in the body is the one that touches your wallet" offers a humorous but accurate reflection of how people often respond when financial stakes become personal. Money carries emotional weight. It represents security, independence, and a measure of success. So, when financial commitments are on the table, reactions can be outsized: fear, anxiety, defensiveness, or hesitation are all common responses.

I have seen this phenomenon in PE materialize in several key moments. One example is the requirement for PE professionals to invest personal capital into deals, often through carried interest or direct co-investment. Another is the expectation that founders will roll a portion of their sale proceeds back into the company after a transaction, maintaining some equity stake in the next chapter.

Speaking from experience, putting personal capital into a deal definitely sharpens your diligence. When it is your own money on the line, not just your firm's or your LPs', your risk radar becomes very well calibrated. The scrutiny intensifies, as does the sense of accountability.

On the other side of the table, a founder's willingness or reluctance to reinvest is a powerful signal. It says a lot about their conviction in the business. I recall attending a deal team meeting where a founder had been pushing back on rolling even a modest portion of proceeds into the company. A partner at the table, clearly unimpressed, leaned back in his chair and said dryly, "His hesitation says it all. *The most sensitive nerve in the body is the one that touches your wallet.* If he truly believes in the upside, this shouldn't be a heavy lift."

That comment stuck with me. It was a message that financial alignment speaks louder than pitch decks or passionate speeches. If a founder wants to completely cash out and walk away the moment a deal closes, it is hard not to wonder what they know that we don't. Some might call that view cynical. I would call it cautious. Either way, a founder's reluctance to reinvest tends to raise questions. And for me, it certainly never inspires confidence.

130. GOAT RODEO

After a meeting with the management team of a potential acquisition target, a PE colleague and I were debriefing on the flight back to Boston.

He leaned back in his seat and said, "I like the business. They are in a good niche with real potential. But this company is a total *goat rodeo.* We would have to replace most of the management team. It would be a serious project."

I nodded. "True, the team is rough around the edges. But the business is growing despite itself. My take? If this company had even moderately seasoned leadership and mature processes in place, it would be growing at twice the rate."

He didn't hesitate. "They're riding a wave, but waves crash. There's no management control system. No budgeting discipline. The controller is basically a staff accountant with a new title. It's pure reactionary chaos…everything is fly by the seat of your pants."

I had never heard the term "goat rodeo" before, but I immediately got the picture. It is one of those expressions that does not require much explanation. It conjures a vivid image of uncoordinated people and processes pulling in opposite directions, resulting in disarray that feels more comic than tragic, at least until you try to clean it up.

In business, a *goat rodeo* is what happens when dysfunction becomes the norm. Everyone is busy, but no one is aligned. Systems are absent, accountability is murky, and leadership is reactive rather than intentional. Left alone, it is a slow-motion train wreck. But with the right leadership, governance, engaged PE team and Board of Directors, it is not necessarily fatal.

Goat rodeos are messy, but they are not hopeless. They just require patience, a strong plan, and a management upgrade that can actually corral the goats.

131. BABY IS UGLY

In PE, diligence often uncovers flaws or vulnerabilities that the founders and stakeholders of a business simply don't see. This leads to one of the more uncomfortable dynamics in dealmaking: the gap between a founder's valuation expectations and reality.

One of the more colorful phrases I have heard in these situations is, "We need to tell them their *baby is ugly*." It is a slightly humorous, deeply awkward metaphor for delivering tough but necessary feedback about a business someone has poured their heart into.

Any time a deal requires a valuation reset or revised structure after a Letter of Intent is signed, a scenario often called a "retrade", tensions are bound to rise. These conversations can derail a deal entirely or, at the very least, erode trust. Still, when diligence reveals serious issues, it becomes essential to confront them directly.

The metaphor works because founders, like parents, are emotionally attached to what they have built. Criticizing their "baby" can feel personal, even when the intention is purely constructive. Maybe there is customer concentration risk they never considered, or margin degradation they have rationalized away. Maybe the leadership bench is thin, or the reporting infrastructure is hanging together with duct tape and goodwill. From the inside, these can look like quirks. From the outside, they can look like risk.

One colleague once put it bluntly after a diligence session: "I like the founder, but someone has to break it to him. The baby has a lazy eye and a crooked smile, and we are the ones who have to point it out."

Uncomfortable? Absolutely. But sugarcoating reality helps no one. Providing clear, respectful, and data-driven feedback is critical, not just to protect our investment but to give the founder a chance to fix what needs fixing. It is not about being harsh. It is about being honest.

In the end, tough conversations are a core part of the value creation process. If we cannot tell someone their *baby is ugly*, we probably are not the right partner to help it grow up strong.

132. BURN THE SHORTS

Short-selling is a trading strategy where investors borrow shares of a stock and sell them, hoping to buy them back later at a lower price. If the stock price drops, the short-seller profits by pocketing the difference between the sale and repurchase prices. But if the price rises instead, the short-seller must repurchase at a higher cost, locking in a loss.

During my time at OPKO Health, following their acquisition of Claros Diagnostics where I had been CEO, I frequently joined Dr. Phillip Frost, the billionaire entrepreneur and OPKO founder, at major investment banking conferences. I had a strong working relationship with Dr. Frost, a man widely respected in financial circles for his past successes and unconventional strategies.

At the time, his vision for OPKO was to create a diversified health-care platform with multiple business verticals, including therapeutics, diagnostics, and services. Some of these verticals were interdependent, and the structure was complex, often drawing skepticism from analysts and investors. Still, Dr. Frost's track record spoke volumes. Regardless of the questions raised, he was revered for his instincts and long-term thinking.

After our investment banking conference presentations, we would often head into breakout sessions with individual investors. What I did not initially realize, and what Dr. Frost later pointed out, was that many of these investors were shorting OPKO's stock. They had shown up not just out of interest but because they were actively betting against us.

Some of these one-on-one sessions were tense. The tone could shift quickly from curious to confrontational. But Dr. Frost never flinched. He remained composed, gracious, and always professional. Behind the scenes, however, he was monitoring the short interest closely. When he saw a spike, he would quietly start buying OPKO shares himself, creating upward pressure on the stock price.

One day, I asked him about this approach. He gave me a knowing smile and said, "I love to *burn the shorts.*"

The phrase "burn the shorts" refers to when a stock's price unexpectedly rises, forcing short-sellers to scramble to buy back shares at a loss, further fueling the price surge. For long investors like Dr. Frost, it is a moment of quiet victory. It is not just a financial outcome but rather a strategic move that turns the tables on those betting against you.

That moment captured a lot about Dr. Frost's mindset. Patient. Calculated. And always one move ahead.

133. DEALS IN FLIGHT

The term "deals in flight" in private equity refers to investment opportunities that are actively moving through a firm's pipeline. These transactions are in progress and may be at different stages of evaluation, diligence, or negotiation. When a PE firm says it has multiple "deals in flight," it typically means the team is juggling several potential investments, each with varying levels of traction and complexity.

My first exposure to the term came early in my PE experience, when we chose not to pursue a particular opportunity that didn't quite meet our criteria. After the meeting, a colleague remarked, "It's just not worth chasing, especially with the number of *deals in flight* we've got right now. This one doesn't crack the top three."

That comment resonated as it underscored an important reality in PE: resources and attention are finite. A firm may have several promising targets under review, but only a few will make it across the finish line. Many fall away due to red flags in diligence, breakdowns in negotiations, shifts in market conditions, or a simple reprioritization of strategic focus.

The phrase "deals in flight" may sound exciting, but it is also a reminder of the dynamic and uncertain nature of dealmaking. Not every takeoff ends in a landing.

134. YOU DON'T HIT STRETCH GOALS IF YOU DON'T HAVE THEM

In every CEO role I've held, I've implemented a Management by Objectives (MBO) program. This results-oriented management approach aligns organizational goals with individual performance objectives. At its best, it involves a participative process where employees and managers work together to define goals that are specific, measurable, achievable, realistic, and time-bound, also known as SMART goals.

However, I've seen MBO programs fall flat when objectives are handed down without collaboration or feedback. In my experience, the key to success is not just the structure of the program, but the spirit of it: open communication, mutual buy-in, and a shared commitment to achieving meaningful outcomes.

Because bonus compensation is often tied to MBO outcomes, I've always advocated for objectives that are framed as "stretch goals." Base compensation should reflect the fulfillment of core job responsibilities. Bonuses, in contrast, should reward individuals for pushing beyond what is expected. Too often, I've reviewed MBO plans packed with objectives that mirror an employee's day-to-day job description. That may make bonus attainment easier, but it completely defeats the purpose.

I once discussed this philosophy with the founder of a newly acquired portfolio company as we prepared to implement an MBO program. I was encouraged to hear that he shared the same mindset.

When I asked about his view on using stretch goals as the foundation of the program, he smiled and said, "Look, *you don't hit stretch goals if you don't have them.* I'm not interested in setting people up for failure, but we should be able to map out a real path to get there. I don't have a problem stretching. Let's go for it."

That kind of mindset is exactly what MBOs are meant to foster. When executed properly, they build a culture of accountability and achievement. By setting ambitious but attainable goals, encouraging active engagement, and rewarding meaningful performance, MBO programs can drive productivity, strengthen alignment, and elevate an organization's overall effectiveness.

135. NOSEBLEED TERRITORY

As a kid, some of my fondest memories were occasional trips into Boston on the MBTA Orange Line with my cousin, Mike DiModica (RIP), to catch a Boston Bruins matinee at the old Boston Garden. We would pool our paper route earnings and scrape together just enough for upper balcony seats, usually under ten dollars. Smoking was still allowed back then, so those cheap seats were often blanketed in a haze of cigarette and cigar smoke, adding a gritty charm to the whole experience. That section was affectionately known as the "nosebleeds," a term that suggested you were so high up you might need oxygen, or at least a better view.

Years later, during due diligence for a PE acquisition opportunity, that term came back to me in a very different context. We were deep into evaluating a business with a compelling management team, strong sustainability factors, and real growth upside. Our investment thesis was solid. But it was a competitive process, driven by investment bankers representing the seller and drawing in both strategic and financial buyers. Since our initial conversations, the banker's valuation guidance had climbed steeply.

As we debated internally whether we should stretch to meet the new price expectations, one of my colleagues cut through the optimism with a dose of reality.

"This is getting out of reach," he said. "I can't get comfortable here. The EBITDA multiple is higher than I've ever seen in this segment. We're in *nosebleed territory* on valuation."

His comment nailed it. The valuation had climbed so far it felt like we were sitting in the last row of the Garden again, only this time the smoke was from the friction of inflated numbers.

Disappointing? Yes. But it also brought back a vivid memory of youth, high hopes, and the unmistakable feeling of being way up in the cheap seats where the air is thin and the view is distant, but the experience still teaches you something valuable.

136. MELTING ICE CUBE

Over the years, both as an operator and in private equity, I became very familiar with the annual ritual of budgeting. Like clockwork, financial budgets would be hammered out during the fourth quarter for the upcoming calendar year. Ideally, the forecast and final budget would be approved by the end of November, setting the stage for performance comparisons at every quarterly board meeting that followed.

Of course, reality has a way of challenging even the most carefully laid plans. Sometimes the forecast needed adjusting up or down based on year-to-date performance or shifts in the business environment. But one particular portfolio company managed to turn this into an annual tradition of disappointment.

No matter how optimistic the initial plan, we could count on them to walk into the mid-year board meeting with a downward reforecast. One year, as we were preparing for yet another round of this, a fellow Board Director summed it up with memorable clarity.

"Let's not act surprised when the numbers drop again," he said dryly. "Their budgets are like a *melting ice cube*. I've decided they just can't forecast the business with any confidence. Hell, I'm not sure they can forecast what they're having for lunch tomorrow."

His "melting ice cube" analogy hit the nail on the head. The issue wasn't just market unpredictability or shifting industry demand, although those played a part. The real story lay deeper, in the leadership's inability to instill discipline, the organization's lack of accountability, and a culture that treated budgeting like an exercise in hope rather than a management tool.

137. WHACK-A-MOLE

The phrase "whack-a-mole" refers to a metaphorical scenario where problems or challenges keep popping up in quick succession, each demanding immediate attention. The term originates from the classic arcade game in which players use a mallet to strike toy moles that randomly appear from different holes. In a business context, a *whack-a-mole* situation arises when solving one issue leads to another springing up almost immediately, creating a never-ending cycle of problem-solving.

I have encountered whack-a-mole scenarios across scientific research, operational environments, and within PE settings. These situations are typically symptoms of deeper systemic issues, broken processes, or a reactive management style that lacks forward-looking discipline. The phrase is often used in business circles to describe times when teams are overwhelmed and firefighting takes the place of strategic action.

My first real taste of this dynamic in PE came with a portfolio company that manufactured capital equipment for the healthcare market. The "moles" in this case included recurring production glitches, supply chain bottlenecks, quality control failures, and malfunctioning production machinery. No sooner had we resolved one issue than another would appear, often more urgent than the last.

That experience was a wake-up call. It made clear the need for a top-tier executive team, a robust operational backbone, and a cultural shift toward proactive problem-solving. We could not afford to keep swinging blindly at symptoms. We had to slow down long enough to identify root causes, implement preventive systems, and establish real accountability.

Breaking free from a business whack-a-mole cycle requires more than quick fixes. It takes thoughtful pattern recognition, process improvement, and an investment in organizational maturity. Most importantly, it requires a culture that prizes continuous improvement over reactive heroics. Only then can a company move beyond putting out fires and focus on building lasting value and sustained growth.

138. THE VIEW ONLY CHANGES FOR THE LEAD DOG

The phrase "the view only changes for the lead dog" is often used to emphasize the importance of being out front, of leading rather than following. In a literal sense, when a team of sled dogs is harnessed together, only the one at the front sees open trail ahead. Everyone else has a more limited view. The metaphor applies in business as well: those who lead gain access to new perspectives, greater opportunities, and tougher challenges. Followers may still be part of the journey, but their vantage point and influence is more constrained.

I first heard the phrase when I was an undergraduate, and it stuck with me. Over time, I saw its relevance as an executive and again in PE, especially when it comes to building companies that aim for market leadership.

While studying chemical engineering at Northeastern University, I was fortunate to participate in the school's Cooperative Education Program, or "co-op." It's one of the reasons I chose Northeastern. The program blends academic coursework with hands-on, professional experience in a student's chosen field. For me, that meant multiple co-op assignments at the U.S. Army Materials Research Command (AMRC).

AMRC was an outstanding place to learn, not just technically, but in terms of mentorship. I was especially fortunate to work under Dr. Jim Sloan, the lab director and my supervisor. Jim was a brilliant physical chemist and a natural mentor. He also broke the mold of the traditional academic. Raised in Brooklyn, he was sharp, irreverent, and allergic to bureaucracy. He had little patience for pomp or posturing and carried himself with a kind of unfiltered honesty that made him both entertaining and deeply effective.

As I approached graduation, I started thinking seriously about going on to earn a Ph.D. in chemical engineering. Jim had always encouraged me to consider graduate school, and when I finally asked for his unvarnished opinion, he didn't disappoint.

"Getting a Ph.D. puts you in an entirely different category," he said. "It's your calling card. It puts you in the lead dog position."

I asked, "What if I work for a couple of years, then go back for the Ph.D.?"

He practically launched out of his chair. Hands flying, eyes wide, he blurted, "Absolutely not! If this were an MBA, fine, maybe. But you've got momentum right now. You're thinking like a scientist. You're in the zone. Go straight through. You won't miss a beat."

Then he paused, leaned in a little closer, and with a wry grin added, "You'll be the expert. The lead dog in your field. And remember, *the view only changes for the lead dog.* If you're not the lead dog, you're spending your whole career staring at the asses of the ones in front of you."

Classic Jim. Raw, insightful, and unforgettable.

His advice had a lasting impact on me. Between 1982 and 1986, Jim's mentorship shaped my thinking in ways that extended far beyond the lab. Pursuing a Ph.D. turned out to be one of the best decisions I ever made. It was challenging, yes, but it stretched me professionally and personally and opened doors I could not have imagined at the time.

Jim's "lead dog" metaphor still resonates. It reminds me that becoming a true expert can transform not only how others see you but also how much of the landscape you can actually see for yourself. There is nothing wrong with being part of the pack, but if you want the clearest view and the chance to shape the path ahead, you need to lead it.

139. EARLY INNINGS

PE investment diligence involves a thorough investigation and analysis conducted during the evaluation of a potential target company. This process typically covers financial, operational, market, and legal aspects, aiming to gather critical information, identify risks and opportunities, and validate the assumptions that underpin the investment decision.

I've often heard PE colleagues describe the early stages of diligence as being in the "early innings." Borrowed from baseball, this phrase signals that the evaluation is just beginning and that there is still a substantial amount of work ahead.

I remember a colleague using this idiom during a firm meeting when asked for specifics about a target company. He replied, "Those are great questions, but we're still in the *early innings*. There's a lot more to learn."

The phrase captures the reality that deeper investigation, data gathering, and analysis remain before detailed diligence questions can be answered or conclusions drawn. PE diligence is inherently complex and time-consuming, demanding meticulous attention to detail, thorough risk identification, and a comprehensive evaluation before reaching a final decision.

140. GREENFIELD MARKET

I have often heard the term "greenfield" used in PE to describe potential market penetration opportunities for a target investment. The term originates from the construction industry, where it refers to undeveloped land with no prior construction or development. Similarly, a greenfield market opportunity represents a space that has yet to be explored: one without existing products, services, or dominant players.

Examples of *greenfield* opportunities appear in emerging industries, new technology sectors, or underserved geographic regions. For instance, the rise of electric vehicles created a greenfield market for companies to develop EV manufacturing, charging infrastructure, and related services.

Greenfield opportunities involve creating a market where none existed before. In these cases, the target company has the chance to shape market dynamics, build customer demand, and set industry standards. With little or no competition, there is a clear first-mover advantage that allows the company to capture market share, set prices, build brand recognition, and establish leadership. While greenfield opportunities come with higher risks due to uncertainty around adoption and lack of an established market, they also offer the potential for significant rewards if successful.

141. WHITE SPACE

In a competitive marketplace, companies often concentrate on serving defined customer segments or solving specific problems. However, there are often gaps or unaddressed areas where customer needs are unmet or competition is minimal. These represent the market "white space." *White space* opportunities can include underserved demographic groups, unmet customer needs, emerging technologies, or unaddressed geographic regions.

While white space can take many forms, I've often found some of the most accessible and productive opportunities come from within existing satisfied customers. Consider companies that successfully deliver a product or service, then disengage once the transaction is complete. This is a missed opportunity. Many of the portfolio companies I work with in PE offer a broad suite of services. When a company has established a successful engagement with a client in one area, there is often significant potential to expand that relationship by identifying and addressing white space within the same client organization. This could involve gaining access to other departments or business units and offering additional solutions already within the company's capabilities.

Establishing new relationships within current clients is a powerful way to access untapped white space. These opportunities also naturally emerge following add-on acquisitions, where a portfolio company expands its range of services. In these cases, the acquired capabilities can often be *cross-sold* to an existing base of satisfied customers. If the company has built trust and delivered strong results, the opportunity cost lies in failing to leverage that goodwill to reach new stakeholders and decision-makers within those accounts.

Pursuing white space opportunities can be a highly effective strategy for companies looking to accelerate growth, enter new markets, differentiate themselves, or strengthen client relationships. The key is understanding the full scope of customer needs, identifying service gaps, and proactively using existing relationships as a foundation for expansion. When executed effectively, targeting white space can drive new revenue, improve customer loyalty and retention, and unlock meaningful competitive advantage.

142. HEADED TOWARD A KILL

As I mentioned earlier, only a small percentage of deals that come across a PE firm's desk ever make it past the Indication of Interest or Letter of Intent stages. PE firms are a discerning bunch, armed with strict investment criteria and a healthy skepticism. We maintain a dynamic pipeline of opportunities that flow through various stages from the first teaser deck to final investment committee approval. It is a perpetual balancing act: sourcing new deals, digging deep into diligence, submitting offers, and closing transactions, all while actively overseeing the existing portfolio and sometimes wrangling a CEO or two.

Along the way, you inevitably encounter some colorful language. The PE world has a rich vocabulary that seems to grow more theatrical the closer a deal gets to being shelved. Early in my PE tenure, while we were discussing whether to move forward with a particular opportunity, a younger associate, with great confidence and absolutely no hint of irony, declared, "This one's *headed toward a kill*."

I blinked. "Headed toward a kill?"

To me, it sounded like a rejected title from a Jason Bourne movie, not something you'd hear in a investment discussion. It was oddly dramatic, especially coming from someone who had been in the industry for approximately five minutes and still needed GPS to find the coffee machine. I half expected him to follow up with a line like, "Code red. Target neutralized."

Of course, what he meant was perfectly reasonable: after some preliminary diligence, the deal was unlikely to progress. But his choice of words amused me. In an industry that loves euphemisms like "reassessing fit" or "not actionable at this time," "headed toward a kill" felt unnecessarily aggressive—like swatting a fly with a sledgehammer.

Still, it was a moment that resonated, a reminder that PE, for all its rigor and formality, is also full of personality. Behind the spreadsheets and term sheets, you'll find a cast of characters, each with their own favorite metaphors and war stories. Sometimes they're poetic, sometimes puzzling, and occasionally, like this one, just plain entertaining.

143. EAT THE ELEPHANT ONE BITE AT A TIME

The phrase "eat the elephant one bite at a time" is a familiar metaphor in business and project management. It captures the idea that large or complex tasks are best approached by breaking them down into smaller, manageable parts and tackling them step by step.

One of the most monumental tasks I have encountered in PE is the integration of a transformative add-on acquisition into an existing portfolio company. These acquisitions are often made with clear strategic intent: whether to expand into new geographies, extend technological capabilities, diversify the customer base, or unlock new market segments. When done right, integrations can drive top-line growth, improve earnings, create operational efficiencies, and open up cross-selling opportunities. But none of it happens by accident. Success requires a methodical, disciplined approach, with multiple strategic and operational workstreams moving in concert.

Of course, integrations can feel overwhelming, especially given their scale, complexity, and the sheer number of moving parts. That is why it is critical to assemble a cross-functional integration team and build a detailed plan that outlines tasks, timelines, and clear ownership across every functional area: finance, operations, sales and marketing, human resources, IT systems, and cultural alignment. That last piece—culture—is often underestimated but can be the difference between friction and momentum.

I remember an integration where I served on the Board of a portfolio company, and we were navigating a particularly complex post-merger plan. During an early breakfast meeting with the CEO and a fellow PE colleague, we were deep in discussion about the path forward. The CEO, someone I had worked closely with and greatly respected, looked tired. He was already feeling the strain and had begun to encounter signs of cultural resistance within the organization.

Trying to offer some reassurance, I said, "We've got a strong team, and you're not expected to pull this off overnight. This is practically a full-time job, and you don't need to go it alone."

My colleague chimed in without missing a beat, "We know it is a big lift. Just remember, you have to *eat the elephant one bite at a time.* Let's walk through the integration plan together, take a step back, and break it into stages."

That moment shifted the tone. You could see the CEO exhale. The metaphor was simple, but it helped. It reinforced that we were aligned, that the work was structured, and that no one was expecting him or his staff to swallow the whole thing at once.

This phrase, while light-hearted, serves an important purpose. It reminds leaders not to get paralyzed by the enormity of the task or discouraged by early resistance. A well-designed integration plan, complete with specific accountabilities and steady communication, allows teams to make meaningful progress one step at a time.

Executing a successful integration in PE is no small feat. It demands planning, disciplined project management, clear communication, and true collaboration between the acquirer and the acquired. There are many variables, personalities, and competing agendas. But when done right, these integrations do more than check boxes, they can ignite value creation on an entirely new level.

144. EAGLES FLY WITH EAGLES

My father once told me, "You are a reflection of the company you keep." He was not talking about corporate affiliations but the people with whom I chose to surround myself. His point was simple and timeless: your friends can shape your behavior, values, and ultimately, your reputation.

I have found the same to be true in business. There are plenty of ways to validate this idea through organizational behavior, corporate culture, and leadership tone, but one of the clearest areas where it plays out, in my experience, is in talent acquisition. Especially in business development.

Some of the most successful business development executives I have worked with, both during my time as a CEO and now in PE, share a remarkably consistent profile. They are deeply knowledgeable about their industry, understand the products or services they are selling inside and out, and can clearly articulate the value proposition. They are relationship-driven, take a consultative approach to selling, and combine that with a laser focus on results. Many are what you might call classic "Type A" personalities: competitive, urgent, goal-oriented, and wired to win.

I remember a Board meeting at one of our portfolio companies where we were discussing plans to build out the business development team. My PE colleague Barry, someone I have worked with for many years, asked the CEO about his recruiting strategy.

"Are you planning to engage a search firm?" Barry asked.

"Yes," the CEO replied. "I've narrowed it down to two and should make a decision shortly. I'm also going to ask Mike to tap into his network for strong candidates."

I chimed in, "I have a few terrific folks from past assignments. I'll check in with them, and I'm sure they'll have strong referrals too."

Barry nodded, smiled, and said, *"Eagles fly with eagles."*

It was a great line. His point was that top-tier talent tends to travel in the same circles. The best people know other great people. It is not just a hiring tactic; it is a truth about how strong professionals operate. They build networks filled with others who match their caliber of excellence, drive, and integrity.

My father was not a business executive. He was a blue-collar foreman. But his wisdom about the company you keep holds just as true in the boardroom as it does on the shop floor. In both worlds, strong people attract strong people. And when you are building a high-performance team, that is exactly the kind of gravitational pull you want to create.

145. AHEAD OF OUR HEADLIGHTS

I have often encountered the expression "getting ahead of our headlights" in PE. It is typically used as a cautionary phrase, a warning not to make decisions or take action before having enough information or a clear understanding of the potential consequences. The analogy is a good one, like driving at night, your headlights only illuminate so far ahead. If you move too quickly without seeing what lies ahead, you risk driving straight into trouble.

One particular situation early in my PE career comes to mind. We were just beginning diligence on a founder-led contract medical device manufacturer. The company had posted steady, if unspectacular, growth over several years and boasted a wide range of capabilities. However, early diligence flagged a potential issue with customer concentration.

Since this was a proprietary opportunity I had sourced, there was momentum to move quickly. One of my colleagues suggested we submit a Letter of Intent to secure exclusivity before other bidders could get involved.

Before we could act, another member of the deal team raised a red flag.

"Guys," he said, "let's not get *ahead of our headlights*. I want to better understand the extent of product-level concentration, the life cycle stage of the devices they are manufacturing, and how long these customer relationships have actually been in place."

He was right to speak up. Committing to a valuation range without visibility into those dynamics would have been risky. Customer concentration alone can carry major implications for future cash flows, valuation durability, and exit optionality.

In my experience, "don't get ahead of your headlights" is one of those deceptively simple phrases that carries real weight in the context of PE investing. It is a reminder that diligence is not just a formality, it is the foundation of disciplined investing. PE demands deliberate, informed decision-making. The temptation to move fast can be strong, especially in competitive processes, but there is no substitute for taking the time to fully illuminate the road ahead.

146. A HIGH TIDE RAISES ALL SHIPS

You've probably heard the phrase "a high tide raises all ships." I have encountered it many times over the years, both as a CEO and an Operating Partner in PE. In business, it typically refers to the idea that during periods of economic expansion or strong market performance, most companies benefit. A rising tide brings with it increased consumer demand, improved purchasing power, and broadly positive market sentiment. The result? Operational expansion, growing headcount, bigger bonuses, and more robust growth across the board. Companies often find themselves with better access to capital, more favorable financing terms, and the confidence to invest in new initiatives.

That said, I learned the hard way as a CEO that it is precisely during these "high tide" periods when critical decisions must be made with the greatest care. I now regularly remind my portfolio companies of this same lesson. While economic tailwinds can lift nearly everyone, seasoned leaders know better than to confuse temporary good fortune with permanent strength. The fundamentals still matter.

As I referenced in a previous section ("It Is Only When the Tide Goes Out That You Learn Who Has Been Swimming Naked"), booming revenue can hide a multitude of sins. Operational inefficiencies, bloated cost structures, declining margins, and eroding quality or customer satisfaction can all be obscured by the illusion of top-line success. The risk is that leadership gets lulled into complacency. Problems that are papered over during a boom can quickly become existential when the cycle turns—and it always does.

So, while a rising tide may lift all ships, the smartest captains are the ones who take that moment not to celebrate, but to reinforce the hull.

147. SINGLE SOURCE OF TRUTH

"The single source of truth" is a widely embraced concept in business and data management. It refers to having one central, authoritative reference point for information within an organization. At its core, it represents the need for a reliable, consistent, and up-to-date source of data that all stakeholders can access and trust. Across nearly every functional area of a business, the importance of this principle cannot be overstated.

In my experience in PE, this concept becomes especially relevant during the post-investment phase, when we're helping portfolio companies build out more formalized business development processes and systems. Because we often invest in founder-owned and operated businesses, it's not uncommon to find that business development efforts, while effective enough to get the company to that point, are largely informal. Growth has typically come from a combination of the founder's network, customer referrals, and word-of-mouth. There is rarely a dedicated commercial team or a consistent mechanism for tracking opportunities or measuring progress.

In these situations, one of our early priorities is to partner with the founder and management team to recruit a Vice President of Sales and Marketing or a Chief Commercial Officer. That person's role is not just to drive revenue growth, but to establish the structure and discipline required to scale. This includes implementing systems for tracking the sales pipeline, forecasting, and aligning commercial activity with operations.

Customer Relationship Management (CRM) platforms like Salesforce, HubSpot, or Zoho become critical tools. They consolidate contact information, sales activities, and deal stages into a single system that enables full visibility across the organization. With the right setup, any authorized team member can pull up a snapshot of current and potential customer interactions. This visibility is essential, not just for managing the pipeline, but for syncing demand generation with production or service capacity.

I vividly remember interviewing a Vice President of Business Development candidate for one of our portfolio companies. I asked about her experience with team building and management control processes. Without missing a beat, she said, "The first thing I do is implement a CRM as a *single source of truth*. Not just for my team, but for the entire company."

She went on to explain how it allowed her to drive individual accountability, improve forecasting, and support better budgeting and resource planning. Her emphasis on that phrase, "single source of truth", stuck with me. It captured the center of what we aim to build in these organizations: a unified, transparent, and disciplined foundation for growth.

148. OFF-RAMP

An "off ramp" in PE refers to a planned or opportunistic path to exit or monetize an investment. Borrowed from driving terminology, just as an off ramp provides a way to leave the highway, in PE it represents a way to exit an investment, either partially or fully, and ideally with your headlights still intact.

Over the years, I've encountered a wide range of *off ramps* in PE investing. One of the most straightforward is a full exit, where the PE firm sells the entire company to a strategic buyer, typically a larger player in the industry, or to another PE firm in what's known as a secondary buyout. This clean break allows the firm to fully monetize its investment and return capital to its limited partners, ideally with a victory lap included.

Another form of exit is a strategic partnership or minority sale. In this scenario, the firm sells a partial stake to a strategic investor or brings in a new co-investor. This provides some liquidity while maintaining a seat at the table and, with luck, adds a partner who can bring additional capabilities or market access. It's a bit like selling the front seat but keeping your hands on the steering wheel.

Going public through an IPO offers a different kind of off ramp, a staged exit where shares can be gradually sold over time. It delivers liquidity while preserving upside, assuming the public markets play along, and no potholes appear in the form of market volatility or analyst scrutiny.

Dividend recapitalizations offer another route. This involves refinancing the company's debt, typically at a lower cost of capital, and using the proceeds to pay a dividend back to the PE firm. You still own the company, but you pocket some early returns. It's like pulling off at a rest stop, grabbing some snacks, and getting back on the road.

In some cases, a carve-out or asset sale makes sense. The firm sells a non-core division or product line, unlocking value and allowing the company to focus on its core business. This serves as an *off ramp* for part of the investment and, occasionally, a reality check on what parts of the business are actually driving the bus.

And then there's the least desirable off ramp: the write-off or wind-down. When things don't go as planned, and sometimes they really don't, a firm may need to cut its losses, write off the investment, or liquidate the company. It's the financial equivalent of pulling off the highway with smoke coming out from under the hood.

I first heard the term "off ramp" used in the wild during a board meeting for a high-performing portfolio company. As we were discussing strategic options, my colleague Matt chimed in:

"It might be early in our hold period, but a dividend recap could be a nice off ramp to recoup a good chunk of our investment."

Another director, Dan, nodded and said, "Yes, we should start testing the waters. Let's reach out to lenders and explore refinancing options."

Matt added, "Given where I think we could refinance today, the recap might get us close to a two-times return."

Dan smiled and said, "A nice *off ramp*. Everything after that is upside—we'd be playing with the house's money."

Ultimately, choosing an off ramp depends on several factors: market conditions, the cost and availability of capital, the company's performance, investor expectations, and the PE firm's appetite for risk and reward. The decision should be deliberate, well-timed, and aligned with the broader investment thesis. Just like on the highway, you want to make sure your exit takes you somewhere worth going.

149. ROB, REPLICATE AND REPLACE

During my time as CEO of a PE–backed medical device company, I identified a significant opportunity to reduce costs by moving manufacturing of our flagship product to China. To navigate this unfamiliar landscape, I hired an intermediary to help with introductions, communication, and logistics involving prospective Chinese contract manufacturers.

My first trip to China was a whirlwind. It included site tours, meetings with company executives, discussions with local government officials, and negotiations around financial terms, engineering capabilities, and performance expectations. It was all new to me, but I remained optimistic. After several days, I identified a preferred partner and planned to continue deeper discussions.

On my flight back to the United States, I happened to be seated next to Ralph, an executive from a Fortune 500 company who had spent the past decade overseeing outsourced manufacturing partnerships in China. As we struck up a conversation, I shared the purpose of my trip and described the promising meetings and potential partners I had encountered.

With a knowing smile, Ralph asked, "Was this your first trip?"

I responded enthusiastically, "Yes. It was super productive. I toured four facilities, met leadership teams, discussed cost targets, and identified a few strong candidates."

He removed his glasses, set them down on the tray table, rubbed his eyes, and said, "I understand. I remember being in your shoes. Feeling the same way."

Curious, I asked if he had any advice.

He leaned back and said, "This is a long road—full of speed bumps, twists, and turns. Be prepared."

When I pressed for specifics, he paused before saying, "Too many lessons to count. But if I had to leave you with just one, it would be this: *nothing is what it seems.*"

I asked him to explain.

He hesitated, then said, "Be skeptical. Don't fall into the trap of *rob, replicate, and replace.* Just remember, nothing is what it seems."

His words stayed with me as I connected through San Francisco on my way back to Boston. I found myself reflecting on a moment from one of the meetings in China. I had asked a local executive named Bin if he needed detailed technical drawings and a bill of materials of our device to prepare a quote. He responded, "You can send them, but I don't need them. All my team needs is one device. We'll create all the drawings and dimensions from that."

In hindsight, it was a clear signal of reverse engineering intentions.

Despite that red flag, I went ahead and finalized an agreement with a Chinese manufacturing partner. To their credit, they exceeded expectations: delivering on time, meeting cost targets, and maintaining high quality standards. We ultimately reduced cost of goods sold by 40 percent, which significantly improved profitability and EBITDA. The company was later sold at a premium valuation.

But Ralph's warning proved to be spot on. Beyond the predictable challenges of import duties, shipping delays, and time zone friction, we also ran into a host of opaque "city fees," "management fees," and miscellaneous charges that often felt like legalized extortion. Most troubling of all, we later discovered that our devices were being distributed and used in China, South Korea, Malaysia, and Singapore without our knowledge or authorization.

Ralph had been right. It was a long road, and in the end, nothing was quite what it seemed.

150. VIOLENTLY AGREE

I debated whether to include this phrase, but since it happens to be a personal pet peeve, I decided it deserved a moment in the spotlight: "I violently agree."

I have always found it amusing, unnecessary, and just a bit absurd. The first time I heard it was later in my PE career, during a Board of Directors meeting. A colleague tossed it into the conversation with all the confidence in the world. I paused, genuinely puzzled. *Violently agree*? What does that even mean? Is there a gentler version I am missing? Passively agree? Agree with mild enthusiasm?

To me, it sounds like an overly theatrical attempt to signal strong alignment. The word "violently" injects a strange and almost cartoonish intensity, as if someone might leap across the table and shake you by the lapels just to prove how much they agree.

If the goal is to underscore conviction, I would suggest swapping "violently" with something more grounded, like "wholeheartedly." It delivers the same sentiment without sounding like an action movie catchphrase.

Better yet, just agree. No need to throw elbows about it.

151. POINT WITH OUR THUMBS AND NOT OUR INDEX FINGERS

The phrase "point with our thumbs, not our index fingers" is one of my favorites. It's a clever way of framing personal and organizational accountability. I've found it to be as relevant in PE as it is in corporate leadership. Too often, when things go sideways, people default to finger-pointing, quite literally. It is always someone else's fault. But true accountability starts with turning that finger around, thumb inward, and asking, "What's my role in this?"

I first heard the phrase during a discussion with the CEO of one of our portfolio companies. We were talking about how to drive cross-functional accountability, especially when it came to growing revenue through deeper engagement with existing customers. She was adamant that sales was not just the sales team's job.

"We need to set clear expectations," she said, "and create a culture where everyone understands they have a role in driving growth. We all must sell—no exceptions." Then she added, "We have to learn to *point with our thumbs, not our index fingers.*"

It stopped me in my tracks. Not just because it was a great metaphor, but because it was so clearly embedded in how she led. No blame games. No silos. Just a clear call for ownership at every level.

I remember thinking, *I wish I had heard that phrase earlier in my career.* It is simple, memorable, and cuts straight to the heart of what it means to lead with accountability.

152. PARKED IN THE WRONG GARAGE

When it comes to talent acquisition, I have developed a deep respect for the enormous impact that the right executive hire can have on an organization. Across my time as a corporate CEO and now in private equity, I have made some excellent hiring decisions and, of course, a few I'd love to have back. These choices hinge on evaluating a mix of hard and soft attributes: track record, leadership style, emotional intelligence, and cultural fit. It is not an exact science, but over the years, I have developed a kind of pattern recognition for executives who thrive in the types of companies where we invest.

One particular hiring misfire, though disappointing at the time, still makes me smile. After realizing that a newly hired executive simply was not the right fit for one of our portfolio companies, a PE colleague summed it up perfectly and memorably.

"This is painful," he said, shaking his head. "We *parked in the wrong garage* with this guy."

It was such a perfect metaphor. Just like pulling into the wrong garage leaves you in the wrong place entirely, hiring the wrong person drops you into a situation that just does not work. Every garage represents a different potential hire, and unfortunately, we had chosen one that looked good from the outside but did not fit once we were inside.

The experience was a lesson that even with all the diligence, interviews, and glowing references in the world, there is no guaranteed formula for getting it right. Ultimately, the real test of a hire comes once they are in the role and the rubber meets the road, which usually does not take long to reveal itself. Sometimes you nail it. And sometimes, well, you have to back out of the garage and start over.

153. ATTRACTIVE FISHING HOLES

In addition to sourcing new investment opportunities through relationships with investment bankers actively marketing assets, PE firms also dedicate significant time to pursuing proprietary deals. These are opportunities that surface without an investment banker representing the target company.

PE firms typically concentrate on specific industry sectors and subsectors, which investment bankers understand and use to guide which firms they approach with deals. While a firm's focus may evolve over time, most have defined targeting projects that identify attractive subsectors aligned with their investment criteria. By pursuing both proprietary and banker-led opportunities within these focus areas, firms increase their odds of uncovering investments that match their strategy. This dual-track approach helps build a more robust and relevant deal pipeline.

During an annual strategic planning meeting, we were reviewing our areas of interest within healthcare, drilling down into each subsector and the respective growth drivers. As we debated whether to expand or shift our focus, a colleague offered a simple but effective analogy: "I wouldn't change our focus. These subsectors are still *attractive fishing holes* for new deals. The markets are still positioned favorably."

The metaphor stuck. Much like a seasoned angler knows where the fish are biting, PE firms concentrate their efforts on "fishing holes" with strong growth dynamics, sustainable profitability, and favorable market conditions. By deploying their time, capital, and expertise in these zones, firms aim to increase their chances of reeling in high-quality opportunities that align with their strategy and offer meaningful returns.

It is a process rooted in strategic sourcing, combining thorough research, industry insight, and a keen understanding of market trends to identify and capitalize on the most promising investment opportunities. In short, success in PE often comes down to knowing exactly where to cast your line.

154. THOSE WHO EXALT THEMSELVES WILL BE HUMBLED...THOSE WHO ARE HUMBLE WILL BE EXALTED

I find it essential to include this expression because it has remained consistently relevant across nearly every professional experience I have had, including in private equity. This biblical proverb carries timeless life lessons and offers powerful management insight. I have witnessed its truth play out many times, often culminating in the classic scenario where the *emperor has no clothes*.

The behavior described in the proverb is rooted in ego, arrogance, and an inflated sense of self-importance. In my experience, it is often exhibited by individuals early in their careers, though not exclusively. It can stem from academic elitism, personal privilege, or simply unchecked ambition. But in almost every case, the outcome is the same: the person is eventually humbled. Sometimes they are brought down a few notches, and in more serious cases, they are removed from their position altogether.

This fall from grace rarely happens overnight. It often unfolds slowly, as the individual remains unaware of how their behavior is perceived. What allows it to persist is typically poor oversight, misplaced tolerance, or a lack of honest feedback from those around them. When left unaddressed, the consequences can be costly, both for the individual and the organization.

On the other hand, I have consistently found that managers and senior leaders who lead with humility, respect, and self-awareness tend to earn lasting admiration. They are recognized for their contributions not because they demand attention, but because they share credit generously and accept responsibility when things go wrong. Their teams respect them. Their peers trust them. And their leadership has staying power.

The expression "Those who exalt themselves will be humbled, and those who are humble will be exalted" is more than a moral teaching. It is a practical guide for how to build credibility and influence. It reminds us that modesty, emotional intelligence, and a grounded sense of self are far more powerful in the long run than self-promotion and ego.

In both corporate and PE environments, humility often commands more respect and yields greater long-term success than bravado. By staying humble and leading with authenticity, individuals contribute to healthier organizations and build careers marked by trust, resilience, and real leadership.

155. TROUBLE RIDES A FAST HORSE

The first time I heard the phrase "trouble rides a fast horse," I couldn't help but picture Clint Eastwood appearing on the horizon, galloping into town with squinted eyes and a dust trail behind him. But over time, I came to appreciate its real-world application far beyond spaghetti westerns. In both my CEO days and in PE, this idiom has proven to be spot-on when it comes to organizational behavior, operations management, and business development.

At its core, the phrase suggests that problems tend to show up quickly and without much warning. In business, that means operational issues can surface suddenly and escalate rapidly if not dealt with decisively.

One vivid example came during a conversation with my PE colleagues about a product being piloted by one of our portfolio companies. Field failures were reported, but initially brushed off by management as statistically insignificant. The early warning signs didn't reach our radar until the issue was verging on crisis. Fortunately, the CEO acted quickly and pulled the pilot before things spiraled.

I later discussed the situation with a colleague, a seasoned manufacturing executive working for a PE firm. He cut straight to the point: "One field failure with a patient is one too many. You acted fast. It was the right move. *Trouble rides a fast horse*, and this could've snowballed into a disaster on multiple fronts."

That phrase stuck with me. The metaphor of the "fast horse" captures how swiftly and unpredictably trouble can hit. One moment everything seems steady, and the next, you're staring down an issue that came out of nowhere and is now bearing down at full speed.

The lesson is clear: leadership must stay vigilant. That means monitoring operations continuously, watching key performance indicators, staying attuned to market shifts, and being transparent about potential risks. When warning signs emerge, they should trigger swift and deliberate action, not wishful thinking or delay.

Ignoring trouble or assuming it will pass only gives it more time to gain momentum. And when it does, no one wants to be the last one standing in its path, wondering how the galloping hooves went unnoticed.

156. BASEBALL-STYLE ARBITRATION

In business, "baseball-style arbitration" refers to a unique method of dispute resolution borrowed from Major League Baseball contract negotiations. Instead of a back-and-forth compromise or a traditional arbitration process, each party submits a final proposal: typically related to pricing, terms, or contractual conditions, and the arbitrator must choose one of the two in its entirety. No middle ground. No tweaking. Just pick a side.

This all-or-nothing setup forces both parties to put forward their most reasonable, well-supported offer. Overreach, and you risk losing it all. It is a high-stakes, efficiency-driven way to break deadlocks, often used in contractual disputes, acquisition offers, pricing disagreements, and other situations where a definitive outcome is needed without the drawn-out slog of negotiation or litigation.

I had never encountered this concept in practice until my time in PE, during a particularly competitive acquisition process for a company we really liked.

A colleague turned to me and said, "This deal has turned into *baseball-style arbitration*. We're not there yet, but we still have a shot."

In this case, the investment banker running the process had narrowed the field to two finalist PE firms and requested final bids. The founders would then choose one offer, with no further negotiation or countering. Whichever bid they selected would set the valuation and terms, period. Winner takes all.

It was a classic baseball-style moment: both sides had to bring their best, most rational offer to the table. There was no room for fluff, gamesmanship, or hoping for post-offer adjustments. From the seller's perspective, it accelerated the process and forced bidders to put their cards on the table. From the buyer's side, it created pressure to be both aggressive and realistic.

In PE, this approach can be surprisingly effective. It avoids prolonged haggling and forces clarity, something both sides can appreciate when time, resources, and competitive tension are in play.

157. STRAWMAN

I have encountered the term "strawman" countless times throughout my career, both before and during my time in PE. It has come up so often, in fact, that it deserves a place in this collection. The origin traces back to the image of a scarecrow used as a stand-in during debate, a flimsy figure constructed not to stand its ground, but to be easily knocked down. In business, however, the term has evolved into something far more useful and nuanced.

In PE, a "strawman" often refers to a rough initial idea or proposal, used as a conversation starter. It is not meant to be final or bullet-proof. Instead, it provides a framework for discussion, giving the team something tangible to react to. I have found it especially helpful when grappling with thorny problems or complex scenarios where trying to get everything right on the first pass would be counterproductive.

One particularly vivid example comes from a post-merger integration effort involving two portfolio companies. During a planning session, someone presented a draft of the new combined reporting structure. It was basic and full of assumptions, but it sparked conversation.

"This is just a *strawman*," the CEO said, sliding the org chart across the table. "We needed to start somewhere. Let's use it to pick it apart."

And that we did. The draft served as a useful foil: something to challenge, reshape, and build upon. The key was that everyone understood its purpose. It was not meant to be right, just directional. That shared understanding made the process far more productive.

Of course, the term "strawman" is not always used so innocently. I have also seen it deployed more strategically, even manipulatively, in negotiations. In that context, it can take the form of an exaggerated or oversimplified position, intentionally crafted to be dismissed or dismantled. It is a tactic: introduce something extreme, allow the other party to shoot it down, and then pivot to a "compromise" that was your real goal all along.

During a consulting assignment, I watched a seasoned executive propose a valuation framework for an acquisition with overly aggressive assumptions. When the counterparty pushed back, they quickly offered a revised model that seemed more reasonable, but in reality, it was the number they had intended to land on from the beginning.

"That first offer was a *strawman*," one of he later admitted. "It anchored the conversation right where I wanted it."

Used responsibly, a strawman is a powerful collaborative tool. Used deceptively, it can steer a negotiation in misleading ways. Either way, understanding its purpose, whether as a sketchpad for ideas or a strategic decoy, is essential in navigating business discussions, especially in PE where the stakes are high and the gamesmanship is real.

158. HEADROOM

When evaluating add-on acquisitions for our PE portfolio companies, we explore a range of investment theses. These often include geographic expansion, technological enhancement, customer diversification, and operational efficiency. In many cases, merging two businesses creates opportunities for product or service synergies, staff rationalization, offshoring, and other value-enhancing strategies.

It was in this context that I first encountered the term "headroom." In PE, I found "headroom" is often used to describe the untapped potential for value creation, growth, or operational improvement beyond a company's current performance.

I remember the term coming up during a deal review meeting. We were assessing a potential add-on acquisition when one of my PE colleagues said, "There's a lot of *headroom* with this business. We could consolidate nearly the entire back office, cross-sell into their customer base, and create an immediate margin lift. The integration is clean, there's no customer overlap. We'd be leaving value on the table if we passed."

That remark was meaningful. The word "headroom" was not just shorthand for upside, it was a signal that the deal had strategic fit, operational synergies, and financial leverage all lined up.

In another deal discussion, someone laid out a rough sketch of projected synergies and integration timing across a few scenarios. One team member asked, "Is this the final plan?" The presenter smiled and said, "No, just a strawman to frame the discussion and get us thinking about how to capture the *headroom*."

In that moment, the language of PE came together: a "strawman" proposal helped frame the possibilities, while "headroom" captured the unclaimed value waiting to be unlocked.

In practice, headroom often translates to EBITDA arbitrage, a favorite term in PE circles. If you can acquire a business at one multiple of EBITDA, integrate it efficiently, and lift margins or growth, you not only grow earnings but also benefit from EBITDA multiple expansion. That's the sweet spot.

Understanding where the headroom is, and how to get there, often defines the difference between a mediocre deal and a great one. Whether it's cost takeout, cross-selling, or platform leverage, headroom represents the delta between what a business is and what it could be with the right strategic and operational support.

159. HUNTING WITHIN THE FARM

Business development strategies often require a multifaceted approach that includes pursuing new clients while also deepening relationships with existing ones. Clients who have experienced successful outcomes can become invaluable advocates. They not only provide positive word-of-mouth referrals to peers at other companies but also open doors to additional stakeholders or departments within their own organization.

In PE, the practice of growing existing customer relationships for portfolio companies is sometimes referred to as "hunting within the farm." It is a simple phrase, but it captures an important idea: there is often untapped growth potential within a company's current customer base. While acquiring new clients and diversifying the customer mix is always a welcome and necessary part of any growth strategy, I have found that some of the most efficient and highest-return opportunities often come from cultivating what is already familiar.

I recall one board meeting where the CEO of a portfolio company laid out a fairly ambitious revenue plan for the coming year. One of my PE colleagues asked, "Is this based on new logos or expansion of existing accounts?" The CEO replied, "Mostly new logos." That sparked some debate.

Another board member jumped in: "We should create an alternative plan that flips that ratio, assuming most of the growth comes from existing clients. There is a lot of value in *hunting within the farm* considering how well our clients like us. You should pressure-test how much wallet share we really have and how much more we could capture."

That kicked off a broader conversation. Within a week, the management team came back with a revised go-to-market plan that combined traditional new business development with targeted account mining efforts. Not only was the updated plan more achievable, but it also had a faster path to revenue and better margins, since customer acquisition costs were lower and the sales cycles were shorter.

Hunting within the farm may not have the allure of landing a major new client, but it can deliver powerful, scalable results when executed well. This approach pairs nicely with a strawman exercise: start with a simple model that assumes growth comes from existing relationships, then iterate based on what is realistic and where the friction lies. In the end, it is often the customers who already trust you that will be the fastest and most reliable source of incremental growth.

160. RUNWAY EXTENSION

Throughout my time in PE, I have frequently encountered the term "runway extension," especially when working with early-stage pharmaceutical companies. The phrase tends to surface most during market downturns or periods of tight funding, when companies need to make every dollar work a little harder. Foundationally, "runway extension" refers to the strategic effort to stretch existing capital as far as possible, ideally just far enough to hit a major milestone before running out of cash or returning to investors with a hat in hand.

In the pharmaceutical world, this often means prioritizing high-value programs, delaying or shelving lower-priority projects, cutting burn rate, and squeezing maximum value from limited resources. It is a balancing act that aims to keep operations moving forward: research, clinical trials, and regulatory work without hitting a financial wall.

I remember sitting in a potential client meeting for one of our portfolio companies in the pharma services space. The CEO of the client company, visibly weary but sharp as ever, said half-jokingly, "Our science is strong, but right now our biggest innovation is in creative budgeting. We are in full *runway extension* mode." Everyone chuckled, but we knew exactly what he meant.

A colleague leaned over and said, "If they can make it to their Phase 1 readout without another raise, they'll have serious leverage on valuation. This extension might be the best return they engineer all year."

The metaphor is fitting. Just like a pilot needs enough runway to get airborne, these early-stage companies need enough time and capital to hit key inflection points. Run out too soon, and it is back to the investor pool at lower valuations and higher dilution.

What I have found particularly interesting from a PE lens is how this dynamic fuels demand for specialized outsourced service providers. Instead of building in-house teams, which requires onboarding, infrastructure, and long-term commitments, early-stage pharma companies often turn to clinical research organizations (CROs), regulatory consultants, or contracted subject matter experts to handle high-skill functions on an as-needed basis. It is a smart tradeoff: access to world-class capabilities without the full-time burn.

From an investment perspective, this outsourcing trend creates tailwinds for the service providers we back. It is common to hear a company say, "We are managing headcount, preserving cash, and buying flexibility. Our CRO partners are key to keeping us moving without breaking the bank."

Runway extension may not be flashy, but it is essential. In early-stage drug development, the winners are not always the ones with the most funding. Sometimes, they are the ones who know how to coast, glide, and squeeze every ounce of momentum from limited fuel until they hit that lift-off milestone.

161. ARROWS ARE UP

I have heard the simple phrase "arrows are up" used often during PE diligence. It is shorthand for a positive outlook and usually signals a green light to keep advancing an investment opportunity.

In my experience, the diligence process moves through a series of gates, and clearing each one typically requires unanimous enthusiasm, or at least no major objections. After one particularly revealing management meeting with a potential acquisition target, a PE colleague summed up his take with, "I was pleasantly surprised. I went in a bit unsure, but my *arrows are up*. I think we should move forward and push toward an LOI."

That phrase, "my arrows are up," is a concise way of saying that the diligence findings have either met or exceeded expectations. It often reflects alignment across financial, operational, and cultural dimensions. On the other hand, when someone says "my arrows are down," it is usually time to hit the brakes. That is PE-speak for "something smells off," and more often than not, it leads to a quiet exit from the process.

Like many idioms in PE, "arrows are up" is part report card, part gut check. And in PE where momentum matters, enough arrows pointing up can be all the signal a team needs to keep going.

162. CLOSE TO SHORE

Being part of PE investment deal teams has given me a front-row seat to the nuanced complexity behind every investment decision. These decisions are shaped by disciplined due diligence, strict adherence to key metrics, pattern recognition honed through experience, and a deep understanding of business dynamics. Beyond the numbers, we evaluate management strength, business model durability, and the feasibility of executing on growth strategies. Yet at the core of it all lies one fundamental requirement: unanimous consensus among the deal team to move forward.

Each team member brings a unique lens to the table, shaped by a blend of personal experiences, risk tolerance, and battle scars from past deals. Some see landmines. Others see opportunity. Personally, I tend to lean toward the latter. I look for what could go right rather than fixate on what might go wrong. That mindset likely comes from my years as a CEO, steering through tough environments and leading turnaround efforts where others may have backed away. So, when evaluating an opportunity, I often find myself focused on the future trajectory: how we can add value during our hold period, what levers we can pull, and whether the risks are ones we know how to manage.

That said, I do not see opportunity everywhere.

We were once evaluating an add-on acquisition for a portfolio company that was facing sluggish growth amid a broader market downturn. The target offered some consolidation benefits that could yield EBITDA arbitrage, but beyond that, the strategic fit was thin. There were no clear advantages in technology, geography, or customer diversification. The value creation story felt like a stretch.

During a deal team meeting, I broke from my usual optimism and said, "I just don't think this moves the needle. Even if the deal is priced right, I'm not convinced we should take this on."

To my surprise, a colleague who typically leans more aggressive chimed in, "Unless the valuation is unbelievably compelling, I don't see the point of charging ahead. I think we should stay *close to shore*. This could distract our management team, and I'd rather ride out the cycle and reassess when the waters calm."

That phrase—*stay close to shore*—resonated. It perfectly captured the moment. We were already navigating through choppy conditions, managing existing challenges, and the idea of adding complexity without a clear upside just did not feel like the right move.

In hindsight, choosing caution over ambition in that situation proved to be the right call. And it served as a warning that even in a business built on taking risks, knowing when not to act can be just as important as knowing when to lean in.

163. HIGH WATERMARK

Although I had heard the term "high watermark" used in broader business contexts, I've come to appreciate its distinct relevance in private equity investing. In PE, a "high watermark" refers to a provision commonly found in fund agreements that ensures a PE fund manager only receives performance fees, often referred to as carried interest, when the fund's value exceeds its previous peak, or "high watermark."

When an investor commits capital to a PE fund, that capital becomes part of the fund's overall pool, which is deployed into various investments, such as acquiring portfolio companies. The goal, of course, is to generate returns through eventual exits.

I first encountered the term in a PE context when a colleague remarked, "This exit will get us past the *high watermark* for the fund, triggering carry for the team." In other words, the successful exit of a portfolio company pushed the fund's cumulative returns above its prior peak, making the team eligible to share in the fund's profits.

The high watermark represents the highest value a fund has reached since inception, factoring in both invested capital and realized gains. It acts as a threshold: if a fund's value dips below this mark, the fund manager must first recover those losses before earning carried interest again. For example, if a fund reaches a $500 million valuation, then declines to $450 million, and later climbs to $525 million, carried interest is only earned on the $25 million above the prior $500 million high watermark.

This structure helps align incentives. It ensures fund managers are not rewarded for simply recovering losses, but rather for delivering sustained, incremental value to investors. The high watermark thus encourages long-term value creation over short-term gains.

In another example, during a discussion with a friend at another PE firm many years ago, he referenced a stalled fund by saying, "We're still underwater from the markdowns last year. Until we clear the *high watermark*, we won't see carry." This candid observation underscored how the high watermark can also serve as a sobering accountability measure, especially in periods of underperformance.

164. HOLDING THE PEN

The PE due diligence process is a comprehensive evaluation conducted when a firm is assessing a potential investment. It involves a deep review of the target company's operations, financial performance, legal and regulatory matters, and other critical factors to fully understand the risks, opportunities, and value creation levers tied to the transaction.

Typically, a General Partner or senior investment professional at the PE firm serves as the primary point of contact with the seller or the investment banker representing the seller. This individual also plays a central role in managing the diligence process, effectively acting as the quarterback for the deal: coordinating internal and external resources, managing timelines, and keeping all workstreams aligned and moving forward.

During one internal deal team meeting, a colleague asked, "Who's *holding the pen* on the investment committee presentation?" Although I had not heard the phrase used in that context before, the meaning was instantly clear. Since then, I have seen it used frequently throughout diligence. Someone might say, "I'll *hold the pen* on the quality of earnings review," or "You *hold the pen* on the customer calls summary."

In this context, "holding the pen" refers to the person who has lead responsibility for a specific workstream or deliverable. It goes beyond drafting content. It signals ownership: coordinating inputs from the team, pushing things forward, and ensuring quality, completeness, and accuracy. It is efficient shorthand used throughout the investment process to establish clear accountability.

On another occasion, while reviewing an early draft of the deal team presentation, a team member remarked, "This version is solid. Who's *holding the pen* for final edits before it goes to the Investment Committee?" That simple question not only clarified next steps, but also reinforced alignment on responsibilities and timing.

In the PE world, "holding the pen" has come to represent more than just authorship. It is a symbol of leadership, accountability, and follow-through, all essential qualities when navigating a deal from diligence to close.

165. HANDLE

My introduction to the term "handle" came while evaluating potential acquirers, both financial and strategic, for a high-performing PE portfolio company on whose Board I served. As we prepared for a sale, we launched a structured process to select the right investment banker to lead the transaction. That meant evaluating several bankers with deep sector expertise, strong transaction experience, and credible points of view on market dynamics and valuation.

We ultimately selected Tony Crisman, formerly of Lincoln International and now Managing Director and Head of Healthcare at Stout, to co-lead the process. Tony brought a combination of deep industry knowledge, a strong track record, and a personable, disarming style that made him both effective and enjoyable to work with. I appreciated his strategic instincts almost as much as his ability to keep a room relaxed, even when the stakes were high.

In one of our early meetings, the term "handle" came up during a discussion of valuation expectations. When someone asked where he believed the company would trade, Tony pulled up a few slides packed with precedent transactions, comparable assets, and valuation ranges. After walking us through the data, he leaned back, smiled, and said, "This company is in a class of its own. They've become the go-to player in the space. You shouldn't even consider an offer without a *four-handle*. That's the bar. We have every reason to believe the market will meet it."

At the time, I had never heard "handle" used this way, but I quickly caught on. In this context, a "handle" refers to the leading digit of a valuation range. A "four-handle" meant Tony expected bids to start with a four—somewhere between $400 million and $499 million. It was a shorthand rooted in conviction, supported by the company's performance, leadership position, scarcity value, and strong buyer interest.

Tony's framing resonated with me. It was punchy, confident, and backed by data. We hired him and his team to co-lead the sale process, and sure enough, the final deal closed squarely within the anticipated four-handle range a few months later.

Since then, I have heard "handle" used in all sorts of contexts: deal pricing, EBITDA ranges, even fund sizes. But I still smile when I hear it, because nothing quite matches the first time someone tells you, with a straight face, that your business is too good to sell unless it starts with a four.

166. HEADLINE NUMBER

In private equity, I've found the term "headline number" comes up most often when discussing the valuation presented to a seller in a Letter of Intent. The LOI serves as a preliminary agreement that outlines the general terms under which a PE firm intends to acquire a company. While non-binding in most respects, it sets the tone for negotiations and provides a roadmap to the final purchase agreement.

In this context, the "headline number" usually refers to the total proposed purchase price or enterprise value. It is the number that grabs attention and shapes first impressions. I vividly remember a meeting with an investment banker representing a seller in a highly competitive process. As we prepared to submit our LOI and asked for valuation guidance, he said flatly, "You need to be at a *headline number* of at least $80 million."

The headline number has optical weight. It is often the first number the seller sees, and it tends to dominate the early conversation. Regardless of deal structure, sellers latch onto it. It can determine whether a bid is taken seriously, especially when expectations have been carefully calibrated by their banker.

But while the headline number is important, it rarely tells the full story. It may not reflect the true economic value of the deal once all the details are considered: working capital adjustments, debt assumptions, earn-outs, escrows, and other structural mechanics. In some cases, the headline number can even be misleading if it's inflated by milestone-based payments or deferred compensation.

LOIs vary in complexity depending on the situation, but they typically include key elements like the proposed purchase price and structure, exclusivity period, diligence timeline, sources of funding, closing conditions, and a framework for reps and warranties.

For example, a PE firm might submit an LOI with a $100 million headline number. But that figure might include contingent earn-outs, be subject to adjustments for net working capital or debt levels, and assume certain closing conditions that may or may not be achieved. The definitive purchase agreement, negotiated after the LOI is signed, is where the actual economic value becomes clear.

In short, the headline number is powerful. It sets expectations and moves the process forward. But both buyers and sellers must look beyond that eye-catching figure to fully understand the substance and structure of the deal. The number on the first page is only the beginning of the story.

161. THROW UP ALL OVER IT

Throughout my career as a CEO and in private equity, I've encountered the colorful expression "throw up all over it." It is as vivid as it sounds and typically describes the instant and overwhelming rejection of an idea, pitch, or investment opportunity. Once that kind of reaction takes hold, there is usually no amount of persuasion or spin that can revive the conversation.

In PE, my colleagues and I have "thrown up all over" more than a few opportunities. The triggers are often familiar: margin compression, dangerously high customer concentration, no post-deal role for the founder or management team, or a revenue trend line that is steadily sloping in the wrong direction. Any one of these can raise red flags. A combination? Cue the dry heaves.

I have also seen this reaction surface during year-end budgeting, an annual tradition where optimism and realism often collide. One episode stands out clearly. A portfolio company management team had submitted its second or third revision of the upcoming year's budget, and it was clear they were sandbagging. Again. Understated growth projections, padded timelines, and vague performance goals that left everyone unconvinced.

During one particularly exasperated moment in a budget review meeting, a colleague put it bluntly:

"If he shows us more of the same in the next version of the budget, I'm going to *throw up all over it*. It'll be dead on arrival."

That line got a few laughs, but it also captured the sentiment in the room. It was not just about numbers falling short, it was about trust eroding. The team wanted a forecast that showed some conviction, not a document engineered to be easily beat.

In PE, "throwing up all over it" may be an inelegant turn of phrase, but it is a useful one. It cuts to the chase. It signals that a proposal has crossed a threshold from "needs work" to "nonstarter," and that it is time to go back to the drawing board. Preferably with a mop.

168. WHERE TO SPEND OUR BULLETS

I have come to appreciate the phrase "where to spend our bullets" as a concise way of describing the strategic allocation of time, effort, and resources. In private equity, it carries weight in both investment decision-making and negotiation strategy. It reflects a resource management mindset and the nuance of effective deal execution, emphasizing the importance of making deliberate, high-impact choices to drive meaningful outcomes.

From a resource allocation perspective, the phrase acknowledges the limits of bandwidth and the high opportunity cost of time, particularly when juggling multiple live deals. Deciding *where to spend our bullets* is about focusing on the opportunities that offer the greatest potential return, rather than spreading teams too thin across a broad set of possibilities.

I remember one internal investment deal team discussion where we were considering several attractive targets. The deal flow was strong, but so was the strain on team capacity. At one point, a colleague said, "We're resource constrained. There are some solid prospects on this list, but we need to decide *where to spend our bullets.* It's a tough call, but we can't chase everything." It was a candid reminder that in PE, discipline is not just about saying yes to the right opportunities, but rather is about saying no to the ones that dilute focus.

In a negotiation context, the phrase has a slightly different shade of meaning. Here, the bullets are a finite set of levers (concessions, points of leverage, and persuasive arguments) that can be used to move the deal forward. It is about choosing your battles wisely. You do not push on every term. You push where it matters most. Knowing which issues to prioritize, and which to let go, often makes the difference between a stalled negotiation and a closed deal.

Ultimately, "where to spend our bullets" is about disciplined prioritization. Whether you are evaluating an investment, structuring a transaction, or negotiating deal terms, it is a reminder to focus energy where it counts. After all, you only get so many bullets. Use them wisely.

169. THE FIRST FLOOR

I first became familiar with the term "the first floor" in the context of executing add-on acquisitions for private equity portfolio companies. While add-ons are not always central to the original investment thesis for a platform, we often pursue them to drive geographic expansion, broaden the customer base, or acquire complementary capabilities and technologies.

Much like platform investments, our add-on targets are often founder-owned, privately held businesses. Rather than seeking full liquidity, we typically prefer that sellers retain a meaningful equity stake by rolling it into the combined entity and staying involved in some capacity. This structure promotes alignment and gives sellers the opportunity to participate in future upside.

Even though these founders are not coming in at the original platform investment stage and are therefore not investing at the ground floor valuation, they are often joining at what we call "the first floor." I first heard the term during a conversation between a PE colleague and the founder of a potential add-on for a portfolio company in which I served on the board. The founder was unsure about selling and hesitant about what it meant to join a larger organization.

My colleague explained, "We invested in the platform two years ago. Since then, we have brought in a Chief Financial Officer, Chief Commercial Officer, launched the first phase of a field sales team, added a VP of Marketing, and made serious investments in operations and infrastructure. By merging with us now, you're getting in on the *first floor*. We've built the foundation, and we're just starting to scale. There's a lot of value still to be created."

I appreciated the phrase as it conveyed a powerful message. "The first floor" signals that while the journey has already begun, it is still early in the broader value creation arc. For a seller, it means stepping into a business with proven momentum and a well-resourced growth plan, but with plenty of upside still ahead. It is both a strategic invitation and a financial opportunity to participate in the next chapter of the company's growth. In essence, getting in on the *first floor* means joining early enough to benefit meaningfully from a platform's scale-up phase, even if the elevator has already left the ground.

110. DRINKING FROM A FIREHOSE

Imagine the rush and intensity of water blasting from a firehose. Trying to take a sip would be laughable. In business, the phrase "drinking from a firehose" is a vivid metaphor for the overwhelming experience of being flooded with information or responsibilities, often at a pace so relentless it's hard to process, let alone manage.

I first heard the expression when I was considering my first professional role in the healthcare industry at a large medical device company. I was anxious about the scope of the position, especially the technical depth and management responsibilities tied to a clinical area I knew very little about. Sensing my hesitation, the Vice President of R&D, who, remarkably, is still a close friend three decades later, looked at me and said with a grin, "Don't worry. You'll be *drinking from a firehose* for the first six months. You'll get there."

That image was difficult to ignore. And it turned out to be entirely accurate.

Throughout my career, I've found myself repeatedly *drinking from the firehose*, especially in the early months of each new role. As I moved across different sectors within healthcare over two decades, I had to absorb new clinical subject matter, adjust to unfamiliar company cultures, and develop technical expertise quickly and under pressure. That learning curve only steepened when I later transitioned into private equity, an entirely new domain with its own language, rituals, and expectations. That leap, and the deluge that came with it, is part of what inspired me to write this book.

Even now, the firehose has not let up. With every new investment opportunity and portfolio company engagement, I dive into fresh business models, uncharted markets, and unique operational structures. Whether I'm part of a deal team conducting diligence or sitting across from a management team post-close, I'm constantly learning. It is demanding, yes, but also deeply energizing and rewarding.

Sometimes I think about people who pursue more stable, predictable career paths, the kind where the water pressure is more of a gentle garden hose. I say that with respect, but also with a knowing smile. For me, the pace, the variety, and the intellectual challenge of *drinking from the firehose* is what makes the journey worthwhile. Just remember to come up for air every now and then.

171. DON'T SHOOT ME, I'M ONLY THE PIANO PLAYER

"Don't Shoot Me, I'm Only the Piano Player" was Elton John's sixth studio album, released in 1973. It became his second consecutive number one album in the United States and his first to top the charts in the United Kingdom. I was ten years old at the time, and I vividly remember my older sister buying the record. She played it often on her turntable, filling the house with Elton's unmistakable sound.

While I enjoyed the music, it was the album's title that really stuck with me. It sparked my imagination, calling to mind the old Westerns I watched on TV. I pictured the classic saloon scene, where a gunfight breaks out and the poor piano player, an innocent bystander in the room, either keeps playing nervously or dives for cover as chaos erupts around him. Elton John was perhaps being tongue-in-cheek, suggesting that despite all the noise and pressure of fame, he was just the musician trying to do his job.

In a business setting, "Don't shoot me, I'm only the piano player" has a similarly useful meaning. It can be a way to preface an opinion or observation while acknowledging you are not the final decision-maker.

It signals humility or even mild self-deprecation, especially in a room full of strong opinions and high conviction.

I never thought I'd get to use the phrase in a professional context, but early in my PE career, the moment arrived. We were in due diligence on a potential acquisition, and I was struggling to get comfortable with several elements of the business. Most notably, it lacked any meaningful recurring revenue and was more project based. I sensed my view wasn't widely shared within the team, and as someone still relatively new to investing, I wanted to voice my concerns without coming across as dismissive or overconfident.

So, during the investment deal team discussion, I led with:

"I've thought a lot about this. *Don't shoot me, I'm only the piano player*, but I'm really concerned about the lack of recurring revenue here."

The phrase earned me a few blank stares. Apparently, the Elton John reference was lost on the under-forty crowd, but the conversation that followed was productive. I laid out my concerns around revenue sustainability and a few other key risks. While I was half-expecting to be politely overruled, the team took the points seriously, and we had a thoughtful debate about the deal.

Later, I realized I was the oldest person in the room. None of my colleagues had been born when the album came out, much less heard of the phrase. That made me smile and admittedly cringe a little. Still, it felt good to sneak a bit of vintage rock and roll into a modern PE setting. I haven't used the phrase since, but I still chuckle when I think back on my attempt to wedge it into the lexicon of dealmaking. Some metaphors just age better than others.

172. THRESHOLD ISSUE

The concept of a "threshold issue" in private equity is closely related to other expressions in this book like "knock-out factor" and "third-rail issue." It refers to a fundamental concern that must be resolved before an investment can proceed. If left unaddressed, a threshold issue can jeopardize both the long-term viability of the business and the success of the investment.

These issues typically surface during due diligence. While they vary depending on the industry and the specifics of the target company, threshold issues are deal-critical. They are the kinds of concerns that can stop a transaction in its tracks, regardless of how promising the financials may appear.

I remember one example clearly from my first year as an Operating Partner in PE. We were in a deal team meeting reviewing a company with solid topline growth and attractive margins. On paper, it looked great. But a seasoned colleague raised a red flag:

"Forget the revenue. What worries me is that the founder wants to walk away the day the deal closes and refuses to roll any equity. That's a *threshold issue* for me. I wouldn't touch it."

His comment shifted the tone of the discussion immediately. It didn't matter how strong the numbers were if there was no continuity of leadership or alignment of incentives.

Over time, I've seen many types of threshold issues derail otherwise promising deals: unstable leadership, intense competitive threats, lack of technology or service differentiation, excessive customer concentration, or a weak go-to-market strategy. These aren't minor red flags you can brush aside or "fix later." They demand serious scrutiny, and if they can't be resolved or sufficiently mitigated, they can and should be deal-breakers.

Raising and addressing threshold issues early is critical for driving internal alignment within the deal team and, more importantly, for setting the investment up for long-term success. You can work through a lot of imperfections in a company, but if you miss a true threshold issue, you may end up owning a problem that no amount of capital or operational expertise can fix.

113. DRY POWDER

In private equity, "dry powder" refers to capital a firm has raised from limited partners (LPs) but has not yet deployed into specific investments. The term conjures the image of unused gunpowder: resources at the ready, waiting to be deployed when the right opportunity appears.

PE firms raise funds with the goal of investing in platform companies or add-on acquisitions that align with their strategy. Until those dollars are committed to specific deals, they sit and are categorized as dry powder. A healthy reserve provides flexibility, giving firms the ability to move quickly on attractive opportunities, take advantage of shifting market dynamics, or pursue strategic acquisitions as they arise.

But too much dry powder for too long can be a red flag. Extended under-deployment might point to challenges in sourcing quality deals, overly rigid investment criteria, or consistent losses in competitive bid processes. In those cases, LPs may begin to question whether capital is being put to work efficiently enough to deliver expected returns in a reasonable time frame.

Dry powder also becomes relevant during reverse due diligence, when target companies diligence the firms evaluating them. Savvy founders often dig into whether a potential buyer has the financial capacity and the intent to follow through. I remember one such founder who, after presenting his company's growth story and vision, paused and asked us bluntly, "So, how much *dry powder* do you actually have ready to invest?"

It was a pointed question. He wasn't just asking about our fund size. He was assessing whether we were serious, credible, and capable of moving quickly if the deal progressed. It was a good reminder that due diligence goes both ways. Just as we assess the readiness of a target company, smart founders are measuring ours.

174. MORE CONNECTIONS THAN LEGOS

With more than 30 years in the healthcare industry, I take great pride in the network I have built along the way. I have always made a point of staying in touch with former colleagues and expanding my circle through industry events, philanthropic work, social platforms, and the kind of conversations that don't feel like networking at all. I genuinely enjoy it. I also love playing connector, introducing people who I think might benefit from knowing each other, whether for business, collaboration, or just good conversation.

This network has become one of my most valuable assets in private equity. It has helped source proprietary investment opportunities and support portfolio companies in areas like business development, executive recruiting, strategic add-ons, and even marketing partnerships.

One moment that still makes me laugh happened during a meeting with the founders of a potential target company. We were explaining how our firm adds value beyond just writing a check, and a colleague introduced me with a grin. "Mike is hands-on with business development and general management. He has helped source some major deals. The guy has *more connections than Legos*."

The comparison was unexpected, oddly specific, and absolutely hilarious. But more than anything, it was gratifying to have one of my favorite parts of the job called out by someone I respect immensely. Turns out, being a professional dot-connector has its moments.

175. YOU ARE WHO YOU PRETEND TO BE

The statement "you are who you pretend to be" carries deep psychological weight and could easily serve as the central theme of an entire book. While I don't intend to tackle such an ambitious undertaking here, I'd like to share a personal experience of how this phrase influenced me and helped build my confidence when facing a new and unfamiliar challenge. The concept extends beyond the earlier "drinking from a firehose" analogy, reflecting a more advanced stage in the learning curve; one that demands the ability to genuinely "walk the walk" and "talk the talk." It has broad relevance, particularly in executive leadership and PE.

After my tenure as CEO of Claros Diagnostics, which was acquired in 2011 by OPKO Health, a publicly traded company with a market cap at the time exceeding $1 billion, I developed a close bond with Dr. Phillip Frost, OPKO's billionaire Chairman and CEO. I remained with OPKO in a senior role, leading the point-of-care diagnostics division and working with Dr. Frost on a day-to-day basis. Our relationship was built on mutual respect, and before long, Dr. Frost invited me to join him in presenting at major investment banking conferences. This was completely new territory for me, especially given the spotlight that comes with representing a public company so closely watched due to Dr. Frost's remarkable reputation and influence.

One memorable experience remains etched in my mind. Dr. Frost and I were scheduled to present at an investment banking conference in the grand ballroom of The Waldorf Astoria in New York City. That morning, over breakfast at The Pierre Hotel with Dr. Frost and other senior OPKO executives, I found myself unusually quiet and more introspective than usual. Although I've always been comfortable with public speaking, this was different. It was my first time presenting as part of a public company, with high expectations riding on the outcome.

My uncharacteristically subdued state during breakfast didn't escape Dr. Frost's notice. As we rose from the table, he gestured for the others to proceed to the waiting car, and he touched my elbow. He asked, "Is everything okay, Michael?"

I nodded, acknowledging his concern, and responded, "Absolutely. I'm just mapping out the presentation in my mind. This is a new experience for me…you know, presenting and addressing questions as part of a public company. I want to ensure it goes off without a hitch."

A reassuring smile crept across Dr. Frost's face, and he imparted his wisdom, "Remember, no one in the audience comprehends the business or technology better than you do."

He then motioned for us to join the others who were already heading to the car, and continued, "And the spotlight of being a public company? You'll get used to it. This is just the first of many of these types of presentations."

As we walked, he stopped and looked directly in my eyes, "Remember, *you are who you pretend to be.* You got this."

In that moment, a wave of calm washed over me. The presentation went on to become one of the best and most memorable of my career.

In my case, the phrase "you are who you pretend to be" wasn't about pretending to be something artificial; instead, it captured the process of stepping up and adapting to a completely new aspect of my role and the expectations that came with it. It reminded me that presenting oneself as knowledgeable, reliable, ethical, and capable is in line with authenticity. Consistently aligning actions with these values builds a credible reputation and underscores the importance of being genuine, embracing your role, values, and strengths in both your career and personal life.

176. SMOOTH SKIES NEVER MADE A GREAT PILOT

I would feel uneasy discovering that the pilot flying my plane had never faced turbulence or bad weather. One of my favorite sayings, "Smooth skies never made a great pilot," captures that instinct perfectly. In business and private equity, it echoes the sentiment behind the "stepping on landmines" idiom I discussed earlier. I firmly believe that confronting adversity and learning from setbacks are not just useful—they are essential. These experiences build resilience, sharpen judgment, and foster the kind of adaptability that separates good leaders from great ones. Just as pilots earn their stripes flying through storms, business leaders become more capable by navigating difficult situations.

I remember this phrase coming to life during a particularly tough situation involving "John," a first-time CEO of a PE-backed portfolio company. He reached out to me and a colleague for advice on a thorny organizational issue. One of his top executives was knocking performance goals out of the park but creating serious disruption in the process. The cultural fallout was beginning to affect team morale and cohesion.

We met for breakfast ahead of a Board meeting where the issue was set to be discussed. Over coffee, I shared a similar experience from earlier in my career and suggested a few immediate steps. First, John needed to engage the executive directly and candidly. Second, we could explore bringing in a management coach. And third, I offered to step in, given my strong and trusted relationship with the executive in question.

We all agreed the individual was delivering on the numbers, and we wanted to exhaust every reasonable path before considering separation. Still, the tension was real, and the clock was ticking. John was a bit hesitant. My colleague, after listening closely, acknowledged the strain John was under but didn't let him off the hook. He leaned in and said, "Jim, you've got to find a way to make this work. *Smooth skies never made a great pilot.* Take Mike's advice and tackle this head-on."

It was the kind of moment where theory meets reality and where leadership is tested not by spreadsheets or strategy decks, but by people, pressure, and the uncomfortable gray areas in between.

177. BRAIN DAMAGE

I've frequently heard the term "brain damage" used in private equity, especially during the due diligence phase of a potential investment. It refers to those situations where a deal starts consuming an inordinate amount of time, energy, and internal resources, often while confidence in the opportunity is rapidly eroding.

You'll hear it in conversations like, "It's just not worth the *brain damage* to keep going," which is shorthand for saying the deal has become more trouble than it's worth. The complexity, friction, and opportunity cost are starting to outweigh the potential upside. In other words, the return doesn't justify the headache.

The term tends to surface when diligence gets especially messy. Maybe the management team is evasive or slow to engage. Maybe the financials are murky or there are looming regulatory or legal red flags. Or maybe there's just a growing disconnect on valuation or deal terms that no one seems motivated to bridge.

I remember one deal early in my PE tenure where our team spent weeks trying to make sense of the revenue model for a tech-enabled services business. We kept requesting data and clarification, but what we got back was either incomplete, inconsistent, or delivered in a format that looked like it had been pulled together during a fire drill. The management team got defensive, the process dragged on, and internal frustration mounted as other, more promising deals started stacking up in the pipeline.

During one particularly memorable deal team meeting, a colleague finally said what everyone was thinking: "Look, we've already spent way too much time on this, and we still don't have conviction. It's not worth the *brain damage*. Let's move on." And just like that, we did.

The phrase may sound casual, but it captures a core truth in PE: knowing when to walk away is just as important as knowing when to lean in. If a deal becomes disproportionately difficult relative to the likely return, the smartest move might be to preserve your team's bandwidth—and sanity—for the next opportunity.

178. SINGING FROM THE SAME HYMN BOOK

A hymn book, also known as a hymnal, is a collection of religious songs traditionally used in churches and other worship settings. These books include lyrics and musical notation for hymns, sacred and spiritual songs sung as expressions of worship, praise, or reflection. Hymn books serve as a shared guide, allowing congregations to sing together in unified voice during services.

I have encountered the phrase "singing from the same hymn book" often used in business as a metaphor to describe alignment across a team. It suggests that everyone is on the same page, delivering consistent messages, sharing the same priorities, and working toward a common goal. It is especially important in high-stakes or high-visibility situations, where any signs of misalignment can undermine confidence and trust.

I have heard the phrase frequently in PE, but the first time it really landed with me was during my time on the Board of Directors of a portfolio company. I had a strong working relationship with the CEO, "Ned," who invited me to sit in on a prep session with his executive leadership team ahead of a key Board meeting. The VP of Engineering was scheduled to present an updated timeline and revised budget for a high-profile project that had been under close scrutiny.

As the team walked through the details, the CFO raised concerns about certain line-item expenses that had grown since the last review. He paused, looked directly at the VP of Engineering, and said, "Before we walk this into the Boardroom, we need to make sure we are all *singing from the same hymn book*. I need to fully understand what is driving these cost increases. If I'm surprised by this now, you can be sure the Board will be even more concerned."

That moment was memorable. It was a clear and effective use of the phrase to highlight the importance of internal clarity and alignment before presenting to external stakeholders.

At its core, "singing from the same hymn book" is about more than just message discipline. It is about credibility. Whether across leadership teams, departments, or investor and management lines, aligned communication builds trust, strengthens execution, and ensures everyone is well-informed and moving in the same direction.

119. IF YOU DISCOVER YOU'RE RIDING A DEAD HORSE, THEN GET OFF

I first heard the phrase, "If you discover you are riding a dead horse, then get off," as a business metaphor for recognizing when an effort is no longer worth pursuing. It found it to be a blunt but effective warning that continuing to pour time and energy into a failing initiative rarely ends well. Whether it is a project, strategy, or leadership decision, knowing when to walk away is a skill. The message is similar to the gambler's trap of chasing losses: driven more by pride, fear, or sunk costs than by rational thinking.

I encountered this idiom early in my PE tenure during an interview with a candidate named Bob. He was being considered for the Vice President of Business Development role at a portfolio company where I sat on the Board. Bob had an impressive track record in which he consistently outperformed quotas, communicated his value proposition clearly, and brought an unmistakably driven, Type A energy to the conversation.

At the time, Bob was working for a healthcare company that had recently been acquired by a PE firm. The firm, with a diversified portfolio spanning unrelated industries, replaced the existing CEO with someone from its own network. From there, things quickly changed. Sales territories were restructured, inside sales were outsourced, the field team was cut, and a premature product launch led to major customer complaints and attrition.

While Bob's motivation for exploring new opportunities was apparent, I asked him to share more about his situation. He leaned in slightly and said, "The company I helped build over the past five years has become unrecognizable. I managed the sales transition well and did fine financially, but it has been hard to watch what happened after the acquisition. I finally realized, *if you discover you're riding a dead horse, you have to get off.* It was time to move on. I was miserable and just burning time."

His honesty struck a chord with me. Bob was not bitter, just clear-eyed. The metaphor he used, *riding a dead horse*, cut through the noise and captured something fundamental about leadership: the ability to assess a situation objectively, acknowledge when it is no longer viable, and act accordingly.

That mindset matters. It is easy to get caught in the trap of defending past decisions or sticking with a failing effort out of stubbornness or inertia. But the most effective leaders know when to cut losses, move on, and redirect energy toward something that actually has a future. Bob did exactly that and his candor in explaining why left a lasting impression.

180. END-OF-THE-RAINBOW ACQUIRER

In private equity, when we invest in a company, our goal is to add value over a defined period, typically four years or more. We aim to help the business grow, create jobs, generate positive impact, and eventually exit the investment with a strong return for the company's leadership, our investors, and ourselves.

During the diligence process for a pharmaceutical services business, we were building financial models to project performance over the next five years. As we explored various scenarios including an aggressive upside case, one of my colleagues began firing off a series of pointed, strategic questions: "What do we know about comparables in the space for exit multiples? Can we reasonably expect a strategic or financial buyer to step up when it is time for us to exit? Once we execute our playbook, who is the *end-of-the-rainbow acquirer?*"

His mention of "exit multiples" referred to the valuation we hoped to achieve at the time of exit, typically expressed as a multiple of EBITDA. But the more colorful part of his inquiry—"end-of-the-rainbow acquirer"—was what stuck with me. It was shorthand for the ideal buyer: the one most likely to pay a premium due to strategic fit, synergies, and growth potential.

The idiom evokes the image of a pot of gold at the end of a rainbow: elusive, valuable, and worth chasing. In the world of PE, identifying that acquirer is more than just a hopeful exercise. It helps shape how we position the company, which levers we pull to drive growth, and how we frame the story when it is time to go to market. Knowing who your end-of-the-rainbow buyer might be is about imagining the best possible outcome and then building toward it with intention.

181. DEAL FEVER

I have become quite accustomed to the term "deal fever" often used in private equity to describe a state of overexcitement or emotional attachment to a particular investment opportunity. When it sets in, judgment can become clouded. Risks get rationalized, red flags are brushed aside, and the focus shifts from objective evaluation to simply getting the deal done. I've witnessed this dynamic more than once and, early in my PE career, I fell into the trap myself.

It happened during diligence on a contract medical device manufacturing company. I was part of the investment team and found myself completely taken with the business. The service offering was compelling, and the founders were charismatic and persuasive. I was so drawn in that I glossed over some fundamental concerns, including heavy customer concentration and the looming expiration of key Master Service Agreements with blue-chip clients.

Interestingly, one of my colleagues leading the deal was equally intrigued, but had the experience to pull back and assess the situation more dispassionately. During one of our deal team meetings, he said, "I know there's a lot to like. Their growth is impressive, their technology is solid, and this is right in our strike zone. But we cannot let *deal fever* blind us to the real issues we've identified. I feel the momentum too, but we need to pump the brakes."

That comment hit home. Seasoned investors know how easily enthusiasm can tip into bias. When *deal fever* takes hold, it often leads to fixation on the upside while downplaying or ignoring the downside. The result is usually a rushed process, incomplete diligence, and a willingness to take risks that would otherwise be unacceptable.

Deal fever can be triggered by any number of forces: intense competition for a hot asset, fear of missing out, or the allure of a seemingly outsized return. But regardless of the cause, the outcome is often the same, compromised judgment and deviation from disciplined investing.

Experienced firms know this and work hard to guard against it. They rely on rigorous diligence protocols, multi-layered investment committee reviews, and cultures that encourage challenge, skepticism, and external input. In some firms, stage-gate approval processes are used to slow things down deliberately, requiring unanimous partner support before an investment moves forward.

Recognizing and managing deal fever is essential not just for protecting capital, but for maintaining credibility, investment discipline, and alignment with long-term value creation.

182. MOTHERHOOD AND APPLE PIE

During my time as CEO of a venture-backed medical device company, our technology was making steady progress through successful clinical trials. The market opportunity was massive—hundreds of millions—and we had momentum. Then, midstream, one of our clinical investigators, "Terry," a world-renowned physician in his specialty, approached me with a new idea.

He had identified a compelling opportunity to expand the device's use from adult patients to an adjacent pediatric indication. It involved treating a rare disease, one with limited commercial potential but clear clinical value. This kind of extension could qualify under the FDA's "compassionate use" or "orphan indication" designations, which sometimes allow for expedited clearance to help patients with urgent unmet needs.

Terry's proposal was thoughtful and ambitious. He suggested we pursue this pediatric application, seek grant funding to support the effort, and aim to publish and present the clinical outcomes. The science was strong, the need was real, and the reputational upside was obvious. Still, I needed Board approval, so I added it to the agenda for our upcoming meeting.

When I presented the opportunity, the response was swift and unanimous. One director smiled and said, "Mike, this is like *motherhood and apple pie*. If you're confident it won't distract from our core mission, then go for it. It helps kids, gives the company positive visibility, and frankly, it's just the right thing to do."

The phrase "motherhood and apple pie" is often used to describe ideas that are universally embraced, inherently good, and nearly impossible to argue against. Much like, well, actual motherhood and a slice of warm apple pie, some things just don't need a hard sell.

In this case, the idea checked all the boxes—ethical, clinical, reputational—and required no further convincing. Sometimes, in a room full of investors and operators, it's nice when something can be both strategically sound and simply... good.

183. BID WILL HUNT

Navigating the private equity diligence process and arriving at an appropriate valuation range is a multifaceted and often nuanced exercise. Over time, I have come to see it as more art than science. While there are objective reference points such as industry deal comps, feedback from investment bankers, and expectations shared directly by founders in proprietary opportunities, crafting a valuation range for an Indication of Interest (IOI) can still feel like a high stakes guessing game.

It is often anxiety-inducing, especially knowing that while you may have a chance to revise your bid later in the process, there is always the risk of being cut early by the seller.

I remember one particular meeting where we were debating the appropriate IOI range for a business based on vague guidance from the investment banker representing the founders. After a thoughtful discussion, we landed on a range that felt balanced. But one of my colleagues was not convinced. He grabbed at his chin, shook his head, and said, "I just don't think our *bid will hunt*."

Another colleague added, "You might be right. Hopefully we'll get another bite at the apple and make it to management meetings, but we run the risk of being left out. We should try to get more guidance from the banker."

In that moment, when he commented on not believing our bid will hunt, it caused me concern since I was feeling very good about the potential for the opportunity. Borrowed from hunting, the expression was a colorful way of saying he doubted our offer had the strength to be taken seriously in a competitive process. The concern was clear: if our bid lacked ambition and did not meet *headline number* expectations, we might not make it past the first cut.

That kind of pushback is valuable. While valuation frameworks and models provide structure, they do not guarantee success. Experience, market feel, and judgment often play just as critical a role in determining whether your bid clears the bar or gets left behind.

184. GREAT AT IDENTIFYING PROBLEMS...NO IDEA HOW TO FIX THEM

Having served as an Operating Partner in private equity for more than a decade, I have seen a recurring pattern across many of the companies we invest in, especially when it comes to building out the executive leadership team. One of the most common functional gaps we encounter is the absence of a professional Chief Financial Officer.

We try to identify these gaps collaboratively with founders during the diligence phase. But time and again, even in founder-led businesses generating over four million dollars in annual EBITDA, we discover financial operations being handled by a part-time bookkeeper (perhaps a family member), junior accountant, or contractor working out of QuickBooks. There is no formal budgeting process, no operating metrics, and no real performance dashboards. It is surprising, and occasionally even a little comical.

When we bring up the idea of hiring a CFO, the reaction from founders tends to follow a familiar pattern: "Why do we need a CFO? What would they do that we are not already doing? Isn't that just an unnecessary expense?"

We explain the value a seasoned CFO can bring: establishing budgeting discipline, producing timely and accurate reporting, managing banking relationships, and creating dashboards with meaningful KPIs. We often share anonymized reports from other portfolio companies to show just how impactful a strong financial leader can be. In many cases, the resistance stems from simply not knowing what they do not know—and that is entirely understandable.

One particular situation still makes me smile. A founder had decided to step back from day-to-day operations and transition into a Board role. We hired a professional CEO, Matthew, a 25-year veteran of the industry. During the subsequent CFO search, we struggled to find someone with both the technical chops and the interpersonal fit to work well with both Matthew and the founder.

Matthew and I had quickly developed a strong and candid working relationship. One morning over breakfast, we were debriefing the ongoing CFO search when he paused, leaned back, and said, "Do you know what I find ironic about hiring a CFO?"

I raised an eyebrow and took a sip of coffee. "Go on."

"We go to great lengths to find someone with the right credentials and pedigree," he said, "but in the end, CFOs are *great at identifying problems—they just have no idea how to fix them.*"

I stifled a laugh. He was not wrong. I had seen that movie more than once.

Matthew continued, "Don't get me wrong, I know we need to professionalize finance. But honestly, what we need even more right now is a COO. Someone who can execute. Someone who gets stuff done."

His point landed. It aligned with our broader strategy for the business, and his frustration echoed something I had heard many times before from other seasoned executives: finance leaders are essential, but execution is what keeps the lights on.

That moment reminded me of something from early in my own career. In a private budget review, the CEO I reported to, who could be harsh and never one to sugarcoat things, grumbled, "I can't believe what a CFO is going to cost us. If you're not responsible for driving revenue, you're dispensable. Finance staff are just cogs sucking on the teats of the company."

I have developed a more balanced perspective since then. But I will admit I still have a soft spot for the folks out there selling, building, and delivering revenue.

185. LISTENING WITH ONE EAR

The COVID-19 pandemic profoundly reshaped the workplace, accelerating the adoption of technology-driven communication, increasing the demands of multitasking, and blurring the lines between professional and personal life. In the face of widespread uncertainty, we adapted to remote work, virtual meetings, heavier workloads, and the erosion of boundaries between home and office.

Remote work brought some clear efficiencies: no commuting, fewer in-office distractions, but it also forced many of us to juggle overlapping responsibilities. Alongside our professional duties, we were managing households, caregiving, and even helping children with remote schooling, often all at once.

Virtual collaboration tools like Zoom and Microsoft Teams quickly became essential. Back-to-back video meetings became the norm, requiring constant mental agility and task-switching. As work hours bled into evenings and weekends, many found themselves perpetually "on," with little room to reset. The result was often fatigue, if not full-blown burnout.

I'll admit, I occasionally gave in to multitasking during virtual meetings, especially when I was not the host. If a call seemed less than critical, I might be half-listening while catching up on emails or knocking out unrelated tasks. I was not alone. You could often spot others doing the same: darting eyes, the telltale glow of a second screen reflected in their glasses, or the unmistakable pause when their name was called.

One moment still stands out. A colleague who was clearly multitasking got caught off guard when asked a direct question. He fumbled, then said, "Apologies, could you repeat that? I was a bit distracted and *listening with one ear.*"

Listening with one ear perfectly captured the fractured focus and constant distraction that defined so much of our pandemic-era work life. It remains a vivid reminder of how dramatically our work culture changed and how many of those changes are likely here to stay.

186. KEEP HIM WARM

I've encountered the phrase "keep him warm" frequently in executive-level recruiting, both as an operator and in private equity. It's often used when a candidate has advanced through initial interviews but has not yet been selected or ruled out. For example, someone might say, "I'd like to see a few more candidates before deciding. Let's *keep him warm* in the meantime."

The expression refers to maintaining a positive, ongoing relationship with a candidate who remains a potential hire, even if they're not currently the top choice. The goal is to keep the candidate engaged and interested, preserving flexibility while continuing to evaluate others.

Tactically, this might include checking references, broadening the circle of internal stakeholders who meet the candidate, or providing periodic updates on the hiring process. These actions convey continued interest without a formal commitment. Often, this period of limbo ends abruptly when the candidate receives another offer, forcing a go-or-no-go decision.

During a portfolio company CEO search, we had a candidate with strong operational skills but limited experience in growth equity-backed environments. The hiring committee was not fully aligned, and one partner said, "Let's *keep him warm*. We'll have the CFO meet him while we continue outreach."

We checked references, shared a recent Board deck for his review and feedback, and kept the conversation casual. Two weeks later, the candidate informed us of another opportunity he was considering. That forced our hand, and we quickly convened to decide whether to move forward or step aside.

187. DIFFERENT SET OF MUSCLES

When evaluating leadership needs and identifying gaps that must be filled to complement the founding team, it is essential that the private equity firm establish a clear process for communication and consensus-building with the founders before finalizing the transaction. Aside from the CFO role, I've generally found that reaching alignment on necessary leadership additions is a relatively smooth process.

In founder-owned and operated businesses, where we often make our investments, it is important to recognize the extraordinary commitment these entrepreneurs have made. They have taken substantial personal and financial risk, often tying a large share of their net worth to the company, and have successfully built it to the point where it has attracted outside investment. That in itself is a significant accomplishment. At the same time, many founders are self-aware enough to acknowledge the limitations of their experience when it comes to scaling the business further.

In a deal team meeting for a founder-led pharmaceutical services company, a colleague raised a thoughtful concern about the founder's ability to lead through the next stage of growth. He put it simply: "The company has the potential to double or even triple revenues organically over the next few years. But that's going to require a *different set of muscles* than he has today. The good news is he understands that and is staying engaged through the CEO search and into the transition. It's great that he'll maintain an active board role moving forward."

The comment was not a critique of the founder's past performance. Quite the opposite. It was an honest recognition of a common truth: founders often have a skill set well suited for launching and growing a company to a certain stage. Beyond that point, the business may require leaders with different experience to execute on a more complex, scaled growth strategy. Founders often remain invaluable in customer-facing roles or strategic advisory capacities, but bringing in a new executive leader with those "different muscles" can be critical to unlocking the next phase of success.

188. WHAT GREAT LOOKS LIKE

When revisiting the topic of leadership gaps in executive teams following a private equity investment, particularly in founder-led businesses poised for meaningful growth, there is often a pressing need to bring in functional leaders with direct experience executing at scale. These additions are not about replacing the founders' vision or passion; they are about complementing that foundation with operational muscle and a blueprint for sustainable performance.

The leadership needs can span across finance, operations, project management, business development, human resources, and other critical functions. In these conversations, I've often heard colleagues frame the challenge by saying, "We need to hire someone who knows *what great looks like.*"

The phrase "what great looks like" captures the importance of bringing in leaders who have experienced true excellence in their domains. These are individuals who not only understand high standards and best practices, but who have also led organizations through the processes required to achieve and maintain them. They know the KPIs that matter, the cadence and discipline required for execution, the systems and tools that drive visibility, and the cultural attributes that reinforce performance.

I recall a conversation during a diligence debrief on a healthcare services business. The company had real momentum but lacked depth in its operating infrastructure.

One colleague noted, "The founder's built something impressive, but the team is thin, and everything's reactive. We need someone in operations who knows *what great looks like*—who's seen a scaled version of this and can help them build toward it."

Another colleague added, "Same for finance. They're managing cash and booking revenue, but there's no real forecasting, no visibility on margin by service line. We need a CFO who's done this before and can put a real framework in place."

Bringing in someone who knows *what great looks like* can be transformative. It raises the standard and helps the organization benchmark itself not against its past, but against what is possible. These leaders bring the perspective, discipline, and credibility needed to define the next chapter: not just in terms of what to do, but how to do it in a way that scales.

Ultimately, these hires serve as both catalysts and culture carriers. They model what great looks like, operationally and behaviorally, and help lift the rest of the team to meet that standard. In a growth-oriented PE environment, that can make all the difference.

189. LINES IN THE WATER

In both my executive leadership roles and private equity experience, I've frequently heard the phrase "lines in the water" used in the context of sales and marketing. It typically comes up in discussions about business development and pipeline health. For example, a commercial leader might say, "We have a lot of *lines in the water* right now," referring to the pursuit of multiple leads, opportunities, or prospects simultaneously.

The expression draws from fishing, where casting several lines increases your chances of catching something. In a sales context, it conveys an intentional strategy of broad outreach and running multiple plays in parallel to improve the odds of converting leads into revenue. Each "line" represents a potential customer engagement, partnership conversation, or proposal under review. While not every line will result in a win, the aggregate activity often signals a healthy, forward-leaning go-to-market engine.

The Chief Commercial Officer of one of my portfolio companies reported during a quarterly board meeting that the team had over 80 qualified prospects in active discussions, many at the "contract in review" stage. The breadth and maturity of those "lines in the water" gave the board confidence in both near-term bookings and long-term pipeline strength. This visibility enabled us to forecast revenue with greater precision, align hiring plans to future demand, and prioritize resources toward higher-probability opportunities.

I remember a conversation that followed between one of my PE colleagues on our deal team and the CCO after the meeting.

"Eighty is a big number," my colleague said. "But how many of those are real? What's your confidence level in the conversion rate?"

The CCO replied, "We've done a lot of scrubbing. These are late-stage conversations, probabilities greater than sixty percent, with defined scopes and pricing. Not all of them will close, of course, but these are high quality *lines in the water.*"

Another board member added, "That's what we want to see, volume with discipline. It's one thing to have lines in the water. It is another to know which ones have a fish on."

In PE, it is not just about activity, but rather it is about intelligent activity. The best commercial teams are not just casting broadly, they are constantly evaluating where to invest time and energy, based on data, engagement signals, and strategic fit. When executed well, "lines in the water" becomes more than just a catchphrase. It becomes a lens through which we assess the quality of the commercial engine itself.

190. TRACTOR PULL

A tractor pull is a motorsport event in which modified tractors attempt to drag a heavy sled as far as possible down a dirt track. As the sled moves, its weight shifts forward, increasing resistance the farther the tractor goes. It is raw horsepower meets slow-motion agony. These events are especially popular in rural communities and are staples of local fairs and festivals. I had the chance to attend one while living in the Midwest, and I still remember the chest-rattling noise, the flying dirt, and the unmistakable smell of diesel and fried food. The further the tractor went, the louder the crowd got—and the harder the pull became.

In PE, the term "tractor pull" gets thrown around figuratively to describe something that feels just as grueling: a long, frustrating, and increasingly difficult due diligence process. One of the best examples is customer diligence, where we try to speak directly with the target company's largest customers. These interviews are critical for validating revenue quality and the strength of customer relationships. But getting access to these customers without spooking them about a potential ownership change? That requires choreography worthy of a Broadway production.

In one particularly drawn-out diligence process, we had been circling a deal for weeks. The team was still debating which customers we should speak with, how many we could reasonably approach, and how to avoid triggering panic. Every time we thought we were close, we hit another gatekeeping snag.

During a late-night Zoom call, the frustration boiled over. One of my colleagues lamented, "We started this thinking we'd glide through diligence in a few weeks. This has turned into a full-on *tractor pull*. Every inch feels harder than the last. There's no way we're going to hit our original deal timeline."

Another teammate deadpanned, "At this pace, we'll be in exclusivity so long we might qualify for squatters' rights."

Laughter aside, the point landed. Like a tractor pull, at times diligence often starts with optimism and momentum but quickly turns into a slog as resistance piles on. Every step forward requires more effort. Progress is slow, success is uncertain, and the engine starts to smoke a little.

The phrase is similar in spirit to "pulling teeth," but with more noise and horsepower. In PE, "tractor pull" has become our shorthand for the kind of painstaking, inch-by-inch process that tests your patience and your deal conviction. And while no one ever wants to be in one, the reality is that the deals worth doing often require exactly that kind of persistence.

191. STACKING PENNIES

Private equity due diligence on an acquisition target requires a close look at customer-specific dynamics. These typically include the length of client relationships, historical and forecasted revenue, profitability by account, customer concentration, the number of active programs, and average revenue per product order or service engagement.

It is not unusual to find companies with impressive top-line growth and sizable customer contracts but a heavy reliance on just a few clients. That kind of concentration introduces significant risk. On the flip side, some companies boast a broad and diversified customer base but struggle to grow quickly because the average order size is small or engagements are short in duration.

During one investment deal team meeting, we were evaluating a company that had strong customer diversification but a flat growth profile. As the team debated the merits, one colleague chimed in with a clear-eyed assessment:

"Look, the service is valued, and they've done a nice job spreading risk across customers. But growing this business is going to be like *stacking pennies*. The data shows shorter engagement durations than we expected, and revenue per customer per engagement is low."

Another colleague offered insight, "There are a lot of logos, but each one adds just a sliver to the top line. I don't see that changing any time soon. If we pursue this, we need to be fully aligned on what we are signing up for."

In that moment, "stacking pennies" became the phrase that stuck. It captured the nature of the opportunity perfectly: steady but incremental revenue gains that require consistency and patience, not big leaps. There is nothing wrong with this model, especially if the underlying business is defensible and cash generative. But it demands a long-term mindset and an acknowledgment of the opportunity cost. While the *pennies* can add up over time, the time itself might be better spent chasing dimes—or dollars—elsewhere.

192. SINGLE SHINGLE

A successful investment strategy, particularly in the private equity sector where I have operated, often hinges on identifying companies with distinctive niche products or services that are well positioned to gain market share through disciplined execution. That execution typically includes strengthening executive leadership, improving operational efficiency, expanding field and inside sales teams, and launching targeted marketing initiatives.

One concept that frequently comes up in these situations is the presence of the "single shingle" competitor. These are small, independent operators, often referred to as "mom and pop" businesses, that can signal both market fragmentation and opportunity. In many cases, they offer a compelling target for displacement by a more professionalized player.

I encountered this dynamic firsthand while serving on the investment deal team and later the Board of Directors for a national provider of revenue cycle management services for physician practices. Before our investment, the company had built an impressive track record relying almost entirely on word-of-mouth referrals. There was little formal marketing or sales infrastructure in place. Yet, despite that, the business was growing at a steady double-digit pace, a clear indicator that its service offering was both differentiated and valued. A physician's referral to a colleague was essentially a warm introduction that often converted directly into a new client.

During diligence, we took a closer look at the competitive landscape and quickly realized that the company's main competition for its target customer, small to midsized physician practices, was typically a *single shingle* provider. These were small firms, often family-run, delivering highly localized services. While they benefited from long-standing personal relationships with clients, they generally lacked the scale, technology, and regulatory sophistication required to serve a growing, compliance-conscious healthcare environment.

In one internal discussion, a partner summarized the opportunity well:

"These *single-shingle* operators are hanging on with legacy systems and relationships, but they cannot compete with a more scalable, professional platform. If we can modernize the sales engine and tell our story clearly, we should be able to win these accounts consistently."

That became a central part of our investment thesis. By leveraging a broader service portfolio, more advanced technology, deeper compliance capabilities, especially in data security and patient privacy, and a more structured approach to client service, the company was well positioned to replace outdated incumbents.

The presence of single-shingle competitors in a market is often a sign of untapped potential. For a well-capitalized and professionally managed business, these fragmented landscapes offer the chance to consolidate share, standardize quality, and deliver meaningful value to customers who are ready for a better solution.

193. LONG PUTT

The term "long putt" comes from the world of golf, a game many of us claim to enjoy for the challenge, the fresh air, and the occasional perfect shot that tricks us into coming back. Personally, I have never played often enough to be much of a threat on the course. More often than not, I find myself on the green after too many strokes, staring down a daunting putt from a considerable distance. It's a situation that requires focus, finesse, and a fair amount of luck.

In PE, a "long putt" refers to an investment opportunity that comes with high execution risk and a meaningful degree of uncertainty. Much like the golf version, sinking it is possible but far from probable. These deals usually carry speculative upside, multiple layers of complexity, and a whole lot of "ifs."

I first heard the term used in a PE setting during a review of a particularly tricky investment opportunity. As we wrapped up the financial model and discussed next steps, a colleague, Pete, leaned back and asked, "So, what do we think of the opportunity overall?"

Amy replied, "It's interesting. The platform checks some boxes, but the team is light, and the tech still hasn't been fully validated."

I added, "Yeah, and there are real questions around client attrition. I'm not convinced the customer relationships are as sticky as they look on paper."

Pete nodded. "So, we're agreed. This is a *long putt*."

"Exactly," Amy said. "High risk, high reward. If we move forward, we'll need a serious post-close plan to de-risk execution. And with other deals in the pipeline, I wouldn't prioritize it."

These types of investments are often riddled with headwinds: broken internal processes, gaps in leadership, intense competition, regulatory uncertainty, or questions about sustainability. Pursuing a long putt requires not only conviction and a strong stomach but also a playbook that accounts for heavy lifting from day one.

That said, when these deals work, they can be game changers. Precisely because others shy away, the upside can be substantial. Just like in golf, sinking a long putt is rare but when it happens, it feels like magic. Or at least enough magic to keep you playing the game.

194. SCAR TISSUE

Embarking on due diligence for a PE investment, especially with a founder-owned and operated company, requires a careful balancing act. The goal is to rigorously evaluate every functional aspect of the business, but it is just as important to maintain self-awareness and emotional intelligence when engaging with the founder and executive team. These are, after all, the same individuals you hope to partner with after the deal closes. Push too hard, too early, and you risk damaging the very relationship you're trying to build.

One instance stands out clearly. We were conducting diligence on a founder-led business that had no investment banker involved on the sell side. We had agreed on a timeline for closing, but the sellers were falling behind in pulling together key materials required for our Investment Committee approval and lender underwriting. It became clear we would need to extend the timeline.

During a tense deal team meeting, one of my colleagues summed up the situation perfectly:

"We can only push so hard. I'm starting to worry we're going to create too much *scar tissue*. If we keep pressing at this pace, we might do real damage to the relationship."

The phrase *scar tissue* was spot on. It captured the lingering resentment and post-close friction that can arise when the diligence process becomes too aggressive or impersonal. Even if the deal gets done, that early damage can show up later, especially when you're asking that same founder and leadership to lead the charge on post-close initiatives.

The reality is, timelines are often contingent on the completeness and accuracy of the information provided. In banker-led processes, much of that is prepackaged in a well-organized data room. But in proprietary deals, where there is no banker quarterbacking the process, things tend to move slower. Founders are still running the business full time, and the idea of spending hours on diligence requests might feel foreign, if not burdensome.

Unlike a formal sell-side process, proprietary deals lack clearly communicated expectations around how demanding diligence can be. As a result, it falls on the PE team to manage that dynamic with care. Patience, empathy, and thoughtful communication go a long way.

There is no perfect formula. But reminding the sellers early that the proposed closing timeline depends on the pace of information flow, and making room for the reality of their day jobs, helps set a more collaborative tone. In founder-led deals, where relationships matter as much as financials, avoiding scar tissue is not just good manners—it is good business.

195. FULL EEYORE MODE

In the PE portfolio companies with which I have been involved, annual budget planning typically kicks off in the fourth quarter of the calendar year. During this period, the management team prepares and presents a draft budget to the Board of Directors. What follows is often a spirited back-and-forth, with multiple rounds of revisions as the board challenges assumptions, probes the underlying logic, and pushes for refinements to the plan.

These discussions can get intense, especially since management bonuses are often directly tied to hitting the year's financial targets. Tensions may arise when perspectives diverge. Management might present the budget as an ambitious stretch plan, while the PE team suspects it is a sandbagged forecast designed to set the bar low enough to ensure bonuses are paid. It is also common for management to highlight emerging risks or uncertainties that could impact performance in the year ahead.

One particularly memorable moment came during a heated budget review session. I had the pleasure of serving alongside an independent board member named Jack, known for his animated, unfiltered style. During a tense exchange with the CFO, Jack put his hands on the back of his head, smirked, and said, "Why does it feel like every year around this time you guys go *full Eeyore mode* when it comes to building a budget?"

The room cracked a smile, tension eased, and the message landed.

For context, Eeyore is the gloomy, slow-talking donkey from A. A. Milne's Winnie-the-Pooh, always expecting the worst, even on a sunny day. Jack's comment, though lighthearted, carried weight. While prudent risk awareness is appreciated, the board expects a budget grounded in realism, not pessimism. Especially when bonuses are on the line, the goal is to strike the right balance between credible forecasting and healthy ambition.

In these moments, humor can diffuse tension, but the underlying message remains clear: the board is looking for a balanced and honest budget, not one clouded by excessive caution or an aversion to committing to stretch goals, particularly when bonus incentives are involved.

196. EAT YOUR OWN DOG FOOD

As a former CEO, I'm well acquainted with the phrase "eat your own dog food," which refers to the practice of confidently using your own company's products or services. The premise is straightforward: if you believe in what you're selling, you should be willing to use it yourself. There's no substitute for firsthand experience when it comes to understanding user satisfaction, product quality, and areas for improvement.

A friend once told me about his early days as an engineer at a major international soft drink company. According to him, employees were expected to exclusively drink the company's beverages, and it was rumored that being spotted with a competitor's beverage could put your job at risk. Harsh? Maybe. But the message was unmistakable: if you're part of the brand, you'd better live the brand. No Pepsi in a Coke office.

In PE, I've seen the phrase take on a slightly different meaning. Here, "eating your own dog food" often refers to living with the terms you negotiated in order to win a deal. The PE environment is fiercely competitive, and winning a deal sometimes requires uncomfortable concessions; whether that's agreeing to aggressive earn-out structures, granting founders or key executives unusually generous employment terms, or accepting governance frameworks that are less than ideal.

Once the ink is dry, though, those terms are yours to live with.

I remember one portfolio company review call shortly after we had closed a deal. We were discussing the inevitable complications created by a founder's unusually protective employment agreement, something we had reluctantly agreed to in the final stretch of negotiation. Tensions were rising.

A colleague finally shrugged and said, "Look, we knew what we were signing. We wanted the deal, and this clause was part of the price. Now we need to *eat our own dog food* and figure out how to manage through it."

It was a blunt but effective wake up call. In this world, once you commit, there's no sending the plate back to the kitchen. You own the deal, warts and all. So, grab a fork and dig in—even if the dog food is a little tougher to chew than you hoped.

197. ADDITION BY SUBTRACTION

When a pivotal member of a leadership team, someone perceived as critical or even irreplaceable, unexpectedly resigns, it can send shockwaves through an organization. PE investors may initially react with urgency, even panic, focused on quickly filling the perceived gap. In some cases, that urgency is warranted. The impact is real, and it takes time and careful planning to backfill the role. But in other situations, the disruption is far less severe than expected. Occasionally, the departure turns out to be a blessing in disguise.

Over the course of my career, I have come to believe that no one is truly irreplaceable. Some people are certainly harder to replace than others, and their absence can create meaningful challenges in customer relationships, team morale, and market perception. But businesses adapt. Teams evolve. The show goes on. As leaders and investors, we must learn to navigate change without losing momentum.

One example stands out. I was serving on the board of a PE portfolio company that had recently completed a major add-on acquisition. Several months after the merger, one of the co-founders of the acquired business, "Ryan", abruptly resigned. During diligence, he expressed enthusiasm about staying engaged and driving long-term value. His departure caught us completely off guard. Ryan had been highly engaged during diligence, played a visible role with customers, led business development efforts, and had been instrumental in recruiting talent. He had also just realized substantial generational wealth from the transaction.

So, when Ryan announced he was leaving to pursue "personal endeavors," goals he said he had long deferred, we were stunned. Our initial reaction as board members was to try to retain him. We assumed his absence would leave a major void. But when we regrouped with his co-founder and the broader executive team, we encountered a very different perspective.

To our surprise, no one else seemed particularly rattled. It turned out Ryan had been resisting integration efforts, clashing with the new operating model, and had developed a reputation internally for being emotionally volatile and high maintenance. Even his original co-founder, who was now thriving in the combined business, admitted the departure might be for the best.

As one executive put it, "You know, this might actually be *addition by subtraction*. It'll be a heavy lift in the short term, but long term, I think we'll be stronger without him."

That was the first time I had heard the phrase "addition by subtraction" in a business context, though I had certainly lived it before with both employees and customers. With respect to the latter, sometimes the most demanding customers consume disproportionate time and energy, creating drag on morale and value. Letting them go, while uncomfortable in the moment, often clears the way for better focus and stronger performance.

Losing a key executive is never easy, and it can introduce real risk. But not every departure is detrimental. Sometimes, the exit of someone once seen as essential becomes a catalyst for progress. It is a helpful reminder: not every resignation is a setback. In some cases, it is exactly the turning point the organization needs.

198. SET THE MARK

I've always associated the term "mark" with the target of a practical joke or scam. In that context, it's often used by con artists to describe the individual they intend to deceive or manipulate. So, when I first heard the phrase "set the mark" during a PE meeting, specifically referring to valuation, I was understandably confused.

In PE investing, however, the term "mark" takes on a completely different meaning. It refers to the valuation or fair market assessment of an investment, or a portfolio of investments, at a particular point in time. Marks are critical because they establish the current worth of the investments held within a PE fund's portfolio.

Because PE firms invest primarily in private companies without daily public market prices, they must periodically assess the value of their holdings, typically quarterly. The "mark" represents the fair value assigned to each investment, considering factors such as the company's financial performance, comparable company analysis, industry trends, and prevailing market conditions.

I remember one of my earliest experiences in PE was sitting in a meeting when a colleague casually said, "We need to *set the mark* on this one before the end of the quarter. Given the revenue trajectory and comps, we might need to take a modest write-up." At the time, I was still thinking "set the mark" meant picking a victim, not assigning a valuation.

Once the *marks* are established, they are aggregated to calculate the fund's Net Asset Value or Assets Under Management (AUM). These figures provide an estimate of the total value of the fund's investments and are regularly reported to limited partners (the investors in the fund), through detailed performance updates.

It's important to understand that setting the mark is not an exact science. Some subjectivity is involved, although PE firms follow established accounting principles and valuation standards to ensure the marks are reasonable and defensible. Often, third-party valuation firms are engaged to provide independent assessments, which helps maintain credibility with limited partners and auditors.

Finally, marks are not static. They fluctuate over time based on changes in market conditions, company performance, and broader economic factors. This dynamic nature highlights the importance of ongoing evaluation and vigilance in the PE world.

199. MOVEMENT ISN'T ACTION

We've all met people who seem perpetually busy yet fail to deliver meaningful results. They get caught in a cycle of constant activity without making real progress. Early in my career, while reviewing the performance of individual field sales representatives with a mentor, I received a piece of advice that stuck with me:

"Don't confuse being busy with being successful. *Movement isn't action.* Some of these folks are constantly on the move, cold calling all day, but they lack clear objectives."

That insight fundamentally shaped how I came to understand and value effective sales and marketing strategies and later, how I coached individuals in those roles.

In sales and marketing, the phrase "movement isn't action" highlights that busyness alone does not guarantee meaningful outcomes. It draws attention to the crucial difference between activity for activity's sake and purposeful action directed toward clear, strategic goals. People might look productive sending emails, making calls, attending meetings, creating content, but without thoughtful execution aimed at specific objectives, these efforts often fall flat.

Over the years, both as an operator and in PE, I've seen sales teams struggle because they couldn't clearly articulate how their product or service stood out from the competition. Many relied heavily on building personal rapport with prospects, hoping relationships alone would eventually translate into sales. Unfortunately, that approach usually leads to the same disappointing result: missed bookings and revenue targets. Busywork may create the illusion of productivity, but only deliberate, focused action drives meaningful results; not just in sales and marketing, but across every critical function.

For example, rather than indiscriminately blasting out a high volume of cold emails without personalization, a skilled sales representative takes intentional steps: crafting targeted, compelling messaging; leveraging LinkedIn connections; following up diligently with engaged prospects; and rigorously tracking responses to refine their approach. Here, "action" means taking deliberate, measurable steps that directly support key sales and marketing goals, whether that is generating leads, nurturing prospects, closing deals, or building brand awareness.

200. DEAD SOLDIERS

During my college days, I was familiar with the term "dead soldiers" as a humorous reference to empty beer bottles often left scattered after a party for someone else to clean up the next morning. Later, in a business context, I learned the phrase was used informally to describe ventures or companies that had tried and failed. Delivered with a mix of humor and cynicism, the term captures the casualties of competitive markets, where promising ideas often fall short of becoming sustainable businesses.

I first encountered the term professionally while considering a CEO role at a company in the point-of-care diagnostics space, focused on oncology. My own diligence suggested the company's technology was groundbreaking, but I was less certain about the dynamics of the broader sector. To gain perspective, I met with a respected venture investor, "Doug", known for his strong track record of early-stage investments in the pharmaceutical industry, a field notorious for high risk.

Doug's advice was measured and cautious. He summed up his feedback, "I can see the attractiveness of the technology you describe. There's a real value proposition here, but, bottom line, there are a lot of *dead soldiers* in point-of-care diagnostics. I would hesitate to pursue this. I'd stay away."

His warning gave me pause. I've never shied away from risk or from leading pioneering technology companies where outcomes can be binary. Yet Doug's caution intrigued me. From my perspective, pharmaceuticals had an even higher failure rate than diagnostics. I suspected that Doug's view, shaped by his medical training and comfort with clinical indications and therapeutics, may not fully reflect the realities of technology innovation and execution from an engineering standpoint.

Ultimately, I accepted the CEO role. Doug chose not to invest, a decision he would later regret, as the company achieved a highly successful exit, delivering outstanding returns to its investors.

201. ESCAPE HATCH

An "escape hatch" traditionally refers to a specialized emergency exit on ships, designed to allow crew members to quickly evacuate in situations like fires, flooding, or other critical damage. These small, strategically placed openings connect to larger passageways, lifeboats, or emergency rafts, offering multiple routes for rapid, orderly evacuation. Their design and placement are carefully planned to maximize crew safety during a crisis.

I first encountered the term "escape hatch" in a business context both as a company executive and later in PE investing. One memorable example came during my time as CEO of a medical device company, while executing a sale transaction. As we reviewed the Letter of Intent (LOI), the document outlining the framework for the eventual purchase agreement, I was joined by our corporate attorney and one of my board members, a Partner at a PE firm.

During the discussion, my board colleague remarked, "We need to incorporate an *escape hatch* in case they fail to close the deal on time."

The attorney asked, "What are you thinking would be appropriate based on discussions?"

My colleague responded, "We're granting them exclusivity for sixty days under the LOI. At a minimum, we should include a break-up fee if they back out."

In business agreements, an "escape hatch" refers to a provision that allows one or both parties terminate the agreement under specified conditions, often before the original term ends. These clauses are designed to provide flexibility and protect against unforeseen developments like failed diligence, shifting strategic priorities, or deteriorating deal terms that could make completing the transaction undesirable.

The specifics of an escape hatch vary depending on the deal structure, the priorities of the parties involved, and the legal or regulatory framework. Carefully negotiated and clearly outlined in the agreement, escape hatches not only safeguard the interests of both buyer and seller but also create a structured path to unwind a deal cleanly if necessary. Including them shows thoughtful deal-making and balancing commitment with a healthy dose of contingency planning. After all, it never hurts to know there's a door when you need one.

202. TRUST AND INCENTIVIZE

When acquiring founder-owned businesses in PE, there is always an inherent risk that the founder may depart prematurely after the transaction, leading to unforeseen organizational and business challenges. Naturally, we assess the strength of the broader executive leadership team and evaluate the key-person risk associated with the founder.

My experience in this realm has been somewhat unique: the founders have consistently remained involved post-transaction, either as CEOs or in supportive roles such as Board members or business development leaders. In every case, they retained a meaningful equity stake, signaling a vested interest in the company's ongoing success. However, there's always the risk that a founder might change course or in the worst-case scenario, misrepresent their intentions during diligence, complete the deal, and then exit with their financial gains, despite their minority stake.

I recall a particularly memorable discussion with my PE colleagues during a competitive acquisition process. As we debated how to improve our offer to win the deal, we also found ourselves scrutinizing the founders' true intentions. Although the founders were critical to the business's future success, they were poised to receive a significant payout at closing, which raised concerns, especially given emerging challenges with one of their largest customers.

We explored various structuring options, including milestone-based earn-outs, retention bonuses, and a seller's note with an attractive coupon, designed to tie future compensation to ongoing performance. During the conversation, one of my more skeptical colleagues, alluding to the substantial upfront payment and the risk it posed to the founders' continued commitment, remarked bluntly,

"They have eighty million reasons to tell us what we want to hear."

"I understand our business requires a degree of trust," another colleague added, "but we must *trust and incentivize*. There's just too much risk here otherwise."

The idea was that by structuring the deal to include backend payouts contingent on performance and founder retention, we could both strengthen our bid and test the founders' true commitment. If they resisted conditional terms, it would signal potential misalignment.

While I'm generally less cynical in these situations, I couldn't disagree with my colleague's cautious approach, especially given the size of the upfront payout on the table. I lean heavily on building relationships during diligence, drawing on three decades of experience and gut instincts to size up founder character. But no matter how careful you are, surprises still happen. Thoughtful management of this dynamic needs to be a constant thread in every founder-led transaction.

203. CORNER CASES

After executing a PE Letter of Intent (LOI) for the acquisition of a business, thorough due diligence is just the beginning. Closing the transaction demands far more work: negotiating and documenting critical agreements like the stock purchase agreement and employment contracts for key executives. It often includes securing debt financing, which is a challenge all on its own. Purchase agreements, in particular, are complex and require careful attention to a variety of possible scenarios.

In one deal, working against a tight deadline, negotiating the purchase agreement took on an urgent tone. During a conference call with our attorneys reviewing the seller's feedback on our initial draft, we tackled the major terms first, then turned our focus to secondary but crucial contingency terms, some of which were quite unconventional. A colleague leading negotiations stressed the need to dig deep into what he called the "corner cases," emphasizing their potential to derail the deal if overlooked.

He said, "I'm confident we're aligned on the main terms, but we absolutely have to run the *corner cases* to ground. They're subtle, but their implications can be huge."

In this context, "corner cases" are the rare, exceptional conditions or triggers that could materially affect the acquisition terms. These fall outside the usual framework but must be addressed to create a durable, air-tight agreement. While such cases often involve regulatory approvals or breaches of seller representations, my experience shows they most frequently arise around milestone-based earn-outs where additional payments to sellers hinge on future performance. Disputes can quickly spiral if those milestones and conditions are not clearly defined from the start.

Because of this, it is essential to vet these scenarios thoroughly during pre-close legal diligence and to document clear, enforceable resolution paths in the agreement.

In summary, while "corner cases" are less common, they can carry significant risk if not properly anticipated and addressed. Building mechanisms into the agreement to manage these scenarios is critical to protecting both parties' interests and ensuring the long-term success of the transaction.

204. EVERYTHING DOESN'T TASTE LIKE CHICKEN

PE firms often review hundreds of investment opportunities each year. In my experience, we screen more than 300 healthcare deals annually. To make that volume manageable, we rely on a consistent set of evaluation metrics right out of the gate. These include the strength of the management team, sustainability of the business model, organic and inorganic growth potential, customer profiles and revenue concentration, pricing dynamics, and other core indicators.

Over time, patterns inevitably emerge. Certain red flags or green lights tend to repeat. But I have also learned that while patterns are helpful, they can lead to premature conclusions if you're not careful, especially when evaluating a proprietary opportunity that is not part of a formal investment banker-led process. In these cases, it pays to stay curious.

One meeting stands out in particular. We were reviewing a new opportunity when a colleague gave the materials a quick scan and seemed ready to pass based on a few surface-level concerns. Before the discussion could end, another team member spoke up.

"I'd like to turn over the next card on this one," he said. "You have to remember, *everything doesn't taste like chicken.* There's more here than it looks like at first glance."

Another colleague chimed in, "I like the fundamentals. There's real differentiation and some interesting growth angles. I think it's worth digging in."

The "tastes like chicken" comment earned a few laughs. It was a lighthearted message that when something unfamiliar comes along, we often try to fit it into a familiar mold. But in PE, assuming every opportunity fits a standard framework is a mistake. Each deal has its own quirks, risks, and upside. Treating everything like a flavor you've already tasted can cause you to overlook a truly distinctive company.

Yes, efficiency matters when you're screening 300-plus deals a year. But, given the scarcity of proprietary opportunities, I have learned the value of pausing to consider what might not be obvious at first glance. Keeping an open mind, especially when the opportunity is unique or outside the norm, can reveal hidden potential that the metrics alone might miss. It is often the willingness to look past the familiar that leads to the most rewarding investments.

205. RETRADE

In PE, a "retrade" refers to the renegotiation and modification of deal terms after the execution of a Letter of Intent (LOI), often occurring during or toward the end of an exclusivity period. This renegotiation can involve various changes, such as the PE firm seeking a lower purchase price, revising financial covenants, adjusting milestone based earn-out provisions, or modifying other terms based on newly discovered information or unforeseen developments during due diligence.

Although I have heard retrades can be derived by unethical behavior of PE firms, I have never experienced this as a buyer. Instead, they often arise from legitimate concerns uncovered during diligence, such as the discovery of financial or operational issues, changes in customer contracts, shifts in market dynamics, or other unexpected developments that impact the perceived value or risk profile of the investment.

Effectively managing a retrade requires careful handling, as it can strain trust with the sellers, even when the concerns are valid. In some cases, I have experienced situations where, to preserve goodwill and maintain a strong foundation for future collaboration with sellers who would remain involved post transaction, we decided to proceed with the original deal terms despite uncovering issues that introduced discomfort. These issues were not material enough to break the deal but required thoughtful post-close planning to mitigate risk.

I recall a particular situation where we were deep into exclusivity on an acquisition and our diligence team uncovered a meaningful, but not catastrophic, decline in a key customer relationship. During an investment team meeting to review the findings, the debate turned toward whether we should attempt a retrade.

One colleague said, "We're under exclusivity and I hate to *retrade* unless it is absolutely necessary. This is not something that kills the deal, but it definitely shifts the risk-return equation."

Another responded, "Agreed. But we have to protect our downside. I think we need to be completely transparent and approach them with the thought of introducing an earn-out structure into the deal. We're not blowing up the deal, we are just being fair based on new information."

Another member of the deal team weighed in, "We have to be very careful here. If we retrade, it'll leave a bad taste, and these guys are critical to the future success of the company. Is this issue big enough that it really warrants a change in deal terms which will be viewed as a price reduction? Or do we just accept it and build it into our operating plan?"

Ultimately, we decided not to pursue a retrade, opting instead to address the customer risk through aggressive post-close initiatives. The long-term relationship with the sellers, who would retain a stake and play an important role post transaction, was deemed too valuable to risk damaging over a modest adjustment in purchase price.

Retrades are relatively common in PE and can serve as an important tool to protect the firm's interests and ensure a fair acquisition. However, how a retrade is approached, justified, and communicated can significantly influence the outcome of the deal and the strength of the ongoing relationship with all parties involved. Maintaining a long-term perspective is essential to balancing short-term risk mitigation with long-term value creation.

206. YOU PAY FOR YOUR SUCCESS IN ADVANCE

In my experience, entrepreneurs from whom we acquire businesses in PE are remarkable and distinctive individuals. What unites them is their extraordinary willingness to embrace risk and make substantial personal sacrifices in pursuit of building a successful business. This journey demands an unwavering work ethic, often requiring them to forgo vacations, sacrifice time with family and friends, and essentially never switch off. These entrepreneurs do not simply clock out at five o'clock and forget their responsibilities until the next morning. Even when they manage to step away, they remain tethered to the demands of their business. I have witnessed this countless times and lived it myself in professional roles prior to joining PE.

In some cases, I have encountered founder-led businesses where, after decades of sacrifice and dedication, the founder has positioned an heir in a leadership role largely because of nepotism. These heirs, often seeing themselves as the natural successor, sometimes exhibit only a fraction of their parent's work ethic or commitment.

One example stands out vividly. The founder had spent forty years building a highly successful company. He still arrived at the office before sunrise, driving a well-worn Honda Accord. His son, who held the title of President, would roll in around ten, casually park his Porsche Carrera out front, and make a swift exit by two. While the father had poured his life into the business, the son's engagement was more symbolic than substantive. In the end, the founder chose to sell the company to a strategic acquirer rather than risk its legacy under his son's eventual leadership.

Fortunately, there are far more inspiring examples. One that has stayed with me is Sam and Robin, a husband and wife team who launched a technology-enabled healthcare services company straight out of college. Over the next thirty-five years, they grew it into a thriving enterprise. When it came to involving their children, they took a very different approach. There were no golden tickets or fast tracks. Their kids started in the mailroom and worked in data entry during high school and college. After graduation, they had to earn their way into the business, proving themselves through performance and building respect from their colleagues along the way.

I once complimented Sam and Robin on their approach, telling them how rare and refreshing it was to see that kind of discipline in succession planning.

Sam smiled and said, "Nobody handed us anything when we built this company. There was a lot of blood, sweat, and tears. We told our kids, if you want to be part of this business, then *you pay for your success in advance*. We wouldn't have it any other way. They had to earn the respect of the senior team, many of whom have been with us since day one."

That phrase—"you pay for your success in advance"—has stuck with me. It is a timeless truth. Whether in business, education, sports, or the arts, success rarely comes without effort. Personally, not having started life on third base heading for home, I have yet to find a shortcut to anything worth achieving. The dues must be paid. Without that investment, success remains just out of reach, more illusion than outcome.

207. RESERVATION PRICE

When submitting an initial Indication of Interest (IOI) for the acquisition of a company, I have found it prudent to take a somewhat conservative approach to the proposed valuation range. This early range serves as a starting point and is typically refined as we progress beyond the IOI stage.

As we engage with the seller's management team, conduct deeper due diligence, and build a more complete picture of the business, our understanding evolves. We may gain increased confidence in certain aspects or uncover new risks that warrant caution. These insights directly inform our valuation assumptions and help guide our next steps.

Depending on what we uncover, we either decide to walk away or build enough conviction to submit a formal Letter of Intent (LOI) with a well-supported offer. However, even after gaining comfort with the fundamentals of a business, setting the upper limit on valuation can be subjective. It depends on a variety of factors, including financial modeling, forecasted returns, and comparable transaction data.

During an investment deal team meeting, as we were discussing financial forecast models and potential deal structures for a target company, we found ourselves at an impasse regarding the appropriate valuation range. The conversation grew tense, with some advocating for a more aggressive bid while others urged caution.

At that point, one of my colleagues, sensing the need for clarity, asked a key question directed at a senior team member who held significant decision-making authority:

"What's our *reservation price*?"

There was a pause in the discussion. Until then, I had not encountered the term "reservation price" in this context. My immediate association was with classic car auctions, where a "reserve price" refers to the minimum price a seller is willing to accept before completing a sale.

However, in PE, a "reservation price" means something quite different. It represents the maximum price a PE firm is willing to pay for an asset. If the negotiations or seller expectations push the valuation beyond that limit, the firm must be prepared to walk away from the deal, regardless of how attractive the business may otherwise appear.

The senior team member answered without hesitation:

"If forced to give a number today, then I would say our reservation price is seventy-five million based on our models. Beyond that, the risk and return profile no longer makes sense for us."

That simple statement reframed the discussion. It anchored the rest of our decision-making process, helping the team align on deal structure, negotiating strategy, and ultimately, discipline around value.

Understanding and adhering to a reservation price is a critical discipline in PE investing. It ensures that emotional attachment, competitive pressure, and seller persuasion do not cause a firm to stretch beyond its risk tolerance or return thresholds. In my experience, knowing your reservation price and respecting it can often be the difference between making a good investment and suffering a regrettable one.

208. HYGIENE

It is fitting that the word "hygiene" often follows the phrase "hair on the deal." After all, when a deal is hairy, someone has to clean it up. In PE, "hygiene" is the polite way of saying, "This is a bit of a mess, and we need to get it in order."

I first came across the term in this context during diligence on a target company. The business had shown strong growth, but it was operating with the kind of informal structure that might make a CFO break out in hives. The company had never created a formal budget. Forecasting? Also absent. The founders were laser-focused on serving customers and growing revenue, which they did well. But they had little in the way of structured management control, and that lack of financial discipline quickly raised red flags.

As we dug into their projections, one of my colleagues, after a long sigh and a look at the jumbled spreadsheet in front of him, said, "This forecast needs *hygiene*. We need to scrub the assumptions, challenge the customer growth expectations, and unpack every line in this P&L."

Another colleague added, "We're going to need a power washer."

His point was clear. "Hygiene" in this context referred to more than just fixing a model. It meant rolling up our sleeves and cleaning up the underlying financial practices of the business. It meant asking tough questions, documenting rational assumptions, and establishing processes that could withstand scrutiny. Without that hygiene, it was impossible to trust the numbers, much less make an informed investment.

To be clear, hygiene is not just a diligence box to check. It is often the first step in building a culture of discipline and accountability in a founder-led company. It gives investors basic confidence that projections are grounded in something real, not just a hopeful glide path on a slide deck.

In short, if there's hair on the deal, you are going to need some hygiene. And probably a good brush.

209. CONTRACQUISITION

The term "contracquisition" is a clever hybrid I have encountered exclusively in PE. A mashup of "contract" and "acquisition," it describes a niche deal structure that can create real value with relatively low complexity. I first came across it during a transaction involving one of our portfolio companies in the technology-enabled healthcare services sector.

We were approached by the elderly founders of a small business who were ready to retire. Instead of selling their company in a traditional transaction, they offered us the chance to acquire their customer contracts. Their idea was simple: hand off the relationships, walk away, and let us service the clients through our much larger platform company.

During an internal deal team meeting, one of my colleagues summed it up neatly:

"There is no heavy lifting with this. We just drop the company's contracts into our platform and take over from there. This is a textbook *contracquisition* play. We should be able to move quickly."

In this structure, we would absorb the customer relationships, assume responsibility for servicing them, and compensate the sellers with a percentage of the revenue we generated from those contracts over a defined period. There was no upfront cash, no transition of employees, and no integration of legacy systems. Just a clean transfer of value.

Depending on the specifics, contracquisitions can be highly attractive. They allow a portfolio company to diversify its customer base, enter new markets, or boost recurring revenue, all while minimizing financial risk. When structured thoughtfully, they offer a creative path to inorganic growth with limited downside and plenty of strategic upside.

210. LAY DOWN THE BREADCRUMBS

Most of us remember the classic German fairy tale *Hansel and Gretel*, popularized by the Brothers Grimm. The story follows two siblings, children of a poor woodcutter, whose wicked stepmother convinces their father to abandon them in the forest during a famine. The first time, Hansel overhears the plan and cleverly gathers white pebbles to leave a trail home. It works. But the second time, caught unprepared, he uses breadcrumbs which are promptly eaten by birds, leaving the children lost in the woods. The tale eventually turns grim (pun intended), but the concept of leaving a trail to follow stuck in the modern lexicon. Today, we have terms like "breadcrumbing" and "laying down breadcrumbs" to describe guiding someone subtly toward a destination or decision.

In the world of PE, I first encountered the breadcrumb metaphor in a much more corporate setting, thankfully without any witches or gingerbread houses. One of our portfolio company CEOs was describing how she managed to convince a key employee to move from engineering into a business development role. He was a sharp technical mind with real potential in client engagement, but the transition was far from obvious.

"It took time," she said. "I had to *start laying down the breadcrumbs* months in advance. Just planting the idea here and there, showing him how much his communication skills stood out, giving him small wins on the client side. Eventually, he came to see it as his idea."

This kind of patient influence of guiding without pushing is often more effective than top-down mandates, especially when dealing with experienced professionals. "Breadcrumbing," in this context, is about strategy and subtlety. It is the art of shaping someone's path through a series of thoughtful nudges, rather than dragging them toward a destination they are not yet ready to see.

Much like Hansel and Gretel navigating the forest with limited resources and a lot of creative thinking, the best leaders use breadcrumbs to help their teams find the right path—one carefully placed clue at a time.

211. GROWING SMALL

At first glance, the term "growing small" might sound contradictory, but in PE investing, it can reflect a very sound strategy.

I first heard the phrase while working with a portfolio company that provided technology-enabled healthcare services to physician practices. When we acquired the business, the majority of its clients were small practices, typically groups of five to ten physicians.

After the investment, there was a natural impulse to move upmarket and go after larger practices. Bigger clients typically mean bigger contracts, and that can be enticing. But this company had spent the better part of a decade carving out a strong niche in the smaller practice segment. They understood the unique needs of these clients, tailored their offering accordingly, and built a competitive moat around that expertise.

That did not mean they could not eventually win larger clients which indeed, they did, but early on, we had to resist the temptation to sprint away from the very segment that had fueled their success. As we evaluated our go-to-market strategy, the debate over whether to immediately pursue larger practices grew more intense.

One colleague offered a perspective that cut through the noise:

"There is still a lot of runway in the small practice segment. I think we need to lean into what we already do well. It might not sound glamorous, but *growing small* could be exactly what this business needs right now. We are already winning here. Why walk away from a winning hand before we have played it out?"

That insight stuck with the team. We doubled down on what was working. The business continued to grow profitably by targeting small and midsized practices, and in doing so, we built a stronger foundation. At the same time, we professionalized the business development function and brought in new leadership with experience in more complex sales. Over time, we expanded our reach and began successfully targeting larger physician groups.

Interestingly, the value proposition that worked so well with small practices also resonated with larger ones. But the sales process was different. Bigger clients meant longer sales cycles, more decision makers, and a greater need for enterprise-level validation. Still, because we had not abandoned our core segment too early, we had the revenue, case studies, and operational confidence to take that step when the business was ready.

In retrospect, "growing small" was not a compromise. It was a smart, focused strategy that let us scale from a position of strength.

212. TEASE OUT

When PE investment professionals refer to "teasing out," they are talking about the deliberate and often painstaking process of uncovering key insights that are not immediately visible. The phrase captures the idea of pulling threads, sometimes subtle, sometimes tangled, in order to surface hidden risks, overlooked opportunities, or essential facts that can materially impact an investment thesis.

It is less about what is on the surface and more about what lies underneath. In diligence, surface-level data may tell you what is happening, but *teasing* things out helps you understand why it is happening, and whether it is sustainable.

I remember a specific example involving a target company that had grown rapidly in recent years. During a deal team discussion, a colleague raised a red flag:

"We need to understand more about their lead customer. They represent nearly a third of current revenue and a significant chunk of the future sales pipeline. We have to *tease out* the depth of that relationship: how many active programs they are running, how long they have been a customer, pricing trends over time, and the expected life cycles of the products we're supplying."

That comment launched a deeper inquiry. We reviewed contracts, conducted customer reference calls, studied order patterns, and even spoke with former employees. What we uncovered was nuanced. The customer relationship was strong, but some of the programs were approaching end-of-life, and pricing pressure was starting to creep in.

None of that was obvious from the headline financials. It had to be *teased out*. This kind of rigorous analysis is at the heart of PE diligence. Teasing out the details is not just a matter of curiosity, it's essential to building conviction. It helps you validate what you think you know, challenge assumptions, and avoid costly surprises after the close.

Whether you are investigating revenue concentration, operational scalability, regulatory exposure, or cultural fit, teasing things out is often the difference between a well-informed investment and an expensive learning experience.

213. BODY SHOP

During my time in PE, I have spent countless hours knee-deep in due diligence, especially with companies in the pharmaceutical services segment of our healthcare portfolio. One particularly memorable experience came while evaluating a proprietary opportunity involving a company that provided highly specialized expert advisory services to pharmaceutical and biotech clients.

This company had almost one hundred professionals on staff, most of whom were scientists and engineers with advanced degrees and deep experience in the pharma industry. Their bios read like a Who's Who of regulatory and development expertise. It was clear that this was not your average staffing firm. But not everyone saw it that way.

During an early review meeting, one of my colleagues, whose default setting tends to be "no" unless proven otherwise, took a quick glance at the materials and declared, "This is nothing more than a *body shop*. I wouldn't be surprised if the EBITDA is significantly lower than what they are reporting."

The tone was definitive, the shrug almost audible.

Thankfully, our team had a strong interest in the sector and a healthy skepticism of snap judgments, so we committed to a full diligence process. What we uncovered told a very different story.

Far from being a *body shop*, a term in consulting that usually implies a commoditized, high-churn staffing model, we found a company built on long-standing client relationships, high-value expertise, and mission-critical project delivery. In fact, their EBITDA turned out to be higher than the founder originally reported. The discrepancy was not due to inflated forecasts but rather a generous helping of accounting disorganization.

As our diligence progressed, we developed real trust with the founder, ultimately negotiated a Letter of Intent, and moved forward with the investment.

For context, in the consulting world, "body shop" is not a compliment. It usually refers to firms that supply large numbers of generalist consultants to plug short-term holes. These firms often compete on price, focus on quantity over quality, and are less concerned with strategic outcomes than with filling open seats. Clients engage them when they need warm bodies fast, not when they need deep expertise or long-term partnership.

The company we evaluated was the polar opposite. Their professionals were not interchangeable contractors but respected specialists with decades of domain experience. They commanded premium billing rates and worked on long-term projects where depth of knowledge and continuity were essential. Their clients were not just buying time but instead buying insight, judgment, and reliability.

If there is a moral to the story, it is this: just because a firm has a lot of people on staff does not make it a *body shop*. And just because someone says "body shop" with confidence does not mean they are right. Teasing out the truth, not jumping to conclusions, is where the real value lies in diligence.

214. TARGET RICH ENVIRONMENT

Private equity investments in platform companies typically begin with rigorous due diligence to ensure the business can deliver targeted returns on a standalone basis. In most of the deals I have worked on, our investment thesis has not relied on mergers and acquisitions to hit our goals. That said, while we do not assume add-on activity as a requirement, we certainly do not ignore the opportunity. Add-on acquisitions can enhance geographic reach, expand capabilities, diversify a customer base, and more. Evaluating the landscape for potential acquisitions is a critical part of our diligence process. It helps shape a growth strategy that we can pursue post-investment to further increase enterprise value.

When investment bankers present companies for sale to PE firms, their offering memorandums almost always include a section dedicated to growth. This typically outlines both organic strategies such as building out internal business development teams or forming strategic partnerships, and inorganic strategies through add-on acquisitions. Often, there is a slide showing a blinded list of potential add-on targets. These may include a few bullet points on each company's products or services, revenue, EBITDA, location, and the status of any prior discussions.

I remember one particular meeting with an investment banking team representing a company for sale. As we were reviewing the growth opportunities, the banker pulled up a slide that matched this standard format almost to the letter.

"These are the companies that management believes are the most appealing add-on acquisition candidates," he said. "As you can see, this sector is reasonably fragmented and presents a *target-rich environment.*"

The banker's colleague added, "There are more companies out there than what we are showing here. These are simply the ones management finds especially compelling and with whom some initial conversations have taken place."

In this context, a "target-rich environment" refers to a market with an abundance of potential acquisition candidates that align with a PE firm's strategy. It signals opportunity: a wide playing field with options that can be evaluated, prioritized, and selectively pursued. This type of environment can be highly advantageous. It gives investors flexibility and leverage and helps mitigate the risk of overpaying. If, on the other hand, the sector lacked viable add-on targets, competition for a limited pool of companies would likely drive prices up and shrink potential returns.

So, while we may not depend on add-on acquisitions in our initial thesis, knowing there is a robust pipeline of targets gives us confidence that we have room to grow and options to get creative after the ink dries.

215. BID THE BOOK

In the context of a company sale process led by an investment banker, a Confidential Information Memorandum (CIM), commonly called the "book", is prepared and distributed to PE firms. As discussed previously, the CIM is a comprehensive document that provides a detailed overview of the business for sale. It typically includes market context, industry analysis, company history, financial performance (both historical and projected), information about the management team, key customers, growth opportunities, and other data relevant to a potential buyer.

When a PE firm expresses interest in the opportunity, it first signs a confidentiality agreement. From there, it begins its diligence process, which includes reviewing the CIM and often consulting with industry experts and advisors to develop a well-informed perspective on the company, sector trends, competitive positioning, and reputational standing. At this early stage, firms usually have good access to the banker and may even have the opportunity to speak with the management team before submitting an Indication of Interest (IOI), which typically includes a valuation range.

However, in a broad sale process, when the banker reaches out to a large pool of potential financial and strategic buyers, management access is often restricted until after IOIs are submitted. Rather than burdening the company's leadership with dozens of preliminary meetings, the banker and management will typically review the IOIs first, narrow the field, and then invite a select group of bidders to engage in deeper diligence and meet the management team. For example, a company may receive fifteen IOIs, and only the top five to ten groups may be advanced to the next phase. These groups are granted management meetings, access to additional data, and the chance to submit formal Letters of Intent (LOIs). The process then moves toward exclusivity and, ultimately, deal closure.

Over the years, I have been through this process many times. But I still remember the first time we were not given access to management or even informal valuation guidance from the banker before submitting our IOI. It was an odd experience. We had deep sector experience, and yet we felt like we were being kept at arm's length. At the time, I assumed that meaningful dialogue with the founder or CEO was essential to craft a thoughtful and credible IOI. These individuals were, in many ways, inseparable from the company's value proposition.

What I later came to understand is that, in broad processes, this sequence is fairly standard. The management team is protected early on, and initial bids are expected to be submitted using just the CIM and any limited commentary the banker is willing to provide.

During a deal team meeting to prepare our IOI, we were voicing our frustration.

"Are we going to get a chance to speak with the founder before we submit?" I asked, still holding out hope.

One colleague replied, "Not likely. They're running a broad process. If we make the cut, we'll get a real shot in the next round."

Another chimed in with a shrug, "We'll just have to *bid the book* on this one."

Until that moment, I had never heard the phrase "bid the book," but I understood it instantly. It meant submitting our IOI based solely on the CIM and whatever scant insights the banker was willing to offer. No meetings. No founder pitch. Just a well-packaged PDF and our best guess.

It was a good lesson that in PE, process dynamics often matter just as much as the numbers, and sometimes, you have to make your move before you get the full story.

216. RULE OF 40

During an investment deal team meeting with the CEO of one of our healthcare portfolio companies, one of my colleagues made a lighthearted comment about the company's performance relative to its budget. It was the end of the first business quarter, and the company had delivered exceptional results.

He quipped, "The numbers look terrific. Now if we could just achieve the *Rule of 40*, we'd really be in business. At this pace, I think you might actually pull it off."

The room laughed, but I found myself a little puzzled. I had never heard of the "Rule of 40."

As I quickly learned, the Rule of 40 is a commonly used benchmark in PE, particularly when evaluating technology and software-as-a-service businesses, though it can apply more broadly to other recurring-revenue or subscription-based models.

The formula is simple:

Rule of 40 = Revenue Growth Rate + EBITDA Margin

Both inputs are expressed as percentages. The idea is that a healthy company should either be growing quickly, highly profitable, or strike a solid balance between the two. If the sum of the revenue growth rate and EBITDA margin equals or exceeds 40 percent, the company is considered to be performing very well.

For example, if a business is growing revenue at 25 percent annually and has a 15 percent EBITDA margin, it hits the Rule of 40 right on the nose. A company with a 10 percent growth rate could still qualify if it boasts a 30 percent EBITDA margin. Conversely, a high-growth company with thin margins might also pass the test, as long as the combined figure reaches the threshold.

The Rule of 40 serves as a shorthand to assess whether a company is managing the trade-off between growth and profitability in a healthy way. It helps investors gauge whether a company is pursuing sustainable expansion rather than burning cash or growing at the expense of long-term financial health.

Of course, like many benchmarks in PE, the Rule of 40 is more of a guiding principle than a hard-and-fast rule. Its relevance may vary depending on the company's size, maturity, and business model. Some investors of course blend it with other metrics to form a more comprehensive view, but as I discovered that day in the meeting, it is one of those terms that can slip into a conversation and sound perfectly casual, until you realize it is actually carrying a lot of analytical weight.

217. PULLING ON THE OAR

The typical structure of a PE diligence process centers around a "deal team" that drives the opportunity from initial introduction through transaction close. In many cases, that same team remains actively involved post-investment, often serving on the company's Board of Directors.

In my role as an Operating Partner, I have worked alongside deal teams usually composed of two General Partners, a Partner, a Principal, a Vice President, and an Associate. Over time, I have come to recognize a familiar pattern within these teams. There is always one person who becomes the de facto quarterback of the diligence effort, responsible for the daily grind of pushing the process forward.

Earlier in the book, I described this individual as the "swan", gliding gracefully on the surface while paddling furiously beneath the water. This metaphor remains one of the most accurate ways to capture what it feels like to run point on diligence.

I vividly recall a team meeting where we were divvying up responsibilities for a new investment opportunity. As we reviewed the workload, one of my colleagues nodded toward a team member and said, only half-joking:

"He'll be *pulling on the oar* to drive the diligence process forward. Let's kick things off with a full diligence request list."

The image stuck. Just as a crew team depends on coordinated effort and relentless rowing to stay on course, the person "pulling on the oar" in PE diligence is expected to bring energy, focus, and organizational muscle. This role involves everything from corralling internal stakeholders to managing external advisors, collecting and coordinating data analysis, preparing investment committee materials, and making sure that no rock is left unturned.

It is a demanding role, often thankless in the moment, but essential to getting the deal across the finish line. And like any good rower, the best ones make it look far easier than it actually is.

218. PUNCHING ABOVE OUR WEIGHT CLASS

The phrase "punching above our weight class" comes from boxing, where a fighter faces an opponent who is bigger, stronger, and more skilled, clearly stacking the odds against them. I have found the phrase has become a handy metaphor for any situation where a company or individual tries to compete against players operating at a higher level.

As a CEO, I have experienced it in those moments when my company stretched beyond its usual capabilities. Maybe competing against much larger, well-established rivals or bidding on projects that demand more resources than we typically had on hand.

In PE, the idea of *punching above our weight class* often plays out when a firm pursues an acquisition well outside its typical deal size. Suddenly, you are going toe-to-toe with bigger funds that have deeper pockets. That's when resourcefulness and creativity become the secret weapons. Maybe you offer unique deal terms, invite some Limited Partners to co-invest, or propose a milestone-based earnout that ties part of the purchase price to future performance. These moves can help level the playing field.

I remember a deal team meeting where we were debating whether to chase a target larger than our usual range.

One colleague summed it up perfectly: "This one is definitely a stretch. We'll be *punching above our weight class* for sure. But if we stretch on value, get creative with the deal structure, and bring in a couple of LPs as co-investors, we actually have a real shot at winning it."

That line perfectly captured the mindset we needed: face the challenge head-on, but don't forget to lean on innovation and teamwork to compete.

Whenever a PE firm finds itself punching above its weight class, success rarely comes from trying to out-muscle bigger competitors. Instead, it comes down to clever deal-making and finding ways to turn perceived disadvantages into strategic advantages.

219. TAKE IN ALL OF THE GROCERIES IN ONE TRIP

I vividly remember the first time I heard the phrase "take in all of the groceries in one trip." It came up during a conversation about a colleague in PE who was juggling a staggering number of critical responsibilities. He was overseeing several portfolio companies, some of which I was deeply involved with, managing new deal diligence, traveling constantly, and somehow trying to keep it all afloat.

The toll was obvious. His calendar was a nonstop blur of back-to-back meetings, his voicemail was perpetually full, and his energy looked like it had been drained dry. He was clearly overwhelmed, running on fumes, and teetering on the edge of burnout.

One day, during a catch-up with a fellow member of a deal team, the topic of our colleague came up. Never one to mince words, he looked at me and said, "Have you seen him lately? He looks like he's been through the wringer."

I nodded, knowing exactly what he meant.

"He can't keep this up forever," my deal team colleague added with a sigh. "He's trying to *take in all of the groceries in one trip*. It's not just bad time management. He's maxed out and looks sick."

The comment hit home. The problem wasn't just poor scheduling or misplaced priorities. It was about hitting a hard limit on capacity. Our colleague needed more resources, more help, and a healthy dose of delegation before everything came crashing down.

It was a warning that no matter how capable someone is, trying to do everything solo is a recipe for disaster. Even in PE, where hustle is king, sometimes you've got to put some bags down and make multiple trips. Otherwise, you risk dropping the groceries entirely.

220. LAND THE PLANE

Navigating the investment deal process in PE can be a tricky dance, especially when negotiating valuation and deal terms in a competitive sale process managed by investment bankers. In my experience, reaching agreement on valuation is usually the biggest challenge. Yet, hammering out the details on exclusivity, milestone-based earnouts, employment agreements, reps and warranties, and closing timelines can be just as demanding.

I've often heard the phrase "land the plane" tossed around in PE circles. It perfectly captures the critical moment when all parties come together to finalize terms and seal the deal. Like a pilot carefully guiding a plane onto the runway after a long flight, it's about bringing negotiations to a safe and successful close.

One deal that stands out in my memory involved a particularly complex acquisition. The negotiations had dragged on, with disagreements flaring up repeatedly. We were close, but there was still a gap between us and the seller that needed a final push.

One of my partners, who had been deeply involved from the start, decided to step away from the group emails and calls and meet directly with the seller. After that one-on-one, the tension visibly eased. The remaining details fell into place quickly, and we headed toward closing.

On our final group call, the investment banker representing the seller said, "That conversation was absolutely necessary. He had to step in and *land the plane*. Without that personal touch, I don't think we'd have made it."

Later, my partner shared what he told the seller: "At a certain point, it stops being about term sheets and redlines. You have to sit down, look someone in the eye, be completely transparent, and say, 'We want this to work. Here's how we can move forward together.' It changes everything. It breaks the stalemate."

In PE, "landing the plane" is about more than just closing a deal. It's about the leadership, judgment, and interpersonal skill needed to navigate complex negotiations and get everyone safely on the ground. Sometimes, that's exactly what it takes to turn a near-miss into a touchdown.

221. LONGEST POLE IN THE TENT

Before my time in PE, I often heard the phrase "longest pole in the tent" used in project management circles. It referred to the element of a project that was expected to take the most time and effort to complete. In other words, the critical path item that would ultimately determine the timeline for everything else.

The phrase resurfaced during a particularly involved investment diligence process, when one of my colleagues chimed in during a weekly team update.

He said, "We've made good progress on finance and legal, but the *longest pole in the tent* right now is customer diligence. It has taken far too long to get the CEO meaningfully engaged. At this point, I'm not sure if we need a nudge or a cattle prod."

There was a short laugh, but the point landed clearly. Despite everything else moving forward, this one item was holding up the entire timeline. And in PE, when you are trying to hit a closing window, identifying the bottleneck early can make all the difference.

The "longest pole in the tent" is not just a clever phrase. It is a tactical reality. It signals the part of the process that will dictate when the deal can actually close. Ignoring it, or failing to escalate it, can derail even the best-managed timelines.

In this case, we did manage to get the CEO fully engaged after a bit of senior-level intervention, and customer calls proceeded in earnest. But the experience reinforced a key lesson: knowing where the drag is happening is half the battle. The other half is figuring out how to shorten the pole without collapsing the tent.

222. IF YOU SNEEZE, THEN WE ALL GET A COLD

The phrase "if you sneeze, then we all get a cold" has been one of my favorites for more than thirty years. It was first lobbed in my direction by a colleague while I was leading a high-stakes project early in my career. The meaning stuck with me: when one person is carrying too much weight, the entire system becomes vulnerable. I've since used the phrase strategically and occasionally for dramatic effect throughout my career. In PE, I find it especially relevant when engaging with founders and executive teams of our portfolio companies.

These companies are often founder-led and generating real revenue and cash flow, but they are still early in their business maturity. They usually have lean management structures, leadership gaps that need filling, and ambitious growth plans that outpace current capacity. In these environments, where each individual on the leadership team carries outsized responsibility, the phrase becomes more than just colorful language. It is a strategic insight.

One moment comes to mind from a portfolio company board meeting. We were discussing the CEO's growing list of responsibilities. He was effectively acting as CEO, COO, head of sales, and occasionally chief therapist for the team. I turned to one of my colleagues and said, "Right now, *if he sneezes, then we all get a cold.* We've got to start thinking seriously about how to build a real bench around him before this becomes a bigger issue."

The room was quiet for a second. I could tell the phrase had landed, probably new to most of them, but the message came through loud and clear.

My colleague nodded and responded, "Totally agree. Let's not wait for that. I think we prioritize a strong CFO and head of ops in the next ninety days. That gives us a buffer and him a lifeline."

Everyone nodded in agreement. It was one of those moments where a metaphor clarified the risk in a way that a slide deck never could.

In PE, identifying and addressing key-man risk early is critical to scaling a business. If the success of the company hinges on one person showing up healthy and on time every day, you do not have a business. You have a single point of failure. And in our world, that's a cold we cannot afford to catch.

223. ONLY AS FAST AS OUR SLOWEST RUNNER

I had the honor many years ago of being elected co-captain of both the indoor and outdoor track teams at Malden Catholic High School. Whenever I have heard the phrase "you are only as fast as your slowest runner" in my role as an executive or PE investor, my mind instantly flashes back to those relay races.

For the record, I was not one of the fast ones. I threw the shot put and spent far more time in the weight room than on the track. I left the sprinting to teammates who were much quicker and leaner than me.

What I remember most vividly is our head coach, Brother Myles McManus, C.F.X. On the day of a big conference championship, he stood at the front of the team bus, fists clenched by his sides, and addressed our sprinters with a calm intensity that commanded attention.

"Gentlemen," he began, "we are *only as fast as our slowest runner*. You don't want to be our slowest runner. You don't want to be the weak link. Everyone must give their personal best tonight. I cannot ask more from you. And you cannot ask more from yourself."

That moment resonated deeply. The phrase, rooted in the fundamentals of relay racing and the sequential nature of performance, translates powerfully into the business world. I saw it as a CEO, and I see it regularly in PE. It speaks to the importance of teamwork, coordination, and shared accountability. Whether you are executing diligence, managing a portfolio company, or preparing for a sale, success depends on how well each team member performs and how tightly the group moves in sync.

I was reminded of this during the sale process of one of our portfolio companies. We were holding a readiness meeting with the investment banker representing the company. As we walked through the workstreams and deliverables, he said, "We are going to have to complete a quality of earnings analysis, among many other things, to prepare the data room. We need to get ahead of this. We are *only as fast as our slowest runner*. We need to get this kicked off now."

That line instantly brought me back to Brother Myles on the bus.

In deal processes, a delay from any contributor, whether financial diligence, legal review, customer reference work, or lender prep, can hold up the entire transaction. One bottleneck can ripple through the timeline and jeopardize momentum. The same logic applies in managing portfolio companies. A delayed operational improvement, a slow response to a crisis, or a lag in financial reporting can affect the entire organization.

Preparing for an exit is no different. The coordination between the deal team and portfolio leadership needs to be airtight. If the CFO is not ready with audited financials or the CEO is behind on management presentations, it can impact buyer perception and valuation, or even cause a deal to slip.

The phrase reminds us that PE is a team sport. The strength of the team is not defined by its star performers but by its slowest contributor. Our ability to drive performance, create value, and execute successful outcomes hinges on aligning and empowering every member of the team to deliver their best consistently and on time. There are no gold medals for almost finishing the race.

224. EBITDA GOVERNOR

"EBITDA" is an acronym for earnings before interest, taxes, depreciation, and amortization. These are standard line items on a company's income statement and balance sheet. EBITDA is widely regarded as a key measure of financial health and a proxy for cash flow. In my PE experience in the lower middle market, it often serves as the foundation for valuing companies, with acquisition prices commonly expressed as a "multiple of EBITDA." For example, a company might be valued at ten times its EBITDA.

Within PE-backed companies, EBITDA is not just a valuation tool. It is often the central metric used to evaluate executive performance and determine annual incentive compensation. Bonus programs are frequently structured around Management by Objectives (MBOs) programs, which tie a portion of executive pay to specific, pre-agreed goals. These programs are designed to promote focus, reward accountability, and align leadership behavior with business outcomes.

In practice, EBITDA performance is usually the most heavily weighted component of the MBO. Other metrics such as new business bookings, service quality, and employee retention may be factored in, but they typically carry less weight. For instance, a CEO's annual bonus opportunity might be structured with 80 percent based on EBITDA results and 20 percent tied to a growth metric like bookings. If the company hits its EBITDA target but misses the bookings goal, the CEO earns 80 percent of the potential bonus.

Early in my PE career, while working with a deal team to finalize CEO objectives for a new portfolio company, I came across the term "EBITDA Governor" for the first time. Until then, outside of politics, I associated a governor with something that limits the speed of an engine, the device that keeps your go-kart from flying off the track.

As we reviewed a draft MBO plan, one of my colleagues said, "We have to set an *EBITDA governor* here. We don't want to be in a position where EBITDA tanks, we trip a debt covenant, and we're still writing bonus checks."

Another teammate chimed in: "Exactly. We need a hard floor. No matter how well someone hits their other objectives, if EBITDA falls below a certain threshold, bonuses don't get paid."

The concept was simple but important. An EBITDA Governor sets a minimum level of financial performance that must be met before any incentive bonuses are triggered. If actual EBITDA falls below that floor, bonuses are off the table, even if individual MBOs were technically achieved.

This kind of safeguard is especially important in PE, where companies are frequently leveraged with significant third-party debt. Loan agreements often include covenants that require the company to maintain minimum EBITDA levels. A miss on EBITDA can put the company in breach of those covenants, risking technical default and potentially triggering serious consequences from lenders.

That is why understanding the financial structure is essential when designing executive compensation in leveraged companies. An EBITDA Governor is typically set as a percentage of the company's EBITDA budget, providing a margin of safety to ensure covenant compliance. For example, if the budgeted EBITDA is $20 million, the governor might be set at 90 percent of target. Fall below $18 million and no one gets a bonus, regardless of other performance metrics.

Incentive plans often incorporate additional structure in the form of "scales" or "ratchets," allowing for partial bonuses if EBITDA lands above the governor but below target. These mechanisms reward incremental progress without compromising the company's financial health.

In PE, designing thoughtful and responsible incentive compensation plans is part art and part engineering. A well-structured plan with an EBITDA Governor at its core ensures alignment across management, investors, and lenders. It sends a clear message: we are here to grow value, but not at the expense of financial discipline.

225. TURF IT UP

Sourcing companies for PE investment, commonly referred to as generating *deal flow*, can come from two primary paths: through investment bankers or via proprietary efforts. The latter has always been a particular focus of mine. Proprietary sourcing involves actively identifying and pursuing opportunities that are not part of a formal banker-run sale process. It requires persistence, creativity, and a healthy dose of legwork. That means attending industry-specific conferences, poring over attendee and exhibitor lists, reaching out cold to potential targets, building founder relationships from scratch, and leveraging subscription-based market intelligence platforms.

At the center of this approach is something I genuinely enjoy: building relationships with founders and entrepreneurs. Many of these relationships evolve slowly over time. It is not uncommon for years to pass between a first conversation and a founder's willingness to explore PE as a partner. Eventually, the trust builds. They become more comfortable with me, and in turn, with the idea of outside investment.

My engineering background and experience as an operator often help differentiate me. In a world where many investors speak the language of finance, I speak fluent technology, business development, product roadmap, and operational headache. That tends to resonate, and more often than not, it earns me a warmer reception and deeper access, a crucial edge in developing proprietary opportunities.

I remember one particular moment during a meeting with my PE colleagues. We were reviewing a newly surfaced, attractive, and actionable investment lead, and someone asked a simple question: "How did this deal come about?"

Without missing a beat, a colleague responded, "Mike *turfed it up*. Another one for him. Amazing."

I had never heard the phrase "turfed it up" before, but I immediately loved it. It felt oddly accurate. These types of deals are not just found. They are *unearthed*. They come from digging through industry soil, turning over rocks, and cultivating relationships with the patience of a gardener and the persistence of a gold prospector.

In the world of PE, when someone says you "turfed up a deal," it means you did the hard work of discovering and developing an opportunity that was not already polished, packaged, and presented in a banker's pitch deck. You got out in front, took initiative, built trust, and helped create a pathway to partnership that otherwise might never have emerged. And in an industry where differentiated access and early insight can make all the difference, there are few compliments more satisfying.

226. CHANGE MANAGEMENT MUSCLE

My experience in PE primarily involves acquiring majority stakes in lower middle-market healthcare companies. These businesses are often founder-owned and exhibit strong growth, recurring revenue, and healthy profitability. They are not distressed assets. Rather, they have reached an inflection point where founders are seeking significant liquidity, want to retain meaningful equity, and are ready to partner with us to unlock the next phase of growth. At the time of our investment, these companies typically generate between $12 million and $50 million or more in revenue, with EBITDA exceeding $3 million as a floor.

In many cases, the founder stays on as CEO. Sometimes, they prefer to begin a succession process and shift into a new role, such as a board position or a focus on business development. Either way, aligning with the founder and the executive leadership team on the growth strategy is critical before we close the transaction.

Post-investment, value creation involves executing a range of strategic initiatives: enhancing leadership, expanding business development, professionalizing financial planning, scaling operations, entering new markets, or pursuing add-on acquisitions. These initiatives must be implemented thoughtfully to preserve the company's entrepreneurial culture while introducing meaningful operational infrastructure and process. Employees often become anxious when they hear the phrase "private equity," so I rely heavily on my own operating background to foster transparency and set realistic expectations when given the opportunity. It also helps that my firm earned a strong reputation over three decades as a founder- and management-friendly PE firm.

At a banking conference, I had a conversation with a General Partner from another PE firm during which we compared approaches to investing in the lower middle market.

He said, "We are completely aligned in our approach. In every investment, we have to identify executives with real *change management muscle*. They have to be able to hit the ground running and rally the organization."

That phrase, "change management muscle", captures perfectly the leadership capacity required to drive transformation and overcome resistance within an organization.

For example, after acquiring a healthcare services platform, we completed an add-on acquisition of a smaller regional competitor. The integration of the acquired company demanded a CEO with strong change management skills. He and his team had to unify not only systems and processes but also two distinct company cultures. The acquired employees were understandably cautious, unsure of what it meant to be absorbed into a larger organization. The CEO exhibited real *change management muscle.* He held town halls, restructured reporting lines, and introduced a 90-day integration plan with clear milestones and accountability. His ability to combine empathy with decisive leadership proved critical in aligning the organization and refocusing attention on the broader mission.

In PE, executives with true change management muscle are invaluable. They bring stability during periods of disruption while still pushing the business forward. Their ability to execute and embed strategic initiatives, whether operational upgrades, system overhauls, or cultural shifts, can make the difference between an average outcome and a transformational one. Without that capability, even the best-laid growth plans are at risk.

227. 20-SECOND SHOT CLOCK

In basketball, the "20-second shot clock" refers to the time limit a team has to take a shot before giving up possession. In PE, a similar dynamic kicks in during the due diligence phase following an accepted Indication of Interest (IOI). Once your IOI is greenlit, the countdown begins. The PE firm enters a defined window to complete diligence and decide whether to proceed with a formal Letter of Intent (LOI). From there, the goal is to secure exclusivity and close the deal. This stage requires speed, coordination, and clear decision-making, all under timelines negotiated with the seller and their investment banker.

The phrase "20-second shot clock" captures that urgency perfectly. Once diligence begins, the clock is ticking. The team must quickly collect and analyze financials, legal documents, operating data, and market intel. There is no strolling through the process. Move fast, or get boxed out by a competing buyer.

I remember one particular deal team meeting where the target's data was trickling in just fast enough to feel like a drip from a leaky faucet. A colleague, trying to rally the team, said, "We are deep into the *20-second shot clock*. We've wrapped most of the commercial and financial diligence, but if we want to submit an LOI and stay in the game, we need to pull this together by early next week. The clock is down to five seconds."

In another case, we had positioned ourselves well for a particularly attractive opportunity, and our IOI had just been accepted. My colleague leading the deal gathered the team and said, "Let's not lose momentum. The data room is open, and there are others circling. The *20-second shot clock* started the moment we got the nod. We need to submit the LOI in 14 days or we risk losing the pole position."

This analogy speaks to a fundamental truth in PE: diligence must be thorough, but it cannot be slow. The pressure to synthesize insights, validate assumptions, and move to an LOI within a narrow timeframe is a hallmark of competitive deal-making. And the tempo does not slow after the LOI is signed. Marching to close requires the same urgency and precision.

In the end, firms that succeed are those that can balance analytical discipline with decisive execution. Because in PE, just like in basketball, the best opportunities go to the team that gets the shot off before the buzzer sounds.

228. CAREENING AUTOMOBILE

A careening automobile swerves unpredictably from side to side, often at high speed, creating a vivid sense of danger, instability, and lack of control. The driver seems unable to steer effectively, and the vehicle feels just moments away from crashing. In my experience, both as an executive and in PE, this image is often accurately used to describe a business operating without structure, discipline, or clear leadership.

The "careening automobile" analogy captures the essence of a company in disarray. These are businesses that may be growing, but in a way that feels chaotic and unsustainable. Decisions are made without strategic alignment, performance metrics swing erratically, and there is little evidence of systems or processes that create stability. From the outside, they may look like they are moving forward; from the inside, it feels like no one is driving.

I remember evaluating a potential add-on acquisition where this metaphor came to life. The target company had cycled through three CEOs in five years. Leadership turnover was high across key functions. There were no formal financial controls, no strategic planning discipline, and forecasting was more guesswork than analysis. Customer demand fluctuated wildly from quarter to quarter, with no coherent explanation.

During an internal diligence review, one of our deal team members summed it up perfectly: "This company is a *careening automobile*. There are no brakes, no steering, and nobody seems to be watching the road."

Another chimed in: "Their leadership team chases whatever seems urgent that week. It is all instinct and no data. The service itself is solid, but the lack of operational discipline makes this a high-risk play. It would be a huge lift to bring this under control."

In companies like this, the issues are rarely confined to one area. The chaos is usually systemic. Roles and responsibilities are unclear, decision-making frameworks are inconsistent, reporting is underdeveloped, and accountability is lacking. Even when the product or market opportunity is promising, the absence of foundational management practices puts everything at risk.

That said, these businesses can still hold significant potential. But unlocking it requires experienced leadership and a steady hand. Stabilization is more than just a turnaround effort. It means putting in place the processes, team cohesion, data discipline, and strategic clarity that have been missing. It is about getting the car back on the road, pointing it in the right direction, and making sure someone is actually driving with both hands on the wheel.

229. SEARCHING FOR LIFE ON MARS

I have encountered the phrase "searching for life on Mars" most often in the context of venture capital investing in life sciences and thought worthy enough to share. It is typically used to describe companies, often after multiple rounds of financing, that cling to valuation expectations disconnected from performance, market reality, or investor sentiment. It captures the futility of insisting on numbers that simply are not supported by the facts, like hunting for signs of life on a barren, unexplored planet.

To unpack this, it helps to understand the dynamics of an "up-round," when a company raises capital at a higher valuation than its previous round. Up-rounds signal progress and investor confidence. They are usually driven by real achievements like regulatory milestones, IP wins, positive clinical results, or clear signs of commercial traction. These rounds tend to lift the spirits (and term sheets) of both existing and new investors.

Down-rounds, on the other hand, are a tougher pill to swallow. They signal a decrease in valuation and can stem from missed milestones, shifting market conditions, leadership churn, clinical trials that did not successful endpoints, or simple overreach. Down-rounds are often necessary but can be emotionally and financially painful. Founders face dilution, ownership gets reshuffled, and the terms can start to feel more like a rescue mission than a celebration. However, it beats the alternative.

Over dinner, an investment banker friend of mine, Rob, recounted a pitch from a biotech company preparing for a Series C raise. The company focused on biomarker development in oncology. Great science, solid leadership, but they had missed key milestones promised at the time of their Series B, and the biotech market was cooling fast.

Rob described the standoff: "They're behind schedule. The sector is pulling back. Capital is skittish. But the CEO insists this next round must be an up-round. I finally told him, 'You're *searching for life on Mars*.' We can run a process, but someone's going to have to land back on Earth."

He paused, then added shaking his head in disbelief, "Sure, we could push for a higher valuation, but it would come with heavy preferences and term sheet gymnastics. Sometimes, it is cleaner and smarter to take a flat or even a down-round and live to fight another day."

I have found that this concept carries over well into PE, especially when working with founder-led businesses. I have been in plenty of conversations where founders, often anchored by past growth or industry lore, detachment from competitive reality, hockey stick forecasts, and more, hold tight to inflated valuation expectations. Even if the business has plateaued, margins are compressing, or market multiples have come back to Earth, they remain fixated on a number from a different time and context.

In one case, a founder insisted his business deserved fifteen times EBITDA based on a few peer deals he had heard about. But revenue had flattened, customer concentration was increasing, and gross margins were sliding. During our internal meeting, a colleague dryly remarked, "If he thinks he's getting that, he's *searching for life on Mars*."

We ultimately approached the founder with respect, walked through the data, and found common ground. But the phrase stuck. It remains one of the most useful and vivid ways to describe the challenge of bringing valuation expectations back to earth—whether in venture capital or private equity.

In these moments, "searching for life on Mars" becomes more than a quip. It resonates with me as it reflects the emotional and strategic gap between aspiration and reality. In venture capital, setting the right tone early is critical. In PE, where control stakes are on the line and alignment with leadership is essential, bridging that gap takes financial rigor, emotional intelligence, and a well-timed reminder that while ambition is valuable, gravity still applies.

230. POST-AND-PRAY

In my private equity experience in the lower middle market, we frequently invest in companies led by strong, visionary founders but with incomplete or underdeveloped executive teams. This is not unusual. These businesses have typically scaled quickly, often without the time, structure, or resources to build out a fully formed C-suite. One of our first priorities post-investment is to partner with the founder or CEO to assess leadership gaps and prioritize key talent acquisition.

This process often involves bringing in experienced executives such as a Chief Financial Officer, Chief Operating Officer, Chief Commercial Officer, or Head of Human Resources. While each company's needs differ based on their growth trajectory and operational complexity, there is almost always a need to upgrade leadership talent. Before closing a deal, we work collaboratively with the founder or CEO to align on these needs and develop a clear roadmap for building out the executive team.

One example that stands out involved a healthcare services company led by a capable and driven founder, "Barry." The business was growing rapidly in a niche segment, and Barry had done an impressive job getting it to that point. But he was stretched thin, pulled into everything from HR issues to back-office accounting decisions to operational firefighting; none of which played to his strengths in business development and client relationships.

To his credit, Barry was self-aware. He knew he needed to surround himself with stronger leaders in areas where he lacked depth. But he was also apprehensive and cost-conscious. Historically, he had resisted hiring full-time executives, instead relying on a patchwork of part-time consultants, interns, and fractional contractors. That scrappy approach had worked in the startup phase, but it was clearly no longer sustainable.

When we started discussing the executive team buildout post-close, Barry expressed strong reservations about using retained executive search firms. He had never worked with one before and had always sourced candidates through informal networks or LinkedIn job posts.

"I can't imagine paying twenty percent or more of someone's salary to a recruiter," he told me. "That's a huge amount of money. I usually just use LinkedIn and *post-and-pray*. Sometimes it works and someone bites. I've filled a few mid-level roles that way, but never a VP or above that has been successful."

His phrase "post-and-pray" made me laugh, but it also said a lot. It captured the randomness of his approach, casting a line and hoping the right fish swims by. While that method had produced a few decent hires, it had also backfired. One senior hire in particular, sourced this way, clashed with the company's culture and created significant internal friction. It took months to undo the damage.

I explained to Barry that while retained search does come with a cost, the bigger risk lies in failed executive hires. A poor fit at the leadership level can stall growth, weaken culture, and shake the confidence of employees and customers. In contrast, a disciplined, professional search process brings structure, rigor, and access to talent networks that most founder networks simply cannot reach.

To his credit, Barry was open to evolving. He agreed to retain a search firm for his first major leadership hire under our partnership—a Chief People Officer. That hire became a game-changer, transforming the company's approach to recruiting, onboarding, and culture. The return on that investment was clear almost immediately: stronger retention, better internal alignment, and significantly improved morale.

In lower middle market PE, upgrading leadership talent is one of the most powerful levers for value creation. Founders like Barry often need more than just help sourcing great people. They need support in shifting their mindset around leadership infrastructure. Moving from "post-and-pray" to a strategic, deliberate hiring process is not just a tactical step forward. It represents a broader cultural evolution, one that sets the foundation for sustainable growth.

231. FIRESIDE CHAT

In my experience across private equity and venture capital, the term "fireside chat" often comes up during early-stage discussions between potential buyers and company leadership, particularly in advance of a formal sell-side process. Investment banks representing a client company will occasionally arrange these informal meetings, sometimes months before a process officially launches, for a small group of well-aligned financial or strategic buyers. These conversations typically happen on the sidelines of annual industry conferences, investment banking summits, or sector-specific events.

From a PE perspective, fireside chats are incredibly valuable. They offer an early and often exclusive window into a company's leadership, culture, operations, and strategic direction long before a Confidential Information Memorandum is shared or a process letter is issued. These early conversations help build rapport with management, surface founder motivations, and establish trust. When the deal eventually goes live, that familiarity can meaningfully differentiate a firm in a competitive process. In addition, it provides a PE investor with more of a foundation at the time of an IOI rather than just *bidding the book* as described earlier.

The metaphor of a "fireside chat" is fitting. While there is no literal fireplace involved, the term suggests a more relaxed, candid atmosphere which is very different from the formal tone of a structured management presentation. These meetings offer both sides a chance to speak openly. PE professionals can probe into organizational dynamics, talent gaps, customer concentration, margin constraints, or product evolution. In return, company leaders often use the opportunity to assess potential partners, asking questions about track records, investment theses, value creation playbooks, and post-close governance philosophy.

I recall one fireside chat with the founder of a specialty contract manufacturer. The company was not yet in market, but they were in discussions with an advisor and beginning to host select conversations. The founder was refreshingly transparent. He talked about wanting to de-risk personally while continuing to scale the business. He also expressed concern about maintaining the company's culture and was looking for a partner who could support operational improvements without disrupting the employee base. That early conversation allowed us to position our firm as founder-friendly and solutions-oriented. When the formal process began months later, we were already several steps ahead. The foundation we had built helped us move faster and more credibly.

Beyond relationship-building, fireside chats offer a strategic advantage. They allow PE firms to begin informal diligence early, gathering qualitative insight on customer relationships, pricing power, regulatory exposure, and margin drivers. By the time the data room opens, much of the deal thesis is already in motion. This early engagement can accelerate internal decision-making, sharpen investment committee materials, and increase confidence in the execution path.

On occasion, these chats can even open the door to a preemptive offer. While investment bankers rarely want to short-circuit a formal process, a thoughtful and credible bid, paired with the goodwill established in these early conversations, can sometimes lead a founder or board to consider a proprietary path forward. Even when that is not feasible, the groundwork laid during a *fireside chat* often shapes how management perceives potential partners and can tip the scales in a close auction.

In short, fireside chats are more than casual conversations. For PE firms, they are a strategic tool to build trust, shape early impressions, and lay the foundation for competitive advantage before the formal process ever begins. They often set the tone for everything that follows.

232. ELEVATOR PITCH

The term "elevator pitch" is so widely used that I debated whether to include it. Still, I appreciate the cleverness of what it implies and believe it remains relevant, especially for readers early in their business education or careers. Before I came across the term, I was already familiar with the phrase "executive summary," which I often used to describe a one or two-page overview of a business. The executive summary is designed to clearly articulate why a business represents an attractive investment or partnership opportunity.

The purpose of an executive summary is to give the reader a concise understanding of the key attributes of a business. This typically includes a description of the company, its products or services, the core technology or differentiators it relies on, the size and potential of the market it serves, its stage of adoption, and how it compares to competitors. It often highlights financial performance and projections, growth opportunities, the strength of the leadership team, and any plans for future funding or a potential exit. A full business plan would explore each of these areas in greater depth.

An *elevator pitch* is essentially a shorter, verbal version of the executive summary. It is meant to communicate the same core value proposition in about thirty seconds to two minutes; the length of a typical elevator ride. The goal is to quickly and clearly convey why your business matters and why someone should want to learn more. This kind of pitch is especially useful at networking events, conferences, or any situation where time is limited and attention spans are short.

One example comes to mind from a conversation with a PE colleague after he attended a regional medical device conference. While there, he was introduced to the founder of a startup developing an AI-powered point-of-care diagnostic tool for cardiology.

He said, "I met a founder working on AI-based diagnostic tools for cardiology. It was the most impressive technology I saw at the conference. He delivered a strong *elevator pitch*—clearly differentiated, targeting a large addressable market, with meaningful intellectual property. That said, because it is still an early-stage company, it is too soon for us to consider."

233. BURNING A LOT OF CALORIES

Private equity diligence can feel like a mental triathlon. It demands intense focus, sustained effort, and an unwavering tolerance for caffeine. I often hear the phrase "burning a lot of calories" used to describe this phase of the investment process, and while it is not literal, it is surprisingly accurate. The term captures the sheer volume of information being consumed, the complexity of issues being untangled, and the strategic decisions being debated; all in a high-stakes, high-pressure environment.

Much like grinding through a tough workout or sticking to a diet, *burning a lot of calories* during diligence signals that the team is fully engaged and pushing hard. Everyone involved, including deal professionals, management teams, and advisors, is investing significant intellectual energy. Depending on the specifics of the company, the process might zero in on technology risks, customer concentration, pricing trends, regulatory exposure, or competitive threats. Or, if you're lucky, all of the above.

I recall first hearing this idiom when a PE colleague was updating our broader team on the progress of a particularly complex diligence effort. He gave a quick overview and then added, somewhat wearily, "We are *burning a lot of calories* scrubbing the competition. We are trying to map not just the obvious market leaders, but also the smaller, under-the-radar players who could be quietly building something similar. We also have to consider whether any of the big incumbents might eventually pivot into this space."

His delivery made us laugh, but the underlying point was serious: diligence is not just about validating what is visible, it is about anticipating what might be lurking just outside the frame.

In the world of PE, calorie burn is constant. Whether it is diving into customer cohorts, analyzing gross margin trends, modeling unit economics, or negotiating deal terms, investment teams are expected to go deep, move fast, and stay sharp. The process is rigorous for a reason. Getting it right requires more than just intellect. It takes stamina, curiosity, and a high tolerance for late-night spreadsheet sessions.

Ultimately, "burning a lot of calories" is a badge of honor. It reflects the commitment to making informed, disciplined, and strategic decisions. And unlike real workouts, this one comes with closing dinners instead of protein shakes.

234. THROW A VIRGIN IN THE VOLCANO

I first encountered this memorable idiom during a crisis at a PE portfolio company where I served on the Board of Directors. The company was grappling with a serious product quality issue in the field, and responsibility appeared to lie with both internal teams and external component suppliers. To make matters worse, communication from management to the Board had been significantly delayed, even as the situation escalated.

By the time the Board was fully informed, some members reacted with urgency and a fair amount of panic. A few even suggested terminating individuals immediately, despite having no clear plan to address the root cause of the problem.

In the middle of the discussion, a PE colleague cut through the noise with a sharp observation: "There's no magic bullet here. We could *throw a virgin in the volcano* and see what happens, but it's not going to fix this. The company behaved itself into this mess, and it's going to take time to work our way out."

The imagery landed perfectly. The idea of "throwing a virgin into the volcano" captured the futility of seeking a dramatic, symbolic gesture to solve a deeply entrenched issue. In moments of crisis, it can be tempting to look for a sacrificial lamb, someone to blame and remove, but that rarely addresses the structural problems. My colleague's point was clear: this was not a situation that could be solved with theatrics or knee-jerk reactions. The company had made a series of decisions that brought it to this point, and reversing the damage would require discipline, patience, and real work.

In the end, that is exactly what we did. We restructured parts of the management team and executed a thoughtful overhaul of the supply chain. It took nearly a year of focused effort by both the deal team and company leadership to stabilize operations and restore trust with customers and the Board.

It was a powerful reminder that meaningful solutions do not come from symbolic gestures. They come from doing the hard, sometimes unglamorous work of fixing what is broken—step by step.

235. SUSHI BUDGET

I first heard the term "sushi budget" during a Board of Directors meeting at a PE portfolio company, and I could not help but laugh. We were discussing business development strategies, specifically how to deepen relationships within existing clients by getting introductions to decision-makers in other divisions who might also benefit from our services. The logic was straightforward: if a customer already values what we provide based on experience, then expanding within their organization is often a smart and efficient path to growth.

The conversation shifted to one of our largest pharmaceutical clients, a global company with annual revenue north of twenty billion dollars.

One of my PE colleagues asked, "So, how much business are we actually doing with them right now?"

The Chief Commercial Officer replied, "We're expecting around five hundred thousand dollars this year, which is a twenty-five percent increase over last year."

Without missing a beat, my colleague responded, "Five hundred grand? That's their *sushi budget*. That's what they spend on catered lunches and bottled water. We've got to get in there and meet more of the real decision-makers. There's no reason we shouldn't be getting a bigger slice of that pie."

The room chuckled, but the point was crystal clear. The comment may have been funny, but it was also a wake-up call. If a company of that scale values our work enough to engage us, we should be far more intentional about uncovering new opportunities across the organization.

236. DON'T BELIEVE YOUR OWN BULLSHIT

I first heard the phrase "don't believe your own bullshit" earlier in my career during a sale process for a company in which I was serving as CEO, and it has stuck with me ever since. Bias, ego, and the instinct to protect one's reputation can push an executive to exaggerate, rationalize, or twist facts to support a preferred narrative. What may begin as a harmless stretch can snowball into something far more dangerous. When repeated often enough, even the storyteller may begin to believe it.

A well-known example is the rise and fall of Elizabeth Holmes and Theranos. The company claimed it had revolutionized blood testing with technology that could deliver broad diagnostic results from just a single drop of blood. Excitement exploded. In 2015, *Forbes* named Holmes the youngest self-made female billionaire in the United States and valued the company at nine billion dollars.

For those of us with a deep experience in diagnostics, the claims immediately raised red flags. I remember watching one of her television interviews where she described her product, and it was painfully clear she had no grasp of the science. I turned to a colleague and said, "This is complete nonsense." Still, she attracted high-profile supporters like Henry Kissinger, George Shultz, Jim Mattis, and Betsy DeVos. None had the technical background to challenge her claims. As media praise mounted, Holmes appeared to buy into her own mythology. Her confidence grew, but so did the gap between story and reality.

Eventually, investigative reporting and regulatory pressure caught up with her. In 2018, the Securities and Exchange Commission charged Holmes and former COO Ramesh "Sunny" Balwani with fraud, alleging they had raised more than seven hundred million dollars on false claims. Holmes was later sentenced to over eleven years in prison and ordered, along with Balwani, to pay more than four hundred fifty million dollars in restitution. *Forbes* revised its estimate of her net worth to zero and named her one of "The World's 19 Most Disappointing Leaders."

While my first encounter with the phrase was far less dramatic, it resonated deeply. I have witnessed this behavior in the business world and in PE settings. I too came close to falling into this trap during my time as CEO while leading a company through a sale process.

We had partnered with an investment bank, and I worked closely with a managing director named Carl. He ran a broad outreach process that led to more than a dozen meetings with potential acquirers. As is typical, the marketing materials and financial model included aggressive revenue projections and optimistic timelines. At first, the CFO and I were careful to caveat the assumptions. But after pitching the story repeatedly, those projections started to feel familiar—almost real. The caution we once had began to fade.

After one especially strong meeting with a strategic acquirer, Carl and I debriefed over coffee. He said, "Mike, you nailed it. Everything flowed. Your answers were tight and confident. You're in the zone."

"Thanks," I said. "It does feel like it's clicking."

Then he leaned in and said, "Just a word of advice. *Don't start believing your own bullshit*. It's an easy trap."

That caught me off guard. "What do you mean?"

He smiled. "Remember how unsure you were about those revenue forecasts in the beginning? They still carry real risk. You're presenting them well, but if buyers structure the deal around those numbers, they could become the benchmarks for earn-out milestones. And if they are already a stretch, you might find yourself living with a deal structure that is tough to meet."

I nodded as he continued, "You might want to start referencing the underlying assumptions more directly or build them into the model so it's clear what is driving the numbers."

It was the reality check I needed. Confidence is useful in a sale process, but too much of it, especially if built on overly ambitious assumptions, can backfire. That phrase, "don't believe your own bullshit," is a sharp but necessary wake up call to stay grounded. In high-stakes processes like M&A or fundraising, small exaggerations can snowball. What begins as a best-case scenario can morph into the baseline, and once others believe it, you might too. That is when trouble begins.

I later heard a similar sentiment during a PE investment committee meeting. A partner reviewing a management team's projections said, "I'm not saying they're lying, but they've told this story so many times, I think they actually believe it now. They're just not grounded in reality. Not at least what I can see. We need to peel back the layers and figure out what's real."

Whether spoken in jest or as a serious warning, the phrase is a valuable checkpoint. It reminds us to question our own narrative, challenge our assumptions, and avoid mistaking hyperbole for truth. In PE, and in business more broadly, clarity, honesty, and self-awareness are far more valuable than confidence alone.

237. YOU CAN'T PUT A SHINE ON SHIT

I first encountered the memorable phrase "you can't put a shine on shit" from a mentor, David Maupin, who is mentioned frequently throughout this book. While I have found this expression relevant many times when evaluating opportunities in PE, it is worth reflecting on the first time I heard it. That moment occurred during a meeting with the CEO of a company I referred to earlier in the book as "JGYN."

Before the meeting, I was already aware of a critical flaw in JGYN's technology and had also heard about George, the CEO who was smug and had a reputation for arrogance. Despite these concerns, I chose not to share them with David, who was my superior at the time. I wanted him to evaluate George on his own terms and form his own opinion about the exaggerated nature of his pitch. As it turned out, George was a textbook case of the "don't believe your own bullshit" syndrome.

After the meeting, David and I debriefed on George's proposal that JGYN acquire our company. Once I shared my reservations about George and the fundamental limitations of the technology, David responded with a blunt and unforgettable assessment: "No matter how hard he tries with this company, he'll learn that *you can't put a shine on shit*. He may be able to fool some analysts on the street, but in the end, his company is walking dead."

While I credit David for introducing me to the phrase, he never claimed to have coined it. Later research suggests that President Lyndon B. Johnson may have used a similar version—"you can't polish a turd"—when describing the Vietnam War. Books such as *Flawed Giant: Lyndon Johnson and His Times, 1961–1973* by Robert Dallek and *Lyndon B. Johnson: A Memoir* by George Reedy reference Johnson using the expression, although there is no definitive transcript or official record confirming it.

Regardless of its origin, I have found the phrase fitting in many situations, both in and outside of PE. Though I resist using it as often as I'm tempted to, I always recall with a smile the first time I heard it from David. It remains a vivid reminder that no matter how much polish you apply, a fundamentally flawed business or idea cannot be made to shine.

ACKNOWLEDGEMENTS

I am deeply grateful to have been raised in a household where my parents, Frank and Rita, demonstrated unwavering work ethic and resilience. They juggled multiple blue-collar jobs to support my siblings and me, and, above all, instilled in us a strong moral compass, a relentless drive to work hard, and a profound appreciation for education.

Throughout my teenage years and into college, I worked continuously, fully responsible for saving and financing my undergraduate education. While I did not come from financial privilege, I was fortunate to grow up in an environment that emphasized perseverance, entrepreneurial spirit, and the belief that success must be earned in advance. The lessons I learned from my parents shaped the discipline and character that proved essential throughout my academic and professional journey. To them, I am forever grateful.

Over the course of my career, I've had the privilege of learning from remarkable mentors who shaped my path in meaningful ways, though I also encountered a few from whom I could barely tolerate another minute in the boardroom. Lessons came from both, but it is to the former that I owe my deepest thanks.

To James Sloan, Ph.D.—my own "Hawkeye Pierce"—whose extraordinary technical expertise was matched only by his infectious sense of humor. During our time at the U.S. Army Materials Research Command, he demonstrated that even the most intense work environments can be fun.

To Michael Malone, Ph.D., and Richard Farris, Ph.D., who were instrumental in guiding me through my doctoral studies at the University of Massachusetts Amherst.

To Donald Reed, who saw potential in me beyond the laboratory and opened the door to my first steps in general management at Delta Surprenant.

To David Maupin, the most influential management mentor of my career, who not only provided opportunity, but gave me the chance to learn by his side at UroSurge.

To Frank, whose partnership, support, and steady hand were essential as we led RMH / OrthoRehab to an exit beyond anything we had imagined.

To Jonathan Fleming, Rick Geoffrion, and Yuval Binur, Ph.D., at Oxford Bioscience Partners and Accelerated Technologies, who had the foresight and trust to join me on the successful journey at Claros.

To Dr. Phillip Frost, who believed in the vision of Claros and played a pivotal role in bringing 4Kscore™ to market, positively impacting the lives of countless patients.

I am especially grateful to David Belluck at Riverside Partners for giving me the opportunity to take my career in an entirely new and fulfilling direction in private equity—a path that continues to be one of growth and reinvention.

ABOUT THE AUTHOR

Dr. Magliochetti has served over 10 years as an Operating Partner at Riverside Partners, a private equity firm with over $1 billion in assets under management, focused on investing in middle-market healthcare companies. He is a fully integrated partner involved in healthcare pre-investment diligence, post-investment asset management, and proprietary deal origination across pharmaceutical services, medical devices, diagnostics, contract manufacturing, laboratory services, and tech-enabled healthcare services.

Dr. Magliochetti previously spent over 20 years in senior operating roles, during which he executed three successful sale transactions as CEO of Claros Diagnostics, RMH, and UroSurge. Additionally, he has held senior positions with the medical device company Haemonetics and completed an assignment with the U.S. Army Research Command. Dr. Magliochetti serves on the Robert E. Wise Foundation

Board at Beth Israel Lahey Health, and the Board of the Technology Development Fund at Boston Children's Hospital. He has also served on the Board of Overseers of the Boston Museum of Science, as an Adjunct Professor of Biomedical Engineering at the University of Iowa, holds several patents, has authored numerous technical and business publications, served on many professional panels, and has lectured at universities in the U.S. and internationally on entrepreneurship and business development.

Dr. Magliochetti holds B.S. and Ph.D. degrees in Chemical Engineering from Northeastern University and the University of Massachusetts at Amherst, respectively, and an MBA from Northeastern University.